G000118269

POLITICS OF
THE BLACK SEA

The Library of International Relations

Series ISBN 1 86064 080 X
Series Editor: Professor Alex Danchev
Department of International Relations, University of Keele

The Library of International Relations (LIR) brings together the work of leading scholars in international relations, politics and history, from the English-speaking world and beyond. It constitutes a forum for original scholarship from the United Kingdom, continental Europe, the USA, the Commonwealth and the Developing World. The books are the fruit of original research and thinking and they contribute to the most advanced debate in both political theory and practice and are exhaustively assessed by the authors' academic peers. The Library consists of a numbered series and provides a unique and authoritative resource for libraries, academics, diplomats, government officials, journalists and students.

POLITICS OF THE BLACK SEA

Dynamics of Cooperation and Conflict

Edited by

Tunç Aybak

I.B.Tauris *Publishers*
LONDON • NEW YORK

Published in 2001 by I.B.Tauris & Co Ltd
6 Salem Road, London W2 4BU
175 Fifth Avenue, New York NY 10010
www.ibtauris.com

In the United States and Canada distributed by St. Martin's Press
175 Fifth Avenue, New York NY 10010

Copyright © Tunç Ayback, 2001

All rights reserved. Except for brief quotations in a review, this book, or any part thereof, may
not be reproduced, stored in or introduced into a retrieval system, or transmitted, in any form
or by any means, electronic, mechanical, photocopying, recording or otherwise, without the
prior written permission of the publisher.

ISBN 1-86064-454-6

A full CIP record for this book is available from the British Library
A full CIP record for this book is available from the Library of Congress

Library of Congress catalog card: available

Typeset in Baskerville 10/12pt by The Midlands Book Typesetting Co, Loughborough
Printed and bound in Great Britain by MPG Books Ltd, Bodmin, Cornwall

Contents

In memory of Burak

Abbreviations

AO	Autonomous Oblast Region
ASSR	Autonomous Soviet Socialist Republic
ATP	Assembly of Turkic Peoples
BEAC	Barents Europe Atlantic Council
BSEC	Black Sea Economic Cooperation
BSEP	Black Sea Environmental Programme
BSREC	Black Sea Regional Energy Centre
BS-SAP	Black Sea Strategic Action Programme
BSTD	Black Sea Trade and Development Bank
CBMs	Confidence Building Measures
CBS	Council of Baltic States
CEFTA	Central European Free Trade Area
CEI	Central European Initiative
CFE	Conventional Armed Forces in Europe
CIS	Commonwealth of Independent States
COMECON	Council for Mutual Economic Assistance
CPS	Confederation of Peoples of the Caucasus
CRP	Confederation of Repressed Peoples
CSCC	Caspian Sea Cooperation Council
EAPC	Euro Atlantic Partnership Council
EBRD	European Bank for Reconstruction and Development
ECU	European Currency Unit
EEZ	Exclusive Economic Zones
EIB	European Investment Bank
EU	European Union
FRY	Former Republic of Yugoslavia
GATT	General Agreement on Tariffs and Trade
GEF	Global Environmental Facility
GUAMU	Georgia, Ukraine, Azerbaijan, Moldova and Uzbekistan Subregional Grouping
IFI	International Financial Institutions
ICBSS	International Centre for Black Sea Studies
IRPS	Interconnected Regional Power System
ITUR	Italy, Turkey, Ukraine, Russia, Fibre Optic Cable System

KAFOS	Bulgaria, Moldova, Romania, Turkey Telecommunication Link Project
MARPOL	Conventions Protecting the Sea from Ship Based Pollution
MERCOSUR	Southern Common Market of Latin America
OECD	Organization for Economic Cooperation and Development
OSCE	Organization for Security and Cooperation in Europe
PABSEC	Parliamentary Assembly of the BSEC
PCU	Programme Coordinating Unit
PfP	Partnership for Peace
PHARE	Poland Hungary Assistance for Economic Construction
RNCBSEC	Russian National Committee for the Black Sea Economic Cooperation
SAP	Strategic Action Plan
SMEs	Small and Medium-sized Enterprises
TACIS	Technical Assistance to CIS
TBL	Trans-Balkan Line
TDA	Transboundary Diagnostic Analysis
TEU	Treaty on European Union
TRACECA	Transport Corridor Europe, Caucasia, Asia
UN	United Nations
UNEP	United Nations Environmental Programme
USSR	Union of Soviet Socialist Republics
WEU	Western European Union
WG	Working Group
WTO	World Trade Organization

Notes on Contributors

Tunç Aybak is a Research Fellow and Lecturer in South East European Politics, School of Humanities and Cultural Studies, Middlesex University, London

Tor Bukkvoll, Senior Scientist, Norwegian Defence Research Establishment, Norway

Svante E. Cornell is a Lecturer in the Middle Eastern and the Caucasian Politics, University of Uppsal, Sweden

Bülent Gökay is a Lecturer in South East European Politics, Department of International Relations, Keele University, UK

Nikolai A. Kovalsky is President of the Council for the Black Sea Studies, Institute of Europe, Russian Academy of Sciences

Laurence D. Mee, Director, PERC Environmental Policy Unit, University of Plymouth, UK. From 1993-1998 he was the Co-ordinator of the Black Sea Environmental Programme based in Istanbul, Turkey

Eyüp Özveren is a Lecturer in Economic History, Middle East Technical University, Ankara

Plamen Pantev, Director of the Institute for Security and International Studies, Sofia

Preface

On the shores of the Black Sea, there were born a pair of Siamese twins called 'civilization' and 'barbarism'.

Neal Ascherson, *The Black Sea*

The study of the Black Sea as a region is a largely neglected phenomenon within the discipline of international relations. This book is an attempt to remedy this fact. Given the vast area and multiplicity of issues and countries in the Black Sea, this is bound to be an incomplete task. That it is 'incomplete' however does not mean that the issues addressed in this book are inconsequential. We concentrated in this book on specific countries and issues, rather than attempting a complete coverage of the Black Sea countries and related issues. This does not mean that other countries and issues are excluded. They appear briefly, wherever they are relevant to the themes explored. The themes of this volume were carefully selected to reflect current political changes which may have a lasting impact on the reconfiguration of Black Sea politics, in the twenty-first century.

For many decades, the southern and northern shores of the Black Sea remained separated by the division of Europe. The east-west division was the main axis of events and developments, and the politics of the Black Sea was subordinated to superpower rivalries. The Black Sea was devoid of any united function and treated as a barrier and borderline rather than an integral part of pan-European politics. With the collapse of the Cold War, the Black Sea emerged as a region on the physical and intellectual map of Europe. As the chapters in this volume demonstrate, it is now possible to speak of the Black Sea as a region with its own political and economic dynamics. This book, therefore, seeks to build upon knowledge and existing expertise relating to the Black Sea area, providing information and a context within which to make sense of regional issues in a collective way as well as explicitly addressing the question of what these contexts tell us about the place and the future of the region in the new Europe.

The structure and the thinking behind this book developed out of a shortlisted ESRC project in 1998. The final work grew out of the network collaboration of the Black Sea Area Study Group. It started with a few members but, in the process, grew not only in numbers but also in strength, and attracted a number of leading Black Sea specialists from different countries and disciplines. The aim was to bring together a diversity of expertise, national perspectives and disciplines in a single book. This volume represents the outcome of an extended collaboration, among these Black Sea specialists, in which the different approaches and assumptions of political scientists, historians, economic historians and scientists would be examined and tested against the available evidence. Altogether, the book draws on much of the ongoing research on the political economy of the Black Sea. As the following chapters demonstrate we have not reached any single consensus, this was not our intention. This does not mean however that chapters do not constitute the building-blocks of the whole book. Each chapter looks at different issues or national perspectives but the main arch which holds the whole structure of the book together is a focus on the dynamics of cooperation and conflict with reference to the regionalization of political economy in the Black Sea area.

What began as an idea could only develop to a successful conclusion with the cooperation of a number of people. It is therefore a pleasure to express my gratitude to the authors, who contributed chapters to this book. Of course, I take editorial responsibility for interpreting the contents of some chapters. Mistakes, omissions and errors are all mine.

Like any other, this book is a product of a collective effort. Its completion would not have been possible without the support of colleagues and friends, as well as institutions. I would like to thank the following people and institutions who have consciously, and unconsciously, contributed to this book and provided valuable assistance, insights and ideas in different forms.

I would like to thank Helen Wallace, the Director of 'One Europe or Several?' ESRC Research Programme for her initial advice and suggestions about the project. My thanks also go to Iver Neumann, Head of the Centre for Russian Studies, Norwegian Institute of International Affairs, for his inspiring company and his valuable insights about the Black Sea on a short train journey from Keele to London at the time. I would also like to thank colleagues at Keele University, South East European Research Unit, to which I have always been warmly welcomed during my research visits; especially Bülent Gökay for his positive encouragement and contributions which have been invaluable in the completion of this book.

My thanks also go to the General Secretariat of the Black Sea Economic Cooperation in Istanbul, Ambassador Nurver Nureş and his staff have been particularly helpful in providing interviews and crucial documentation. I also thank Namik Güner Erpul, the First Secretary at the Permanent Mission of Turkish Ministry of Foreign Affairs at Organization for Security and Cooperation in Europe. He provided me with research material and official documents and informed me about the developments at OSCE.

At Middlesex University, special thanks are due to the School of Humanities and Cultural Studies, Gabrielle Parker and Heather Deegan for backing the project which helped me to get it off the ground and to colleagues in the Politics and International Studies group, especially Mehmet Ali Dikerdem who gave me unfailing moral support and intellectual encouragement at difficult times. My thanks are also due to I.B.Tauris publishers, the valuable editorial suggestions of Emma Sinclair-Webb throughout; and the keen eye and scrupulous editing skills of Miriam Rivett markedly improved the final manuscript. Without their editorial assistance, this book would not have been completed.

I would like to thank my seven-year-old son Joseph Ayd'n for his inspiring, imaginary poems about the Black Sea which he used to attract my attention when I was completely absorbed in my work; and my partner as well as my best friend Kathryn for her patience, support and faith in my commitments.

Finally I would like to dedicate this book to the memory of a friend who was taken away in the last earthquake in Turkey: Burak Tezdiker, with whom I grew up by the shores of the Black Sea, watching the ships go by. I hope the people of the Black Sea will be living in a peaceful and undivided Europe without the cultural and economic faultlines between east and west in the twenty-first century.

Tunç Aybak

CHAPTER ONE

Introduction

Tunç Aybak

In ancient times, the Black Sea was named the inhospitable sea or *Axenos*. Later the ancients called it the *Euxine* or 'hospitable' sea. These metaphors summarize, in a way, the history of the Black Sea. They also demonstrate how perceptions of geography are closely tied to political and social conditions. Historically speaking, the Black Sea has been a medium for economic and social interaction between different cultures and nations, as well as acting as a barrier between countries. Some Black Sea littoral countries regarded it as the only friendly frontier in a hostile environment, some as an open frontier that might bring raids and unknown enemies from the opposite shores.

The Black Sea has gone through periods of Greek, Roman, Byzantine, and Ottoman dominance. For the greater part of the twentieth century it has remained a divided and semi-closed sea. Under Cold War circumstances, the faultlines dividing the Black Sea were mainly ideological. In the south, Turkey belonged to the Western capitalist camp, whereas in the north, the Soviet Union, Romania and Bulgaria belonged to the Socialist camp. In this period, there was minimal interaction across the Black Sea and it was divided between two rival military blocs. The end of the Cold War, however, has transformed the Black Sea from a dividing mass of water, into a potential regional entity.

The end of the Cold War meant freedom from the conceptual prison of Cold War discourse, but at the same time one of its legacies was uncertainty about the future of security and stability. In other words, the end of the Cold War has not only opened up new potential in regional areas for regional cooperation, but it has also revived the historical sources of ethnic, national and territorial conflicts.

It is a fact that the depths of the Black Sea form the largest mass of lifeless water in the world. It is predicted that if turnover of the water strata were to occur, it would provoke the worst natural catastrophe to strike the earth since the last Ice Age. This demonstrates how fragile the ecological balance in the Black Sea is. This can also be used as a metaphor for understanding the present fragile political ecology of the region. Traditionally the political environment of the region is both fraught with and prone to conflicts, projecting instability for the whole of Europe. It is true, as reflected in the discussions in this book, that the Black Sea is facing a period of instability. The source of this regional instability is a combination of systemic and domestic change. On the systemic level, the collapse of the Soviet Union, and the end of the bipolar world, has created a volatile international environment that has not yet been replaced by more stable structures. On the domestic level, the end of Marxism-Leninism as a ruling ideology, the weakening of the Soviet-era political and economic institutions, the rise of opposition forces and the emerging religious and nationalist forces in the Post-Soviet states, all present challenges to regional peace and stability.

The aim which underlies this volume is to produce an assessment of the emerging patterns of conflict and cooperation in the Black Sea area in the light of the perceptions and policies of the major Black Sea powers. The regional scale of issues as well as the responses to these issues will also be the subjects of analysis in these pages. The book can be read in relation to the themes outlined below.

The Black Sea as a Historical Unit of Analysis

Explanations of the political economy of the Black Sea historically involve a variety of approaches. One may attach primary importance to the North and South axis in terms of the distribution of power in the Black Sea political economy. Another may place the emphasis on the emergence of the Black Sea as a regional unit in the development of world political economy. Yet another rests on the analysis of the Black Sea world as a civilization gulf between the East and West. Grouping all these different approaches together can only be done in a meaningful way by relating them to an analytical framework provided by the Annales School. The work of Fernand Braudel, a leading precursor of the Annales School, is particularly significant, Braudel, a structuralist, sought to identify patterns of structural change implicated in historical processes of transformation. He emphasized the need to distinguish between historical processes in terms of short, medium and long-term change. The short-term refers to the history of events and is mainly connected to the political field, in other words that aspect of history made up by events and personalities which has a short duration. Braudel's notion of conjunctural history adopts a perspective focused on the medium-term and is connected to developments in the socio-economic field, it is of particular use when seeking to produce a historical analysis of the Black Sea region. While Braudel's notion of structural history relates to the slower-moving field of geography and nature, a field which has long-term effects on broader historical processes and structures. It is a notion useful in the construction of an explanation for the historical processes which have impacted on the Black Sea region, in what Braudel terms the *longue durée*.

The assessment of such long and medium-term historical trends in the political economy of the Black Sea region forms the subject of Eyüp Özveren's chapter, which sets the historical scene for other sections of the book. Following the work of the Annales School, Eyüp Özveren looks at the history of the Black Sea world in terms of the Black Sea's status as an independent unit of analysis. In doing so, he produces a critique of different historiographical approaches to the Black Sea as found in the work of historians Braudel, Stoianovich and Bratianau. As opposed to a passive history of the Black Sea produced for the consumption of national collectivities and as a peripheral geography subordinated to larger structures, Özveren offers an emancipatory interpretation, contending that the Black Sea as an entity deserves to be considered in terms of its own regional trajectory. Unlike Braudel, who treated the Black Sea as a 'backyard' of the Mediterranean world, and Stoianovich who focused on the Balkans, rather than treating it as an integral part of the Black Sea basin, Özveren introduces us to Bratianu's Black Sea world. According to Özveren, Bratianu's neglected history is the most instructive of all. In Bratianu's treatment the Black Sea assumes its deserved regional status as an entity.

According to Özveren, the Black Sea enjoyed periods of a regional political economy under the hegemonic powers of the Byzantine and the Ottoman Empires, however this was not without capitalist economic penetration and, at intervals, the political intervention of Europeans. In the wake of the twentieth century , as Özveren observes, the balance along the North-South axis changed, for the first time in history, in favour of the North while the Ottoman Empire collapsed and the Russian Empire reconstituted itself as a Soviet Empire. Much of the second half of the twentieth century was, for the Black Sea, a period of freeze and division under Cold War circumstances. It seems that with the end of the Cold War, the Black Sea has been given another chance to assume the status of a regional political economy in the process of integration into the global political economy.

Turkey and the Black Sea as a Framework of Regional Cooperation

With the end of the Cold War, the course of history has changed and the Black Sea has emerged as an integral part of pan-European political and economic space. The demise of the Cold War exposed European influences. First of all, as a result of the collapse of the Soviet Union, the number of Black Sea countries who wanted to join the European integration project multiplied. Secondly, the political economy of the Black Sea has been opened up to the dynamics of European integration and globalization. Although the Black Sea region is on the margins of Europe, it has now been placed within European intra-relationships. Apart from the structural and conjunctural forms of explanation provided by Özveren, there is Tunç Aybak's consideration of the present political economy of the Black Sea in terms of contemporary political events and the effects of the collapse of the Cold War on the Black Sea region.

One of the consequences of this post Cold War development has been the articulation and formation of new regional groupings and identities within a pan-European context. Since the end of the Cold War six new regional cooperation frameworks have appeared in the pan-European space stretching from the far north, to the Black Sea, these are the Barents European Atlantic Council (BEAC), Council of Baltic States (CBS), Central European Free Trade Area (CEFTA), Central European Initiative (CEI) and the Black Sea Economic Cooperation (BSEC). The emergence of regional cooperation initiatives in the 1990s can be best explained in the context of the sense of isolation for these countries, who felt that they had been left outside the process of European integration. In general, these regional cooperation initiatives were designed to overcome the old east-west Cold War divisions from the Arctic in the far north to the Black Sea in the south. They are by-products of the rapidly opening European political economy. However, each regional cooperation framework operates within a different systemic setting and has its own historical trajectory with correspondingly different geopolitical considerations. Therefore, they need to be assessed on their own merits.

Aybak presents an evaluation of the formation of the BSEC against factors in its regional background. The BSEC was the product of Turkey's, post Cold War, regionalist drive to locate itself at the centre of the Black Sea region, in response to the pan-Europeanization of the regional political economy. In the 1990s, as the regionalization of the Black Sea has increased in salient regional issues such as energy, trade and transportation, the other countries' attitude towards the BSEC has

4

accordingly changed. The other key regional players, Russia and Greece, who were suspicious of Turkey's motivations initially, eventually recognized the BSEC's potential role in building a viable regional economic and political stability. Therefore the future of the BSEC will be determined by the level of interdependence and pattern of cooperation developing between these key players in response to the regionalization process of the political economy in the Black Sea area. Even though the level of institutional cooperation is weak, the high level of actual interdependence in regional energy, transportation, environment and trade issues will determine the future of the BSEC. In addition, Aybak concludes that the recognition of the BSEC by the EU, as a complementary framework to European integration, has also reinforced its status and legitimacy in other countries' quest to join Europe.

The Politics of Oil as a Source of Competition in the Black Sea

While Aybak's chapter assesses emerging patterns of cooperation in the regional economy, Gökay's chapter concentrates on the politics of oil and the wider implications of competition, between rival powers, over the extraction and distribution of oil resources for the Black Region. The management of competition over the oil resources in the Black Sea area remains a critical issue for the future stability of the region.

The retreat of the Soviet Union created a power vacuum in the Black Sea area. According to Gökay, following the collapse of the Soviet Union, Turkey with the encouragement of the US, moved in to fill this power vacuum. However, by 1994, Turkey's ambitious policies towards the former Soviet Republics had proved to be futile. Constrained by its own internal economic and political problems and restrained by the return of Russia to the region, Turkey had to adopt more pragmatic and economically-motivated policies. In addition to this, Iran had gradually entered the regional power equation as a significant player. Despite the emergence of new regional rivalries, the political and economic interdependence between Russia and the newly-independent states persisted. As Gökay puts it 'the general advantage in the current competition between Turkey, Iran and Russia rests with Russia' and remains to be the case in the future of the region.

The politics of Caspian oil is directly related to the Black Sea. Competition between the rival powers, particularly, revolves around the exploration, distribution and transportation of Caspian oil. Given the history of the Caspian Region and the existence of vast reserves of oil, what we are witnessing is, at present, the replay of the nineteenth century "Great Game" between global powers, multinational companies and regional states, all competing for access to the Caspian region resources. The oil and gas reserves in the Caspian Sea area will be one of the most crucial issues this century. Current estimates put the Caspian Oil reserves at 200 billion barrels which is more than in any other region outside the Persian Gulf. Gökay investigates two related and critical regional issues between the competing powers: the dispute over the legal status of the Caspian Sea; the ownership of the oil deposits; the routes of oil pipelines and transport facilities. There are two main arguments in determining the legal status of the Caspian Sea. On the one hand, Russia and Iran regard the Caspian Sea as a giant lake which entitles the littoral states to joint use. On the other, Azerbaijan and Kazakhstan argue that the Caspian is a sea and should be divided into sectors and exploited separately. Apart from the legal dispute, the transportation of oil through pipelines has been a source of competition between the regional powers of Russia, Turkey and Iran. Each power competes over the choice of pipeline routes through which the oil is transported from the Caspian region. Gökay concludes that the return of multipolar regional competition, reminiscent of the seventeenth and eighteenth centuries, can be observed. However, this does not rule out the possibility that new patterns of cooperation might emerge, out of a necessity to resolve the regional issues in trade, investment and infrastructure.

Security Cooperation in the Black Sea

Given the diversity of countries and the conflict-ridden nature of regional politics, building regional security cooperation in the Black Sea is a difficult task. Pantev, in his analysis of security cooperation in the Black Sea basin, looks at the regional background and existing institutional structures in order to assess the prospect of security cooperation in the Black Sea. He adopts a broader definition of the security concept. The Black Sea basin lies at the centre of three strategically crucial sub-regions: the Balkans, the Caspian sea basin and the Caucasus. In this sense, the BSEC plays a central role in the promotion of peace in the region. The BSEC has no security mandate on security issues. Given the existence of sensitive trouble spots in the former Yugoslavia, Nagorno-Karabakh, Transdniestra, Abkhazia and Chechnya it would not be very easy to build a hard security agenda and conflict-resolution mechanisms into the BSEC's structures. Much of the cooperation within the BSEC structures has no direct relevance to security issues. This is not to suggest, however, that the BSEC has no indirect security role. One must bear in mind that one of the stated objectives of the BSEC was 'to transform the Black Sea into a region of peace, freedom, stability and prosperity'. In fact, according to

Pantev, the BSEC deals with soft security issues (i.e. economics, environ-ment, energy), rather than more traditional 'hard' political-military secu-rity issues (such as the management of conflicts or the provision of mutual defence guarantees). Soft security issues indirectly contribute to regional stability. It is suggested that regular contacts between the countries in multilateral forums at different levels of society, exchange of opinions on technical and economic issues, transactions and existing channels of communication all help to build confidence and create cooperative habits in the Black Sea. Indeed, even though the BSEC is not a strictly a security organization, it has the potential to develop into a security organization in the future. The other European security organizations provide concepts and mechanisms for conflict prevention and resolution. Pantev suggests that a broader definition of security and closer cooperation with other European security organizations (EU/WEU, OSCE, NATO/EAPC/PfP) may strengthen the role of BSEC in hard security issues, as well as soft ones, by extending the institutional framework of EuroAtlantic security zone to the Black Sea area. Finally, Pantev adopts Karl Deutsch's 'secu-rity community' concept and describes the necessary preconditions for the establishment of a Black Sea security community. Provided that members of BSEC are committed to cooperation, Pantev argues that the use of military force might be unthinkable in the Black Sea as a result of increasing transactions, regional communications and institutionalization of security in different issues-related areas. This might in time transform the region into 'a security community' of the Black Sea nations.

Russia as an Enduring Black Sea Power

The Black Sea has played a central and strategic role in Russia's history and national identity. For Russians the Black Sea was a vital route and gateway to the warm seas, and its mild climate, fishing stocks and agricul-tural products provided Russians with live resources. With the collapse of the Soviet Union, Russian access to the Black Sea has diminished substan-tially and the common Soviet borders on the sea have been divided between Russia and the newly-independent Black Sea littoral states of Georgia and Ukraine.

Nikolai Kovalsky seeks to represent Russia's national perceptions of the Black Sea. The Russian presence in the Black Sea is a dominant one. But, as Kovalsky's discussion demonstrates, this dominant status does not confer an identity that is an equally dominant, or even a secure one. Since the collapse of the Soviet Union, Russia has been coming to terms with post Cold War Black Sea realities. In this sense Kovalsky's chapter reflects the vulnerabilities of Russia as a result of its diminishing superpower status in the Black Sea.

The presence of large numbers of ethnic Russians in the region, the unsettled character of Russia's southern borders and the increasing secession movements and ethnic conflicts in the Caucasus have created a volatile environment for the Russians' security interests. In addition refugee movements and environmental threats have destabilizing effects on Russia's well-being.

With the emergence of a number of new states in the Black Sea, there are now inter-state problems that need to be resolved. These include, among others, the consolidation of new borders and the resolution of territorial disputes between Russia and Ukraine. Russia's access to energy resources and routes has become another source of concern for Russia, while Georgia's strategic importance in the Black Sea region has increased as an energy gateway from the Caspian Sea.

According to Kovalsky, in the 1990s the greatest Russian concern in the Black Sea has been the increasing physical military presence of the West. He perceives that NATO's expansion to the Black Sea, through partnership agreements with Georgia and Ukraine and association links between the Western European Union and Bulgaria and Romania, is threatening Russia's national interests. The Black Sea also provides Russia with an important link with the Balkans, in particular with Serbia, with which Russia has cultural, historical and religious affinities. Kovalsky contends that recent unilateral military operations in the Balkans have not only excluded Russia from traditional Balkan politics but also set a precedent that can be used against Russia in the future

Given the above Russian perceptions, it seems that Russia regards the multilateral regional economic cooperation in the Black Sea as an integral part of Russia's new foreign policy priorities in its relationship with Europe. The BSEC, from a Russian perspective, has a potential role in transforming the region into a zone of stability and prosperity as opposed to an extension of NATO's military umbrella into the Black Sea area. In this context, Kovalsky assigns a special role to OSCE as a comprehensive and inclusive pan-European organization for building security and stability within which the BSEC can be an important economic component.

Ukraine as an emergent Black Sea Power
With the collapse of the Soviet Union, Ukraine has become an important player in the political economy of the Black Sea. Tor Bukkvoll analyses the

place of the Black Sea in Ukranian foreign policy. Since its independence in 1991, Ukraine has found itself caught between two opposing, although not necessarily mutually exclusive, tendencies. Ukraine's foreign policy agenda was determined by the political desire to join Europe on the one hand and its growing economic and political role in the Black Sea area, in particular in balancing Russia's political weight. Bukkvoll provides perceptive insights into Ukraine's foreign policy towards the Black Sea.

Ukraine has part of a crucial balancing act in the configuration of regional power politics. Since its independence Ukraine has entered into a bilateral agreement with Turkey and developed subregional groupings with Georgia, Azerbaijan, Moldova and Uzbekistan. As a country which is economically dependent on the Black Sea for its trade and resources, Ukraine recognized the political and economic potential of the region as the extension of its pro-European policies.

Ukraine's quest to join European institutions, particularly after signing the Partnership agreement with NATO was not without strategic implications for the region. Ukraine's security policy developed along the lines of strengthening the relationship with Turkey, Azerbaijan and Georgia. This implied that Russia's political influence and its developing relationship with Bulgaria, Greece and Armenia, needed to be counterbalanced. Despite the configuration of the new balance of power politics in the Black Sea, Ukraine has recognized the necessity to build a security dimension into the BSEC structures to avoid the escalation of conflict. As Bukkvoll puts it, maintaining a balance of power with Russia goes hand in hand with security-building mechanisms in the multilateral forums.

Apart from the strategic dimension, the Black Sea is an indispensable economic base for Ukraine. Its shipping routes and industries are located on the Black Sea hinterland. It is also heavily dependent on Russia for its energy resources and it has to rely on nuclear power stations to generate energy. The politics of pipelines and geopolitics are closely interrelated. Ukraine is also trying to diversify, like other energy-dependent countries of the region, and to take advantage of energy transportation routes between the Caspian resources and Europe. The new transportation routes and communication lines may reduce Ukrainian's dependence on Russia and strengthen its infrastructural links with Europe. Ukraine is actively participating in the construction of the Black Sea transportation network.

The collapse of the Soviet Union has created new ethnic tensions in Ukraine. The existence of large Russian ethnic minorities within Ukraine as well as the revival of old Tatar ethnic group identity in Crimea has become another bone of contention with Russia. Bukkvoll looks at the emergence of civil society activities since the collapse of the Soviet Union. Even though the level of civil society engagement is low, it indicates the existence of fertile ground for cross-regional civil society cooperation at the local level in environmental matters.

The Black Sea and the Environment

The Black Sea is a critical and integral subregion of the European ecosystem. The environment is one of the most salient issues in the political economy of the Black Sea. The Black Sea is now regarded as one of the regional seas most damaged by human activity. Its drainage basin covers one third of the European continent including the major areas of 17 countries, 14 of which are undergoing a profound economic and political transition from centrally-planned to market economies. The littoral states of the Black Sea are heavily dependent on the Black Sea not only for its fish stocks, but for its eco-system balance and maritime transportation. For one thing, except for Turkey, all other Black Sea countries are dependent upon the Black Sea as a maritime gateway to the Mediterranean and warm seas. As a result of rapid industrialization, over-fishing and tourism in the second half of the twentieth century, the Black Sea has become a depository for human and industrial waste. Under Cold War circumstances, a coordinated approach to the environmental problems in the Black Sea was almost non-existent. Despite some countries' efforts to coordinate the management of the environment in the Black Sea under Cold War divisions, and to reach effective and multilateral regional environmental agreements, attempts proved futile. However, the collapse of Cold War divisions opened up the way for the conclusion of multilateral regional cooperation. In 1992, the Black Sea littoral States met in Bucharest to sign the 'Convention on the Protection of the Black Sea against Pollution' and common rules and regulations were adopted in order to prevent further pollution.

In this volume Laurence Mee examines the symptoms of environmental degradation and assesses the impact of the implementation of relevant legal instruments and developing regional policies and bodies, for the protection of the coastal and marine environment of the Black Sea. The policies and measures adopted, following the Bucharest meeting, indicate a move towards a more holistic approach. Obstacles, however, remain, not only because of the legacies of the centrally-planned economies but also the failure of the national governments to address the close link between environmental issues and rapid development, which is vital to maintain a sustainable development of the Black Sea economy. There is also a lack of sufficient investment in the Black Sea countries to upgrade the treatment facilities and to build an environmentally-friendly infrastructure. Effective implementation of national environmental policies is necessary to prevent further pollution from land-based sources, generated from agricultural land use (nitrogen and phosphorus-based fertilizers) and municipal sewage.

Discharges, in particular from the Danube and the other rivers flowing into the Sea, lead to the massive and damaging eutrophication of the Black Sea. Therefore, according to Mee, any action to reduce nutrient input into the Black Sea requires an effective basin-wide approach. Furthermore, as opposed to the top-down approach from the governments, there is a need for bottom-up grass root environmental movements and greater public awareness of environmental issues in the Black Sea countries. Even though there are some examples of local environmental campaigns, the formation of civil society groups in environmental matters are still at an embryonic stage. As Mee observes, incentives for individual or collective environmental action at the local level are 'virtually absent' and there is an urgent need for environmental education to create a new generation of citizens who are aware of their entitlements and commitments to a clean environment and sustainable economic development.

Mee concludes that, if the current trends continue, there is a risk that the Black Sea environment's further deterioration will, in the long-term, damage the regional economic growth. Apart from land-based sources, the shipping of new oil and energy resources from the Caspian Sea and Central Asia via the Black Sea poses one of the greatest challenges to the already-polluted environment. The prospect of accession of the Danube and the Black Sea countries to the EU provides an important incentive for the harmonization of the environmental legislation with the EU. Otherwise Mee warns that 'there is a significant risk of creating a new east-west division across the Black Sea, further complicating the implementation of plans to protect it for its own good and that of future generations.'

The Black Sea and the North Caucasus

The North Caucasus lies between the Black Sea and the Caspian Sea and it has been an integral role in the international politics of the Black Sea. In analysing the North Caucasus as a subregional entity within the Black Sea, the effects of geography on relations between states, patterns of cooperation and conflict, ethnic and religious rivalries all need to be taken into account. In this sense, the prospect of stability and instability in the North Caucasus has direct repercussions for the whole Black Sea Region.

Historically speaking, the North Caucasus has been a buffer zone between competing empires and between different religions and ethnic groups. The unsettled southern borders of today's Russia are the products of the historical legacy of centuries of Russian rule. Apart from Russia, Turkey and Iran have security interests regarding the future developments in the region. Finally, the North Caucasus constitutes a geographical bridge connecting the Caspian Sea to the Black Sea. It is an important trading route and is in a strategic position for pipelines to transport oil westwards from the rich oil resources in the Caspian Sea.

It was not until the eighteenth and nineteenth centuries that the region was incorporated into the Russian empire. This was not without the resistance of the peoples of the North Caucasus. However, the legacies of the imperial and Soviet past still have an impact on the ethnic politics of the region. In the Soviet period the titular nations were created by linking territories with dominant ethnicities, generally at the expense of other ethnic groups. The North Caucasian people began to reassert their ethnic and national identity following the Gorbachev reforms in the late 1980s. The dissolution of the Soviet Union inevitably accelerated ethnic violence and secession movements. At the time of writing the continuing dispute between the Russian Federation and the Chechen Republic over its declaration of independence has resulted in severe clashes. Conflicts have occurred between the republics of Ingushia and North Ossetia, between North Caucasian units and central authorities, and between Georgia and Abkhazia. There is also a high risk that the Chechen conflict may spill over to the neighbouring republic of Dagestan, with its volatile ethnic diversity. In this sense, the North Caucasus is at a crucial crossroads, concerning future political developments in the Black Sea.

Svante Cornell gives a detailed account of the regional patterns of conflict and cooperation in the North Caucasus which have emerged in the 1990s. He concentrates on two crucial dimensions of relationships; that of relations among North Caucasian peoples; and that between North Caucasian peoples and Russia. In other words, the ethnic conflict between different groups and centre-periphery relations within the Russian Federation determine the political agenda of North Caucasian politics. In this context, he looks at the background conditions for, as well as the characteristics of, interethnic conflict and Russia's response to the emergence of ethnic conflict and secession movements with particular reference to conflict in Abkhazia, South Ossetia, Chechnya and Dagestan and the relations of these 'republics' with Russian federation.

As Cornell sees it the North Caucasus has, historically, been isolated from the external world and both economically and politically 'peripheralized' within the sphere of Russian influence. This has caused the alienation of these 'republics' from the outside world. As can be inferred from the content of Cornell's chapter, the lack of civic understanding of nationhood and territorial disputes on the basis of historical claims, and the failure to see various intermediate solutions between total submission and total independence are all contributing factors to the North Caucasian conflicts.

Another important element in the politics of the North Caucasus is the return of Islam. As Cornell puts it 'in terms of identity, Islam – just as it has been in the past – might become the unifying force of the North Caucasians.' However, one must not forget that the faultlines in the North Caucasus are not only between ethnic groups but also between Christianity and Islam. Therefore, the politics of Islam could act as a dividing force in the region. The return of Islam, however, carries the risk of being manipulated by the Russian Federation which presents itself as the defender of 'Europe and Christianity in the face of expansionist Islam'. Indeed, as the recent Russian attack on Chechnya shows, the threat of Islam is used to justify Russian military intervention.

On the other hand, the pattern of the relationship in the North Caucasus has not always been one of conflict. Recently, a number of attempts at cooperative movements have been made such as the Confederation of Peoples of Caucasus, which is the most all-encompassing one, as well as other more limited cooperation attempts. The potential for peace exists within the framework of this Confederation. In this sense, Cornell suggests that it is up to the people of the region to build lasting peace. The future of stability in the region is therefore dependent upon the developments in the Russian Federation and its policies towards the region.

At the time of writing, the prospect of stability and cooperation in the North Caucasus is not promising. The existence of authoritarian leadership styles, fragmented administrative structures and the immaturity of traditional local political culture combined with high ethnopolitics prevents the parties from reaching non-violent solutions. As Cornell concludes the stability of the region is dependent upon the restraint of the parties. But Russia, as a hegemonic power, still holds the key to regional peace. Russia not only has interests in but also responsibilities towards reinforcing stability and peace in the region. As recent developments have shown there is little evidence that Russia's policies towards the North Caucasus have so far been constructive ones.

CHAPTER TWO

The Politics of Oil in the Black Sea Area: Turkey and Regional Power Rivalries

Bülent Gökay

If you drew a circle with a 1000-mile radius and Ankara as its centre point, it would encompass both the strategic connection points of the Eastern Hemisphere and the trouble spots of political crisis since ancient times. Of course the circle does not comprise every trouble spot in the world, but every inch of it has been a focus of contention. Within this space empires have been created and demolished. No global power can exist without a coherent policy in this region, it is the Eastern Hemisphere's pivot. To understand this region, it is important to understand the interplay between the region's politics and the grand geopolitics of the global system.

During the Cold War, the focus of geopolitical activity was in the south of this region, south of Turkey. The line running from south-eastern Europe, along the Black Sea to the Caucasus was frozen in place. Nothing was happening on either side of the frontier, apart from a covert 'intelligence war'. The active area of the pivot was directly south of Turkey, in the Middle East. The core issues here included the Arab-Israeli conflict, the status of Lebanon and the Kurds in Iraq.

None of the petty geopolitical issues of the region disappeared. The sensitive balance of the grand geopolitical forces of the Cold War had simply made them inoperable. Those same forces heightened the Arab-Israeli conflict and the conflicts within the Maronite Christian community of Lebanon out of all regional proportions. Today, as a result of historic changes in the balance of global forces, the global significance of Middle Eastern conflicts is no longer the case, although their regional importance is still in evidence. The grand geopolitics of the region changed dramatically, as the Soviet power retreated from its old frontiers.

The Arab-Israeli conflict ceased to be globally significant. Whether the Golan Heights belongs to Israel or Syria is still meaningful for the two countries involved, but not so to anyone else.

At the same time, the rest of the pivot has become extremely important. The area north of Turkey has thawed and the entire Caucasus is in chaos. Events in the region of the Black Sea-Caspian-Caucasus are, potentially, critically important. The collapse of the Soviet Union has resulted in the emergence of several new systems of regional and international relations. The Black Sea-Caspian-Caucasus is one of the most important among them, not just in terms of its many crises but also because of its natural and human resources. To a considerable extent the future of the region seems to be dependent on the management of Caspian oil and gas resources. This situation proceeds under complicated political and economic conditions, territorial and ethnic conflicts, and the competing interests of regional and global forces.

Turkey and the Post-Soviet Space

Euphoria

When the Soviet Union collapsed in 1991, Turkey, backed by the US Administration, attempted to pick up the pieces in the Black Sea and neighbouring regions, Transcaucasia and Central Asia. In this way, Turkey appeared to have revived both the 'Eastern Question' and the old 'Great Game', in which the British and Russian empires had fought each other for political power and military influence in the same region during the nineteenth century. Yet, by 1994, Turkey's policies lay in ruins, forcing Turkish policy-makers to rethink their strategies.[1]

The reasons for this outcome can be summed up under two headings: the first, those which relate to new Russia, and relations between the Russian Federation and Turkey; and the second, those linked to the domestic economic and political problems of Turkey.

Relations between Turkey and new Russia take place in the context of Turkey's failed effort to exploit the collapse of Soviet power in 1991, and to create a zone of influence in the Black Sea-Caspian-Caucasus region and in the former Soviet republics of Central Asia. With the disintegration of the Soviet Union, Turkey engaged the post-Soviet successor states through trade, arms transfers, and economic and defence deals. It competed with Russia for influence in the Black Sea, Central Asia and the Caucasus. In serving its own interests, Turkey also acted on the United States' behalf. In this way, both states' policies and expectations, as well as failures, overlapped to some degree.[2]

When the Soviet Union collapsed and the republics began peeking out from behind the proverbial Iron Curtain, Turkey's relations with the independent states of these regions developed swiftly and in an apparent state of euphoria. Bilateral cultural and economic agreements were signed with each republic, and the Turkish government rushed to recognize all of the republics when they gained independence in the autumn of 1991.

Initially, Turkey's position was considered as being at a distinct advantage in its relations with Central Asian and the Caucasian states. It was ethnically and linguistically related to the Azeris and the inhabitants of the Central Asian republics, except the Tajicks. It shared with many of them adherence to the Sunni branch of Islam. In addition, Turkey prided itself on the secular nature of its political system. Ankara was excited by the new opportunities emerging in its geostrategic space. In the early 1990s, Turkish statesmen looked with pride and confidence to a new world in which Turkey would shine as the star of Eurasia.

The period of euphoria gave rise to all kinds of claims, assumptions and speculations in Turkey and the region. It was assumed that ethnic and linguistic kinship was so strong that Anatolian Turkish could easily be understood throughout Central Asia. For many Turks, this represented an opportunity to recapture the greatness of their distant past. The Central Asian and the Caucasian Muslims, for their part, seemed only to feed Turkish feelings of euphoria. After centuries of Russian colonization and decades of Soviet totalitarian control, initially they were sufficiently carried away to accept the enthusiastic attention of Turkey. Probably, on a more important and more pragmatic level, the Muslims of Central Asia and the Caucasus were optimistic about the practical and particularly the economic aspects of Turkey's attention.[3]

Turkey's economic relations with the states of Central Asia and the Caucasus ranged from planning the establishment of special banks to the regulation of financial relations and to the establishment of barter companies. Creating a transportation and communications system as well as small and medium-sized private enterprises to solve problems pertaining to basic utilities became a short-term goal. Setting up the financial framework for developed trade was given priority by the Turkish government, and a special bank (the *Eximbank*) for this purpose was established in Turkey. In addition, a Turkish Central Asian Bank opened branches in the region.[4]

Teletas, a leading Turkish telecommunications company, signed agreements to develop communications technology in the region. A Turkish construction company, *BMB*, and its local counterpart, agreed on the construction of a natural gas pipeline in Turkmenistan. Another Turkish firm, *Konkur Insaat*, signed an agreement to build a large tourist complex and a cultural centre in Turkmenistan. Georgia has been considered a gateway for Turkey to the regional markets. Although the Georgian economy is in bad shape, the cross-border barter trade has been flourishing and some Turkish entrepreneurs have invested in the fields of small and medium-size manufacturing, food packing and the metallurgical industries. Cross-border trade started with Armenia immediately after the collapse of the Soviet Union. The twice-weekly train running between Kars and Gyumri had not only been transporting goods but was packed with mostly Armenian passengers who had been purchasing various Turkish products ranging from electrical appliances, canned food, beverages, detergents to textile products in exchange for vodka, brandy, livestock and hide.[5]

In this period Turkey launched several initiatives for increased economic co-operation and shared prosperity in Eurasia. The most important of these was to constitute the 'Black Sea Economic Co-operation Zone' for multilateral dialogue and co-operation. In 1992, Turkey introduced the Black Sea Economic Co-operation Project (BSEC). It consists of the member states of Albania, Armenia, Azerbaijan, Bulgaria, Georgia, Greece, Moldova, Romania, and Ukraine. It is still too early to talk about the future of the BSEC. At the moment, the poor infrastructure facilities prevent the countries of the Black Sea from further horizontal economic and social engagement.

As in the other issues, Russia and Turkey are in conflict in the BSEC as well. Russia, together with Greece, has tried on several occasions to prevent the formation of decision-making bodies with the power to discuss political issues within the BSEC.

Turkish expectations, i.e. to lead its BSEC partners towards integration with the EC and thus play a unifying and vanguard role in the Black Sea and neighbouring regions, are not acceptable to Russia. Turkey wants to take the lead in the process of integration and thus in establishing growth and stability in the Black Sea area, such a lead would increase Turkey's influence in the region and beyond.

For the same reasons, Russia appears to be reluctant to see this happen. The Russian administration is not enthusiastic about the BSEC because, it is explained, it was created on Turkey's initiative. And it has been turned into a tool for the expansion of Ankara's political influence in the region.[6]

Reality Comes Calling

The two-year period from 1991 onwards witnessed a radical change in the relationship between Turkey and the new republics. It was a period of unfulfilled expectations and subsequent disappointments. Increasingly, the new independent states grew irritated at some of the assumptions and presumptions of Turkish officials. The Turkic summit of October 1992 marked a turning point. Central Asian leaders made it clear that they neither desired nor envisaged an exclusive relationship with Turkey, or wished to become Turkey's 'younger brothers'. The republics may have been Turkey's 'dreamland'. But realities were likely to be very different. Soon it became clear that Kazakhs, Uzbeks and others were uncomfortable every time the Turks referred to them as 'the Turkic republics'. And rightly, they feared Turkish cultural imperialism.

Turkey was expected, especially by the US Administration, to act as a power broker and arbiter in the Black Sea, Transcaucasia, and Central Asia. Yet, circumstances have made this hard to achieve. By 1994, the insufficiency of its economic, political, and military instruments was becoming obvious. Moreover, Turkey now meets Russia's increasingly overt resistance. Ankara naively underestimated the functional and operational ties that continued to bind the newly-independent states to Moscow. Turkey exulted too soon and assumed too much by thinking that the establishment of a TV station beaming broadcasts to Central Asia would result in immediate outpourings of pro-Turkish sentiments in the region. It was equally a mistake to think that the Turks would be welcome to play the role of a new 'big brother' to the region's Turkic-speaking peoples.

If Turkey thought it could lead the new states of Central Asia and the Caucasus into a new world, it soon found out that its capacities were not sufficient to undertake this momentous project. Turkey's economic limitations, especially in view of a significant Russian role in the economic survival of the new republics, are an important modifier of its influence.[7]

The situation was exacerbated by the fact that Turkey promised more than it could deliver. As a result Turks have learned that limited capabilities mean limited influence. It has been realized that influence building is a more costly and complex process than had been originally anticipated. Today it has been understood that Turkey cannot cope with all the challenges as well as exploit all the emerging opportunities at the same time. Now that the initial euphoria has waned, it has become apparent that Turkey's relations with this part of the world are not necessarily or automatically going to be as strong as once proclaimed. Now, after this initial euphoria, Central Asian and Transcaucasian Muslim states are more wary of Turkish ambitions. They seek to diversify their sources of foreign policy investment to escape dependence on any one state.[8]

Regional Power Rivalries

Naturally, Turkey is not the only country interested in the region. Other regional powers have shown an equal interest in cultivating ties with the new independent republics.

For this reason Iran and four former Soviet republics, Azerbaijan, Kazakhstan, Russia and Turkmenistan, formed the 'Caspian Sea Co-operation Council' (CSCC). The CSCC appeared to be Iran's response to the Turkish-sponsored 'Black Sea Economic Co-operation' scheme. Trade between Azerbaijan and Iran has expanded in recent years and has not been affected by the changes of leadership in Baku. Iran agreed with Azerbaijan to co-operate in oil production and also with Kazakhstan on transportation of goods between the Caspian Sea ports of the two littoral states. The enclave of Azerbaijan and the eastern Azerbaijan region of Iran signed an economic and cultural agreement to set up a common market at the Jolfa border gate.[9]

In addition to Turkey and Iran, a relative newcomer to the region has now become a significant player. The United States and, to a lesser extent, its Western allies have been most visible in the realm of economics, particularly in oil and gas extraction. Since the dissolution of the Soviet Union, the United States has shown great interest in helping to exploit the oil resources of the Caucasus and Central Asia. Five American companies form the backbone of an international consortium that signed a major deal with the Azerbaijani government for the extraction of oil from three major offshore fields in September 1994. This eight-billion-dollar production-sharing deal, 'contract of the century', was a thirty-year contract that provided for the development of a number of offshore oil fields in Azeri, Chirag and the deep-water part of Guneshli.[10]

Despite increasing relations with the other powers, particularly Turkey and Iran, today the most important factor in the economic development of the new states is the critical importance of their relations with Russia. This has made their relations with one another of secondary importance. For the new states of Central Asia and the Caucasus, Russia remains the main force to be reckoned with. Most of the new republic's trade is still with the Russian Federation. They are still dependent upon Russia for transport facilities to export their primary commodities. Military ties remain close. Their political and economic interdependence, together with Russia's determination not to relinquish control over this vast area, means that relations with no other country can command greater priority for Central Asian and Transcaucasian states.[11]

The general advantage in the current competition between Turkey, Iran and Russia rests with Russia. Today it is clear that residual economic and military interdependence connects the newly-independent states to Russia. Even with diminished economic, political, and military potential Russia is still trying to play the role of a hegemon in the Black Sea-Caspian-Caucasus region. The weight of its past political, military, economic and cultural role is everywhere in evidence. It is obvious that it could take a long time for the Turkic countries, and other former Soviet republics, to surmount these vestiges of colonialism.[12]

Caspian Oil and Pipelines

The Caspian-Caucasus region has received considerable attention over the past eight years, both because of its potential as a source of oil and gas for world energy markets, and because of the environmental consequences of such a development for this ecologically delicate body of water and the near surroundings. The Caspian Sea is an enclosed body of water, roughly 700 miles from north to south and 250 miles across, lying directly between the states of Central Asia and the regions of the Caucasus and the Black Sea. It is a salt-water body, connected to the Black Sea by the Volga and Don rivers, the artificial Volga-Don canal, and the Sea of Azov, a branch of the Black Sea.

Since 1991, oil has become a major symbol of the region's potential. During the Soviet period, the Caspian basin was politically closed to the world oil industry. The hydrocarbon potential of the Caspian basin states had been suspected by outsiders, but remained unconfirmed during the Soviet period. Moscow had been unwilling to invest in oil and natural gas development in the region, and the resource base has remained relatively untouched.

History of Oil Development in the Caspian Region

From antiquity to the mid-nineteenth century, the Caspian-Caucasus was one of the best-known oil regions in the world. Before the arrival of the Russians, petroleum extraction was very primitive. For centuries petroleum traders had to extract the petroleum with rags and buckets. The tsarist government anticipated the modern petroleum industry when it drilled a well for oil at what is now the giant Bibi-Eibat field in 1871. It was the end of the nineteenth century before the area had its first contact with Western capital. The rich oil potential in the region attracted important foreign companies. By the late 1800s, two competing families came to dominate Baku's oil industry. The Nobel brothers arrived on the scene first, to be followed by the French branch of the Rothschild family. In 1898 Russia became the largest oil-producing country, and held this position until 1902. At the beginning of the twentieth century, 50 per cent of the world's oil was produced in the Caspian Sea region.

After the Tsarist Empire ended and a revolutionary government was set up in Russia, the Caspian-Caucasus oil region endured a period of turmoil during the Civil War until the Bolsheviks seized control in Transcaucasia in 1920. When Stalin announced the First Five-Year Plan in 1927, the state assumed full responsibility for central planning, determining the sites, method of extraction, as well as the amount of production, and modes of transport. In 1928, oil production surpassed the former 1901 peak. The next year, seismic-refraction methods were applied in the Groznyi area of the North Caucasus resulting in even sharper increases in oil output. Oil industry grew substantially during the First and Second Five-Year Plans. Most of the production came from the Baku-Caucasus region. During the Second World War, Hitler sought to capture Baku, but his army was defeated before reaching the target. After the war, major discoveries were made in several parts of the Volga-Ural region and in the North Caucasus. Achievements during the Fourth, Fifth, and Sixth Five-Year Plans were impressive. Most of the increase came from the new producing regions. By 1958, the Caspian-Caucasus district accounted for 28 per cent of Soviet production. The growth in oil production continued throughout the following years, and in 1974, Soviet oil production became the largest of any nation in the world.[13]

With the collapse of the Soviet power and the emergence of the new independent republics in Central Asia and the Caucasus, the Caspian Sea basin, with its vast resources, has again become an area of great interest as well as of foreign investment. The oil industry has returned to the region after decades of Soviet isolation, hoping to rebuild the Caspian Sea basin into one of the world's great oil-exporting regions.

Current industry estimates put oil reserves under the depths of the Caspian Sea at up to 13 billion tonnes, more than any region outside the Persian Gulf. The oil potential of this colossal territory is so significant that the analytical centres of the world's large oil and refining companies consider it to be more long-term than the unstable Persian Gulf. Such reserves put the region on a par with Saudi Arabia, and it is expected that the Caspian basin will become the second most important source for oil for the world's industrialized centres in the next century.

Since 1991, the oil rush to the Caspian has been underway. Large oil companies are racing one another, eager to invest billions of dollars to tap unexploited hydrocarbon resources of the Caspian Sea basin. The intensifying struggle for control of the vast resources of the Caspian Sea basin is often cast as a replay of the nineteenth-century 'Great Game'.[14]

There are at present two main topics that need to be investigated: the determination of the Caspian Sea's legal status and the ownership of oil deposits, and oil pipelines and transport facilities. Many issues around these have now become a question of intense international rivalry between the regional powers of Russia, Turkey and Iran. The complex relationship between these three states is reflected in their respective stances regarding the status of the Caspian, and in their rivalry over the future location of the pipelines. Superimposed over the activities of the Caspian states, and the rivalries of the other regional powers, are the global geo-political objectives and economic requirements of the United States, other leading Western countries, China, and the large-scale multi-national corporate organizations.

Legal Status of the Caspian

Oil in the Caspian is to be found on land and on the sea shelf and seabed. Land deposits clearly fall under the ownership of appropriate states and are not the subject of any controversy. A much more contentious situation exists with respect to marine oil and gas resources for the reason that a considerable amount of oil is concentrated in the shallow shelf of the Caspian. Therefore it is important that the legal definition of the sea itself be clear. There has been disagreement over the ownership and control of the Caspian Sea's jurisdiction and economic zones.

There is no clear and direct historical precedent which can help to shed light on a solution to the question. As early as the 1920s, the Ministry of Oil Industry of the USSR had arbitrarily divided the Soviet zone of the Caspian between the Russian Soviet Federated Socialist Republic, Azerbaijan, Kazakhstan and Turkmenistan. At the same time, the Soviet and Iranian sectors were delineated along the so-called 'Astara-Gasankuli' line, but never confirmed by formal governmental agreement. There are, however, a number of treaties in the first instance between Russia and Persia and in the second between the Soviet Union and Iran. Most of these were about freedom of navigation, maritime activity and trade in the Caspian Sea. History certainly testifies to a superior Russian naval and military presence in and around the Caspian, with the Soviet-Iranian treaties of 1921 and 1940 still operating for the benefit of Russia today.[15] However, these treaties cannot be used to define the status of the Caspian, for these documents only applied to navigation and fishing, and not to the problem of the exploitation of mineral resources.[16]

The long-held position of the Russian Federation is that the Caspian is an enclosed body of water with a single eco-system that represents an object of joint use for all the Caspian countries.[17] Accordingly, the Caspian should not be taken to mean an 'open sea' possessing the properties of 'continental shelf' and 'exclusive economic zone'.[18] In other words, the judicial norms relating to exclusive economic zones of coastal states drawn by the 1982 United Nations Convention on Maritime laws are not applicable to the states bordering the Caspian. Russia has adopted the 'enclosed body of water' approach to solve the problem of legal ownership rights, which envisaged the use of a 20-mile maritime zone. The sovereignty of the riparian states not only covers the maritime zone but stretches upwards to include the airspace directly above it and downwards to the seabed and all the substances which are found on it and beneath it. Another main point in the Russian position concerns an exclusive economic zone of a further 20 miles. In this zone the riparian states have sovereign rights over the preservation of natural resources, covering the seabed and the bowels of the earth beneath the seabed. In the exclusive economic zone, all states, both riparian and those not having an outlet to the sea, enjoy and have the use of freedom of navigation and flight, the laying of cables or pipelines, and other activities of maritime usage as defined by International Law. The remaining central part of the Caspian beyond the 40-mile limit, made up from territorial waters and exclusive economic zone, is the common property of all the Caspian states. This central area is to be placed under the common control and regulation, with all the decisions concerning the usage of this zone requiring the agreement of all the Caspian states.[19]

The Azerbaijani position differs from that of the Russian Federation in some important aspects. Azerbaijan advocates the concept of the Caspian being a 'border lake' and calls for the division of the Caspian into five state sectors. Accordingly, each sector would be considered and categorized as 'territorial waters' belonging to the state concerned. If this position were accepted the richest oil-bearing areas would be given to Azerbaijan and Kazakhstan who support this position. The 'border lake' proposal is based on current international practice with regard to the Great Lakes between the USA and Canada, and Lake Chad between Nigeria, Niger, Chad and Cameroon. The Azerbaijani proposal implies that each riparian state in its own sector should have exclusive sovereign right over biological resources, water surface, navigation, exploitation of the seabed, beneath the seabed and other activities in conformity with legislation of the riparian state. Azerbaijan is proposing another alternative to the question of the legal status of the Caspian, the concept of an 'open sea'. This proposal is based upon the United Nation's Convention on the Law of the Sea 1982, which came into force on 16 November 1994. According to this each state is to have a 12-mile territorial water limit.[20]

Although Kazakhstan and Azerbaijan are allies over the status of the Caspian, there are some differences in their respective positions. Kazakhstan's position is not strictly in line with the 'border lake' or 'open sea' variants. Instead, Kazakhstan has come forward with another proposal, which envisages the Caspian being subdivided into economic zones in accordance with a central line, which is equidistant from points on opposing shorelines.[21] Generally speaking the approach of Turkmenistan has supported the Russian position. Accordingly, the Caspian is regarded as unique, an area where current practice and norms cannot apply. Each state should have its own border and fishing zone, as well as a defined section of the shelf to exploit the mineral resources. The width of this zone should be determined by consultation with all the riparian states. The remaining part of the Caspian should be determined by the principle of joint exploitation.[22]

The other Caspian state, Iran, has been maintaining a reserved position with regard to the legal status of the Caspian. Iran is not very enthusiastic about national division of the Caspian. To a certain extent, the positions of Russia and Iran could be brought closer by the mutual threat of international oil companies penetrating the Caspian region. Tehran's exclusion from the September 1994 'contract of the century' has made Iran a natural ally of Russia on the issue of joint ownership of the Caspian's resources.[23]

In summary, there are broadly two main positions for deciding the legal status of the Caspian. Russia and Iran formally treat the Caspian as a giant lake, which represents an object of joint use for all the Caspian states. Azerbaijan and Kazakhstan treat the Caspian as a sea, which should be divided into sectors and developed separately.

Pipelines

The issue of oil and gas transportation from the Caspian region has now become one of intense international rivalry between the regional powers of Russia, Turkey and Iran. A number of agreements were signed within the last four years concerning hydrocarbon extraction from the Caspian Sea off the coast of Azerbaijan, and the transportation of oil. The first and the most important one was the so-called 'contract of the century', signed on 20 September, 1994, in Baku, between a consortium of oil companies led by the British Petroleum Company and the Azerbaijani state oil company, SOCAR. This is a thirty-year contract that calls for the production of 80,000 barrels per day early next century.

Political symbols come in many forms in the Caspian, but few are quite so compelling as oil and gas pipelines. The choice of an export route is fraught with political and economic problems. The project has been complicated by long-term ethnic hatreds, massive cost overruns and lasting Cold War rivalries. The question of which route to use for Caspian's considerable reserves has inspired a high-stakes tug-of-war among the countries of the region. The 'contract of the century' antagonized Moscow and Ankara, because two main alternative routes have been promoted by these two states.

Central to the Russian-Chechen conflict throughout the 1990s has been the contest to control the Caspian oil deposits. The embattled city of Groznyi, the Chechen capital, occupies a strategic access point. The key Russian-controlled Caspian oil pipeline passes through Groznyi and Chechnya from Baku and Novorrossisk, and Moscow plans to build a new pipeline through Dagestan to the east, bypassing Chechnya.[24] At present, the only operational oil export route follows the line Baku-Groznyi-Tikhoretsk-Novorrossisk, with a possibility of bypassing Chechnya to the east and joining the Atyray-Novorrossisk pipeline at Komsomolsky. On 2 November 1999, the Caspian Pipeline Consortium[25] announced that the 932-mile Caspian Pipeline project will start in late November 1999. This pipeline is expected to be ready for 2001 and will carry crude oil from the huge Tengiz field in Kazakhstan to a new export terminal near Russia's Black Sea port of Novorrossisk. The cost of the pipeline has been put at 2.3 billion dollars.[26] Oil exports from this route are dependent on tanker transportation via the Turkish Straits.

Turkey is actively campaigning against the Russian-proposed pipeline. The reason for this is probably more related to Turkey's geopolitical calculations than it is to expected hard currency in royalties. If the new independent republics of Azerbaijan and Kazakhstan had to rely solely on the Russian pipeline, Ankara's hopes for mproved ties with these states would be drastically frustrated. The Turkish government argues that the oil storage capacity at Novorrossisk is not sufficient to handle enormous amounts of Russian, Kazakh and Azeri crude oil. It has also suggested that the existing Russian pipeline network should be upgraded or replaced to cope with the expected increase in the output.

As the main alternative to the Russian pipeline, Turkey is actively promoting its own pipeline option, the Caspian-Mediterranean Pipeline. This pipeline too foresees the transfer of Kazakh oil to Baku, either by a pipeline through Russian Caucasus or by a pipeline to be laid underwater crossing from the Kazakh Caspian shores to Baku. From Baku, the combined Azeri and Kazakh oil would be carried by a Turkish pipeline through Georgia, Armenia or Iran to Turkey's Mediterranean oil terminal at Ceyhan. The main shortcoming of the Turkish proposal is related to the question of expenditure. The cost of building a pipeline through the territory of Georgia and Turkey to the Turkish seaport on the Mediterranean will take about 2.9 billion dollars.

The most recent development in the Caspian energy jigsaw is the pipeline agreement signed in November 1999, during the summit of the Organization for Security and Cooperation in Europe, by the presidents of Azerbaijan, Georgia, Turkey and Kazakhstan. This agreement calls for the project of building the pipeline to be completed by 2004.[27] Although this is considered a serious setback for Moscow and a success for US-backed Turkey, the major Western power companies are still unprepared to make a final decision to invest in this project. There are no guarantees that the project, estimated to cost at least 2.4 billion US dollars, will be profitable. Officials at BP-Amoco, the main Western oil company working in Caspian oil fields, have said that early estimates of massive oil reserves in the region may have been over-stated. Azerbaijan currently produces about 100,000 barrels of oil a day, roughly one-tenth of the one million barrels a day that would make the project viable.[28] Therefore, it appears that this political victory may be an interesting example of elegant diplomacy with little application.

Partly in order to increase the appeal of the Turkish pipeline proposal and partly due to a genuine apprehension that the increased use of Novorrossisk would bring about heavy tanker traffic through the Turkish Straits, Ankara decided to impose some restrictions on the use of the Straits waterway by oil tankers. The rules governing navigation in the Straits were originally set out in the Montreux Convention of 1936. The Convention guarantees free passage in peacetime for vessels of any country, carrying any cargo. When the Montreux Convention was signed, however, only a few hundred ships passed through the Straits. Now an estimated 50,000 ships use it annually. The average tonnage of ships is 19 times more than it was back then. The Straits are a zigzagging passage whose blind turns, four strong currents, twelve changes of course, combined with fog, and difficult weather conditions have led to hundreds of accidents over recent years. The new regulations, introduced by Turkey in 1994, require that all vessels entering the Straits take part in the Turkish reporting system. According to this, masters use a qualified pilot, and all ships over 200 metres long navigate the area in daylight. Other countries, notably Russia and Greece, say the new regulations break international law.[29]

Many in the West now hold the opinion that because of the many tensions in the region, instead of concentrating on building one pipeline, several pipelines should be built, including a route through Iran. Currently, US-Iranian antagonism makes the Iranian route seem rather difficult, yet given the commercial realities, any political opening could shift the terms of the pipeline question very quickly. Political obstacles have started to matter less, especially after the French company Total SA had signed a two-billion-dollar gas exploration deal with Iran in 1997. After the Total SA deal, France's Elf Aquitaine and Canada's Bow Valley Energy Ltd. made a 300-million-dollar deal to develop an offshore oil field. Recently, the US State Department was 'deeply disappointed and much concerned' by an 800-million-dollar agreement between Royal Dutch/Shell and the Iranian National Oil Company to develop two Iranian oil fields.[30]

Conclusion

Looking back over these developments, some observers concluded that the hope of Turkish governments playing a leading role in the regions of the Black Sea and the Caucasus, and acting as an important promoter of Western interests, had effectively evaporated. The degree of disappointment obviously depended on the scope of the original expectation. Turkey has not turned out to be a regional superpower. But then Turkey's cautious diplomats could reasonably claim that they never set out to perform such an ambitious role.

Turkey had actually never been in a position to step into Russia's shoes. Turkey's inflation rate, its record on democracy and human rights, the Kurdish uprising going on in the south-east, and the fast-increasing alienation of the secular ruling elite from the religious majority population have all hampered Ankara's attempts to balance Russian influence in the region. Turkey's adoption of slogans about the region from the Adriatic to the Great Wall of China was not only provocative but also unrealistic.

Turkish policy had certainly taken some hard knocks. On the other hand, it was hard to blame the policy-makers in Ankara for all these setbacks. No amount of clever diplomacy by Turkey could have rescued the situation and created a different outcome. In these circumstances, it can at least be argued that Turkey had conducted a reasonably successful damage-limitation exercise. Obviously, Turkey's future policies in the region will be affected by the moves made by other players, and the general political evolution of the region.

Russia remained the dominant power in the area. Stability has been maintained, but only through the continuation of autocratic regimes, dependent on the old Soviet security and economic structures. In the long run, the best hope for the people of this region is that Russian domination might be reduced through the regional countries developing stronger economic links with the West. In this strategy, Turkey would almost certainly be an important element.

Today we are witnessing a return to a multipolar competition for advantage in the region, reminiscent of that which took place in the seventeenth and eighteenth centuries. In addition to Turkey, Russia and Iran constitute the immediate strategic triad. However, unlike their past rivalry, that of today's is cooperative as well as competitive. They all share an interest in trade and the development of natural gas and oil resources and pipelines. All three would also like to encourage foreign investment to help the development of a regional infrastructure of railroads and communications.

Above all regional stability is the most important common interest sought by all the interested parties. The prevention and mediation of regional conflicts seems to be high on the agenda of the three powers. All parties appear to understand the importance of dampening the nationalism of assertive ethnic minorities of fundamentalist groupings, whether they are Azeris, Chechens, Kurds, or religious movements in Tajikistan.

Notes

1   B. Gökay and R. Langhorne, *Turkey and the New States of the Caucasus and Central Asia*, London: HMSO, 1996, pp.1–3.

2   P. M. Carley, 'Turkey and Central Asia', in A. Z. Rubinstein and O. M. Smolansky (eds), *Regional Power Rivalries in the New Eurasia*, New York: M.E. Sharpe, 1995, pp.193–195.

3   B. Gökay and R. Langhorne, *Turkey and the New States of the Caucasus and Central Asia*, London: HMSO, 1996, pp.18–19; P.J Robins, 'Avoiding the Question', in H.J. Barkey (ed), *Reluctant Neighbour*, Washington, D.C.: US Institute of Peace Press, 1996, pp.184–187.

4   B. Gökay and R. Langhorne, *Turkey and the New States of the Caucasus and Central Asia*, London: HMSO, 1996, pp.19–20.

5   ibid.

6   G. S. Harris, 'The Russian Federation and Turkey', in A. Z. Rubinstein and O. M. Smolansky (eds), *Regional Power Rivalries in the New Eurasia*, New York: M.E. Sharpe, 1995, pp.19–20, 21.

7   P. Robins, 'Turkey's Ostpolitik. Relations with the Central Asian States', in D. Menashri (ed), *Central Asia Meets the Middle East*, London: Frank Cass, 1998, pp.129–149.

8   B. Gökay and R. Langhorne, *Turkey and the New States of the Caucasus and Central Asia*, London: HMSO, 1996, pp.32–33.

9   Ibid., p.21.

10   B. Gökay, 'Caspian Uncertainties: Regional Rivalries and Pipelines', *Perceptions,
     Journal of International Relations*, March-May 1998, Vol. 3, No.1, pp.53–54.

11   G. S. Harris, 'The Russian Federation and Turkey', in A. Z. Rubinstein and
     O. M. Smolansky (eds), *Regional Power Rivalries in the New Eurasia*, New York:
     M.E. Sharpe, 1995, pp.3–25.

12   ibid., pp.26–30; P. Robins, 'Avoiding the Question', in H.J. Barkey (ed), *Reluctant
     Neighbour*, Washington, D.C.: US Institute of Peace Press, 1996, pp.187–190.

13   B. Gökay, 'History of Oil Development in the Caspian Basin', in M.
     Croissant and B. Aras (eds), *Oil and Geopolitics in the Caspian Sea Region*, West-
     port: Praeger, 1999.

14   B. Gökay, 'Caspian Uncertainties: Regional Rivalries and Pipelines', *Perceptions,
     Journal of International Relations*, March-May 1998, Vol. 3, No.1, pp.49–66.

15   *Bolshaya Sovetskaya Entsiklopediya*, Vol. 43, 2nd edition, to press 13 August 1956,
     p.443.

16   A. Shoumikhin, 'Developing Caspian Oil: Between Conflict and Cooperation',
     Comparative Strategy, October-December 1997, Vol.16, 4, p.337; C. Blandy, *The
     Caspian: A Sea of Troubles*, Conflict Studies Research Center, September 1997, p.6.

17   Stephen Blank, 'Russia's Real Drive to the South', *Orbis*, Vol. 39, Summer
     1995, pp.369–370.

18   Kamilzhan Kalandarov, *Nezavisimaya Gazeta*, 4 June 1997, p.5.

19   C. Blandy, *The Caspian: A Sea of Troubles*, Conflict Studies Research Center,
     September 1997, pp.7–8.

20   Stephen Blank, 'Russia's Real Drive to the South', *Orbis*, Vol. 39, Summer
     1995, p.370.

21   B. Gökay, 'Caspian Uncertainties: Regional Rivalries and Pipelines', *Perceptions,
     Journal of International Relations*, March-May 1998, Vol. 3, No.1, pp.57–58.

22   C. Blandy, *The Caspian: A Sea of Troubles*, Conflict Studies Research Center,
     September 1997, p.14.

23   ibid., p.18.

24   P. Siren, 'The Battle for Groznyi: The Russian Invasion of Chechnya,
     December 1994-December 1996', in B. Fowkes (ed), *Russia and Chechnya: The
     Permanent Crisis*, London: Macmillan, 1998, pp.101–104.

25   Equity interests in the Caspian Pipeline Consortium are as follows: Russia, 24
     per cent; Kazakhstan, 19 per cent; Oman, seven per cent; Chevron, 15 per
     cent; Lukarco BV, 12.5 per cent; Rosneft-Shell Caspian Ventures Ltd., 7.5
     per cent; Mobil Caspian Pipeline Company, 7.5 per cent; Agip International,
     two per cent; BG Overseas Holdings Ltd., two per cent; Kazakhstan Pipeline
     ventures Llc., 1.75 per cent; and Oryx Caspian Pipeline Llc., 1.75 per cent.

26   *Reuters*, Moscow, 2 November 1999.

27   *The Independent*, 19 November 1999, p.15.

28   *Itar-Tass* via NewsEdge Corporation, Washington, 17 December 1999.

29   B. Gökay, 'Caspian Uncertainties: Regional Rivalries and Pipelines', *Perceptions,
     Journal of International Relations*, March-May 1998, Vol. 3, No.1, pp.59–61.

30   *Reuters*, Washington, 15 November 1999.

CHAPTER THREE

Black Sea Economic Cooperation (BSEC) and Turkey : Extending European Integration to the East?

Tunç Aybak

Given the existence of fragile and conflict-ridden political circumstances in the Black Sea area, the initiation and the following institutionalization of the Black Sea Economic Cooperation (BSEC) has been an important achievement. In fact, with the recent ratification of its Charter in the national parliaments of the Black Sea Countries, the BSEC has completed its formative phase and consolidated its legal status as a proper regional organization. This has recently transformed the political initiative of the Istanbul Summit into its new phase with legally binding obligations for the member states.[1]

The aim of this chapter is to assess the dynamics of regional cooperation in the Black Sea region, as opposed to the patterns of conflicts, and to investigate whether the regional cooperation process can provide a stable systemic environment for peaceful systemic change and facilitate the enlargement of the EU to the Black Sea region. I will try to answer the following questions: Under what circumstances has the BSEC emerged? What were the origins of and motivations behind the formation of the BSEC? What are the emerging characteristics of the BSEC as a regional organization? Which countries are capable of forming the core of regional cooperation? What are the key regional issues of interdependence? What is the significance of the BSEC for the EU enlargement? Finally I will conclude the chapter with some prospect analysis.

The Origins, Motivations and Objectives of the BSEC

The idea of the Black Sea Economic Cooperation was conceived by a senior Turkish diplomat, Sükrü Elekdağ and adopted by the then President Turgut Ozal in 1990. It had been originally proposed by Turkey to Bulgaria,

Romania and the Soviet Union. Initial preparatory meetings took place in December 1990 in Ankara, delegations from Bulgaria, the Soviet Union and Romania participated and prepared the agenda for cooperation.[2] The project was in line with Gorbhachev's vision of a 'Common European House' and had been conceived before the dismantling of the Soviet Union. But as a result of the disintegration of the Soviet Union negotiations lapsed. According to *Pravda*, the new economic regional cooperation was put forward as a 'common economic space of Bulgaria, Romania, USSR and Turkey' but the idea seemed to have no chance of success after the break up of the Soviet Union. A series of study meetings took place in Bucharest in March 1991, in Sofia in April 1991 and in Moscow in July 1991. However, *Pravda* subsequently credited Turkish diplomats with the survival of the idea stressing that their tenacity and persistence resulted in their proposal's eventual acceptance by the foreign ministers of Azerbaijan, Armenia, Bulgaria, Georgia, Moldova and Russia and Turkey in 1992. *Izvestia* quoted the then President Özal referring to Black Sea regional cooperation as part of a process of 'the creation of a new model of regional organization in which the traditional confrontation between the East and the West is being replaced by an increasing rapprochement between countries.' Özal also emphasized that the objective of this regional cooperation 'is to create favourable conditions for a free movement of people, capital and goods' and to accelerate and simplify the transition of former socialist countries to a free market economy.[3] Finally in line with the consensus reached in Moscow, the Heads of 11 states and governments (Albania, Armenia, Azerbaijan, Bulgaria, Georgia, Greece, Moldova, Romania, Russia, Turkey and Ukraine) met in Istanbul in June 1992 to sign a draft framework providing the objectives and principles of the Black Sea Economic Cooperation (BSEC).[4]

In order to understand the background characteristics of and the political motivations behind the Black Sea Regional Cooperation initiative, it is worth explaining the circumstances under which it emerged. The application for EC membership in 1987 and the instigation of the BSEC in 1992 was due to the determination of Turkish foreign policy makers to integrate Turkey fully into the global economy as well as their desire for modernization and transformation from inward-looking to outward-looking economic policies. The end of the Cold War economic trends, the success of the European Community and the Single European Market, and structural changes in the world economy all, in a way, pressed Turkey towards expanded collaboration within regions.

In some circles, it was suggested that the BSEC stemmed from Turkey's disappointment with the European Community's negative response to its application bid for full membership. In other words, BSEC was conceptualized as an alternative regional initiative to European integration. In fact, when one looks at the general trends since the foundation of the Turkish Republic, BSEC can be seen as another natural stepping stone in Turkey's advance towards European integration. From this perspective, the BSEC is designed to maintain continuity between the periphery and the core of the European integration project. Indeed, the Bosphorus Declaration confirmed that BSEC's main aim is to achieve 'a better commercial, financial and legal environment to improve and boost the economy of the region and help it integrate into the European and World Economy.' In a way, BSEC was a part and parcel of Turkey's overall Europeanization strategy to cope with the effects of globalization and regionalization in the post-Cold War period. As one senior diplomat stated, 'In fact since the beginning of the process, the Black Sea Economic Cooperation has been conceived and elaborated as an integral part of Europe's new architecture' and 'as an instrument directed to achieve higher degree of integration to the European and World Economy. It has never been considered as an alternative to any existing groups in Europe.'[5] Having sensed that its Cold War military assets were diminishing, Turkey wanted to situate itself at the centre of subregional cooperation. It aimed to avoid marginalization from European integration. The pull effects of the dynamics of European integration and the process of enlargement compelled Turkey towards regionalization within an Pan-European context. The European character of the Black Sea Regional Cooperation project was reinforced by the references made to the Conference on Security and Cooperation in Europe. The European character of the BSEC was reflected in Article VII of the Declaration which stipulates 'their cooperation will be developed in a manner not contravening their obligations and not preventing the promotion of the relations of the Participating States with third parties, including international organizations as well as the EC and the cooperation within the regional initiative.'[6] The establishment of the BSEC was also welcomed by the European Parliament in the form of a resolution which stated that cooperation would promote stability in the region and foster the development of relations between the states signatory to the BSEC agreement.[7]

The Characteristics of BSEC

Decision Making Structure

BSEC was originally established as a forum or process. It lacked the legal status of a regional organization. With the recent completion of the ratification process of the Charter of the Organization by the member states, initiated in the Yalta Summit in June 1998, BSEC finally acquired its official regional organization status in May 1999.[8] As a result of the ratification of the Charter, the formative stage of BSEC has come to an end. This has transformed the Black Sea Economic Cooperation process into a proper organization. However, its declared objectives must be assessed against its structural characteristics and achievements.

The BSEC is strictly an intergovernmental regional organization. The highest decision-making organ of the BSEC is the Council of the Ministers of Foreign Affairs which meets bi-annually in April and October. (So far there have been 13 meetings.) The Council decides on all issues pertaining to the functioning of the BSEC and considers all matters submitted by the Subsidiary Organs. It can adopt resolutions, decisions, or recommendations. While resolutions are only adopted by unanimity, decisions and recommendations can be adopted by a two-thirds majority vote. The method of consensus is used on substantive issues which include: admission of new members to the BSEC; granting and extending of observer status to third countries and international organizations; creation of new organs of the BSEC; defining, modifying and terminating the mandates of subsidiary organs; adoption and modification of the rules of procedure; financial commitments affecting all participating states. All Participating States should abide by the resolutions on substantive issues. On specific issues pertaining to technical matters or the functioning of the BSEC the Council of Ministers also adopts decisions by two-thirds majority vote. All participating states which vote in favour of a decision have to abide by the provisions of that decision if adopted.[9] Apart from the council of ministers, the Heads of States have had summit meetings. There have been four summits so far.

The bulk of the BSEC's work is being carried out by 20 different subsidiary bodies (standing working groups). Each subsidiary body has a specific mandate endorsed and assigned by the Council of Ministers. Since the foundation of the BSEC several permanent expert working groups and six ad hoc working groups have been established. These groups are assigned to explore different avenues for regional cooperation on specific issues such as transport, energy, banking and finance, trade and industrial cooperation, exchange of statistical data and economic information, agriculture, environmental protection, health care and pharmaceutics, cooperation in science and technology, legislative information, cooperation and tourism and communications. Working groups form their own agendas and adopt their rules of procedure. The working groups play an important role in the decision-making process. Since the foundation of the BSEC there have been over 100 meetings of experts from the BSEC states. The working groups, after a series of sessions and the reconciliation of divergent views, produce recommendations and prepare draft documents for the deliberation of Senior Officials' meetings.

The working style of the decision attracted criticism in several respects: the competencies of the working groups tend to overlap; mandates of the working groups were not clearly defined; some member states have proved reluctant to bear the cost of hosting meetings. Meetings were usually held at junior level. These groups were either ill prepared or lacked the competence to make final decisions. In the light of these criticisms, in 1996, the Foreign Ministers decided to reform the decision making structure by reducing the number of working groups and upgrading the level of the Senior Officials' meetings.[10]

BSEC is a flexible organization and its decision-making style is not limited by rigid rules. Under Article 17, it is specified that the foreign ministers of the member states should meet regularly to assess developments and set new goals as necessary. The member states agreed to avoid the over-bureaucratization of the organization and the rigidity of established rules. In this sense it is not a self-limiting but an open-ended process with a piecemeal approach to the low politics issues of a technical nature. Given that the BSEC consists of 11 countries with different national interests, political and economic structures, this piecemeal approach has advantages over strictly defined rules.

Membership

Even though the BSEC is built around the Black Sea as an organizing principle, its membership is not strictly limited to states with borders on the Black Sea. For instance, Azerbaijan, Armenia, Albania, Greece and Moldova have no borders on the Black Sea. As the Summit Declaration of 1992 provides, the BSEC 'is open for the participation of other interested states recognizing the provisions of this document'. Since 1995, the Former Republic of Yugoslavia and the Islamic Republic of Iran have applied for full membership. Apart from full membership, observer status is granted. At present, Austria, Egypt, France, Germany, Israel, Italy, Poland, Slovak Republic and Tunisia have observer status. The membership of the BSEC is very diverse and broad. The divergent interests and the wide scope of its geographical area constitutes an impediment to the widening of regional cooperation. Despite the fact the BSEC is an open entity, the enlargement of the BSEC is far from being a contentious issue.

While some members, like Russia, favour a more open approach, Romania, Bulgaria and Turkey are in principle against the further enlargement that would slow down the deepening of the cooperation process amongst the existing members. National interests are also reflected in the issue of enlargement. For instance, while Greece vetoed the membership of the Former State of Yugoslavia, Turkey was against the membership of the Republic of Cyprus.[11]

Bottom-up activities in the Black Sea

BSEC has been initiated at the state level. Therefore, the region-building project was imposed from above by state elites and interstate regional cooperation has been the main characteristic of the BSEC. In addition to the top-down approach there have also been bottom-up activities. Not only the governments but also organizations, enterprises and firms of third countries are allowed to participate in the BSEC structures as observers. At present, 16 NGOs have observer status. These include: Black Sea Press, Regional Energy Working Group, Balkan Centre for Small and Medium Enterprises, Black Sea Region Association of Ship Builders and Ship Repairers, Black Sea Universities Network, Turkish Marine Environment Protection Association, Black Sea International Shipowners Association, Euro-Mediterranean Trade, Distribution and Services Initiative, Russian Maritime Register of Shipping, Forum of Architects of the Black Sea Region. As the emergence of regional networks of non-governmental activities indicate, there seems to be an embryonic regional civil society in the making. In time, it is expected that a genuine regional civil society may develop in the Black Sea area.

Since the establishment of the BSEC, there have been increasing activities at the local government level. The first Mayors' Conference of the Capitals of Black Sea Countries took place in Ankara in 1993. The Conference has convened in different Black Sea capitals since 1993. The round table of the Black Sea Capitals' Governors and Mayors held its first meeting in 1994 in Istanbul and in 1995 in Kiev. At the round table meetings, the heads of city administrations discussed a wide range of issues and covered problems such as city transportation, housing, communal services, protecting the environment and municipal democracy. The International Black Sea Club, based in Varna, was also founded in 1992. The members include the representatives of the cities of Burgas, Varna, Ilichevsk, Konstanza, Nikolaev, Odessa, Pireaus, Thessaloniki, Taganrog and Kherson. The aim of the Club is to provide a forum for multilateral and bilateral cooperation and joint activities among the cities of the Black Sea countries.[12]

The establishment of the Parliamentary Assembly of the BSEC (PABSEC) in 1993 has added another dimension to regional cooperation. Its aim is to consolidate parliamentary democracy in the participating states. More specifically, the PABSEC aims to provide the legal ground for the realization of the principles and goals of the BSEC; to promote the rule of law and human rights. The highest PABSEC body is the General Assembly of representatives of the national parliaments. They meet twice a year.[13] The PABSEC is not an integral part of the BSEC structures but its activities are coordinated with the BSEC. Even though its activities are limited and it has a low profile, the annual meetings provide a platform within which the Black Sea Parliamentarians can develop transnational links and exchange opinions in order to learn from one another's democratization experiences.

As the membership structure and activities suggest, the BSEC is a comprehensive and multilayered regional organization. Even though it is the product of top-down state initiatives, the bottom-up regional activities are also gaining ground. The top-down and bottom-up activities are not mutually exclusive as the governments facilitate and encourage the non-governmental activities and transactions.

Key Issues and Regional Interdependence

Trade and Investment

The dynamic role of the regional business associations is seen as instrumental in transforming the region into a regional trade and investment area. Towards this goal the Black Sea Business Council, representing the interests of the private sector as well as governments, was established. The Business Council is designed to promote joint ventures, private business, multilateral, bilateral and country-specific investment projects through international financial institutions. There are also a number of bilateral business association councils set up between Turkey and the other Black Sea countries.[14] The first BSEC business forum took place in Bucharest in April 1996 and others followed. In 1997, there were nearly three hundred businesses represented and meetings took place between them to explore joint ventures and business potential. In addition, several Black Sea International Fairs were organized in different Black Sea countries. These activities were not limited to the Black Sea region but also extended to potential partners from other countries. A conference for Business Opportunities was held in 1993 in Tampa, Florida with the aim of attracting businessmen and investors to the BSEC area.[15] Two inter-regional business conferences between BSEC and Mercosur took place in Kyiv in 1997 and in Buenos Aires in 1998.[16]

The economic character of the BSEC is particularly marked compared to other subregional cooperation projects in Europe.[17] The BSEC assigns particular importance to the liberalization of the regional economy. In 1997, the Council of Ministers adopted a Declaration of Intent to move towards a Black Sea free trade area.[18] In light of this resolution the Ministers endorsed a Plan of Action to explore the possibilities and to produce some recommendations towards the formation of a regional free trade zone. The Plan of Action developed out of the ensuing series of meetings of Working Groups on trade and industrial development, in February in Yerevan and in Istanbul in April 1998. The Plan includes short, medium and long-term measures. The creation of a system of bilateral agreements to establish the basis of free trade between the BSEC members; mechanisms for the facilitation of transborder trade and coastal free trade area zones are put forward as short-term measures. In the medium term, the eventual accession of members of the BSEC to the World Trade Organization as full members; gradual harmonization of customs and trade regulations; conclusion of bilateral agreements between them to attract foreign investment; and the abolition of dual taxation are outlined as necessary to create a conducive environment for the creation of a regional free trade area. Finally, the Plan stipulates long-term measures including the gradual lowering of tariffs and non-tariff barriers in industrial products; the gradual liberalization of trade in agricultural products; and bringing national legislation in line with the Uruguay Round of GATT in trade and measures related to services; mutual recognition of certificates of conformity and harmonization of the applied standards in trade. Given the low level of intra regional trade activities, this is a tall order as the trade barriers are low in some countries and extremely high in others.[19] However, it provides a blueprint for trade liberalization in the region.

The creation of regional free trade remains a difficult task. This issue also directly concerns the EU's bilateral links with some regional countries. In particular, Greece's full membership and Turkey's customs union agreement with the EU prevents them from participating in regional free trade agreements with third parties. In principle, the EU accepts a general trade liberalization provided that this is compatible with the multilateral trade regime and takes into account their existing trade commitments to the EU.[20] Approval of the proposed action plan by the working group on trade liberalization issues has been slow to materialize. In a recent meeting, the parties emphasized that before any approval could be given further consultations are needed with the European Commission. The Greek Government also expressed its reservations stating that 'Greece will

participate in the implementation of the Plan of Action for the establishment of the BSEC free trade area to the extent that this does not contradict the commitments and obligations deriving from its full membership of
the EU'. [21] The same condition normally applies to Turkey.

Other organizations concerned with trade issues have also been active in
the promotion of trade liberalization in the Black Sea area. In particular,
the Commission of the EU, OECD and WTO representatives helped to
organize seminars and discussions on trade liberalization and harmonization of the trade regimes of the BSEC countries. For instance, a seminar
organized by the BSEC and European Commission workshop discussed
measures to facilitate the cross-border trade.[22] An OECD meeting on trade
liberalization and foreign investment regimes in BSEC countries took place
in 1996. The participants discussed macroeconomic policies and structural
reforms in the Black Sea area. Finally, a seminar on trade legislation
arranged by BSEC, the Central European Initiative and WTO, took place
in Kyiv, in 1997. The representatives of these organizations and the BSEC
members discussed the problems arising from the integration of the national
economies into the global trade regime in the light of GATT and Uruguay
Round regulations. The role of small and medium-sized enterprises in the
formation of an active regional economy was emphasized in a meeting held
in Istanbul where representatives of governmental (United Nations
Economics Section) and non-governmental organizations took part.[23]

Despite the free trade discussions within the BSEC, WTO seems to be
a more appropriate framework within which to facilitate the liberalization
of regional trade amongst the BSEC countries. Only Bulgaria, Greece,
Romania and Turkey are full members of the WTO while the other countries have either applied for full membership or are at various stages of the
accession towards the full membership. Full membership of the WTO
would also lay the foundations for multilateral trade and facilitate in the
transition to a regional free trade environment. Except for Greece and
Turkey all other BSEC countries are in transition to a full market
economy. According to a World Bank survey, national economies of the
BSEC countries are far from trade liberalization (particularly Russia,
Ukraine, Azerbaijan, Georgia and Armenia).[24]

Given that the majority of countries are transition economies, foreign
direct investment is needed to promote the regional economy. Since the
early 1990s, there has been some increase in the flow of foreign investment to the Black Sea region. However, this remains at a modest level.[25]
Several factors determine the flow of direct investment into the region
from the OECD countries. These include: the level of the privatization

process, the progress of liberalization in the national economies, the trade linkages of the BSEC countries, as well as the availability of low-cost labour.[26] Despite the relaxation in the legislation concerning foreign investment in the national economies, bureaucratic traditions and other obstacles discourage the investors.[27] Since the collapse of the Cold War there has also been some increase in intra-regional investment flows. Russia leads in investments by the BSEC countries in the Black Sea region followed by Turkey and Greece.[28]

The decision to establish the Black Sea Trade and Development Bank in 1994 was an important step towards generating regional financial resources for investment. The aim of BSTD, located in Thessaloniki in Greece, is to make an effective contribution to the transition process of the member states towards the economic welfare of the region and to finance and promote regional projects, trade activities, investment and development programmes and other banking services for the public and private sectors in the member states of the BSEC. The BSTD benefits from a subscribed capital of one billion Special Drawing Rights (1.35 billion in dollar terms) as the bank's founding capital.[29] However, due to the long national ratification processes and the difficulties in accumulating financial reserves, the operationalization of the Bank has been a slow process. In June 1999, the BSTD finally started its financial operations. Its first lending operation was to provide $12 million to build a gas compressor station in Ukraine for a Trans-Balkan gas pipeline project. This will increase the capacity of the gas pipeline from Russia to Turkey via Ukraine, Moldova, Romania and Bulgaria. It will be implemented by a joint venture company set up by Ukrainian, Turkish and Russian firms. The total cost of the project will amount to $78 million. The project is also financed by the European Bank for Reconstruction and Development (EBRD). This leads us to another key regional issue which is the management of energy resources.

Energy

Energy is another issue that is high on the agenda of the BSEC. Available resources of oil and natural gas are very rich and concentrated in the Caspian Sea area. All the countries of the Black Sea, except Russia and Azerbaijan which have access to energy resources in the Caspian Sea, are heavily dependent on external energy resources. Current industry estimates place the Caspian Oil reserves as being more than those of any other region outside the Persian Gulf. Apart from oil, 27 per cent of the world's natural gas reserves lie in the Caspian region. The management of interdependence in energy issues constitutes the most challenging task in the activities of the BSEC. Demand for energy, with the growing regional economies, is constantly increasing. Some regional states, particularly Ukraine, are heavily dependent on obsolete and dangerous nuclear stations. (For instance, 60 out of 500 nuclear stations operating in the Black Sea area discharge their nuclear waste into the Black Sea.) There are at least 14 redundant nuclear stations in Ukraine. Environmental issues and energy are, increasingly and closely, linked to the management of regional interdependence.

Within the BSEC, energy issues are discussed at a purely technical level while parties are reluctant to discuss the political aspects of, what are, highly contentious energy issues.[30] At the technical level, the Working Group on Energy has held several meetings to discuss energy issues surrounding the Black Sea. These meetings provide an important platform for an exchange of opinions on the state of affairs between those who are dependent on external energy resources and those who are energy exporters. For instance, in the second meeting of the Working Group in Energy, in Athens in 1997, an ad hoc group of experts was formed with the task of producing a feasibility study on the construction of a regional electricity network which in turn produced a study on the interconnection of electric power systems among the BSEC countries. Following this study, a 'Memorandum on Cooperation of the BSEC Participating States in the Field of Electric Power Industry' was signed by the respective Ministers of Energy. Accordingly a Steering Committee was set up to supervise activities related to the project and report on progress to the Working Group on Energy. The energy and electric consumption per capita in the Black Sea countries is growing rapidly. In this sense, this project is the first major regional collaboration towards the rationalization and the efficient use of regional electricity resources. There is an urgent need for policies and programmes to be implemented.[31]

An important institutional development in the regional cooperation in energy has been the establishment of the Black Sea Regional Energy Centre (BSREC) at the beginning of 1995 in Sofia. This project was sponsored by the EU. The main aim of the centre is to reinforce cooperation between the EU and the Black Sea countries in the energy sector. It is believed that cooperation in the energy sector will consequently strengthen political and economic stability and promote peace and greater prosperity in the region. Apart from the BSEC members the EU energy representatives from the Energy Directorate participate in the meetings. The objectives of the BSREC were declared as: to promote energy policy development and application, and energy market reform with reference to the European Energy Charter; promotion of investment, funding and joint ventures in the energy sector of the Black Sea region; provision of easy access to all interested institutions of the European Union and to the energy sector of the Black Sea region countries and vice versa; creation of Black Sea regional initiatives for partnership with the EU; coordination of services on request, the EU's aid programmes (Synergy, PHARE and Tacis programmes) for the Black Sea projects.

These objectives have been confirmed in a subsequent Conference Declaration, jointly organized by the EU and the Black Sea Energy Centre in 1997 in Bucharest. This Conference indicated the significance of the Black Sea region as an energy market for the EU. It was also a critical step towards achieving closer cooperation in the field of energy between the European Union and the Black Sea region. In this Conference, important Black Sea issues such as harmonizing market reforms, implementing agreed energy policies, the interconnection of energy transportation infrastructure as part of trans-European energy networks, the development and transfer of advanced technologies including energy-related issues of environmental protection have been addressed.[32] Particular attention was paid to the realization of joint energy programmes, their financing and measures to promote investment in line with the provision of the European Energy Charter.[33]

As far as the Black Sea countries are concerned, energy is potentially the most important sector, one that will generate functional regional interdependence and cooperation in the Black Sea area.[34] Therefore, the management of energy resources remains a critical issue for the Black Sea countries.

Transport and Communication

The BSEC also claims to lay the basis for a regional infrastructure to generate interdependence and to accelerate regional economic, energy and social flows. The poor regional infrastructure facilities stemming from Cold War divisions had prevented the countries of the Black Sea from horizontal social and economic engagement. In particular the BSEC envisages promoting functional cooperation in transport, communications, energy and raw materials. Towards this goal, communication and transport projects are crucial for the construction of the foundations of regional infrastructures. So the Working Group dealing with transport and communications proposed several important projects with the strategic aim of linking the Black Sea countries within a regional integrated communications network.[35] Some of these projects became operational in 1998. ITUR is the first concrete project in this field, linking Italy, Turkey,

Ukraine and Russia by a submarine fibre-optical cable system of 3200 km, with its landing points in Palermo, Istanbul, Odessa and Novorrossijsk respectively. The second project is KAFOS which provides a telecommunication link from Moldova to Istanbul through Bulgaria and Romania; this has been completed. The third project, the Trans-Balkan Line, links Italy, the Former Yugoslav Republic of Macedonia, Albania and Turkey. Each member state finances its own section. The transport sector is another area of functional cooperation that aims to lay the basis for a regional network. The strategic aim as defined by the Working Group is to create a trans-European transport network to the east extending as far as Central Asia. This will provide a Transport Corridor Europe-Caucasus-Asia (TRACECA). The Working Groups on transportation adopted three important Pan-European transportation network projects. These corridors are: the Baltic Sea in the North to the Black Sea via Central Russia and the Azov Sea (North-South corridor); an East-West link between the Adriatic Sea and Central Asia; and a smaller transportation network linking the Danube, Don and Volga regions. This has also culminated in the adoption of a common position by the BSEC countries in line with the Pan-European transport system at the Third Pan-European Transport Conference in Helsinki in 1997.[36] At this conference, the Black Sea was recognized as an integral part of a wider Pan-European transport network system.

Turkey and other Key Players in the Black Sea

All successful regional cooperation projects develop around politically, administratively and economically-advanced core areas.[37] The crucial question is whether Turkey as the instigator of regional cooperation in the Black Sea will be able to act as the dynamic core in the promotion of regional cooperation. A glance at a map of the region shows that Turkey is in a very critical location on the intersection of the East and West and the North and South divisions of regional power and energy centres. Since history began, all natural lines of communication from the Gulf to the Balkans and from the Black Sea to the Mediterranean passed through the Anatolian peninsula.[38] This was the case under Cold War circumstances and continues to be so well after the collapse of the Cold War order in Europe.[39] It was due to its strategic position that Turkey had been admitted to NATO in the 1950s. Thus, its geographic location is an important independent factor that makes Turkey a likely candidate in the formation of a regional core in the Black Sea area. However, its geopolitical location must be assessed against political and economic factors. Geopolitics alone cannot determine the future of regional cooperation. Other economic factors must be also taken into account.

On the economic front Turkey, like Greece, has a longer history of democratization and liberal economy compared to that of the post-communist Black Sea region. The Turkish economy has grown rapidly in the last two decades with a six per cent average growth rate over the period 1980 to 1997. Turkey's role as a regional economic core is further enhanced by its dynamic link with the EU. The establishment of the customs union link with the EU, in 1995, demonstrated the Turkish economy's ability to cope with the competitive challenge of free trade in manufactured goods, as well as the trade, competition and intellectual property legislation of the EU.[40] The gradual opening of the Turkish economy to the outside world has been an important factor in this change. Turkey has a strong industrial base as nearly 80 per cent of its exports consist of manufactured goods and in some cases it approaches European standards of production.[41] The EU remains Turkey's leading trading partner. In 1997 the EU accounted for nearly 47 per cent of Turkish exports and 51 per cent of its imports. Full integration into the EU remains Turkey's long-term objective. This has been confirmed in the Helsinki Summit of the EU which has recognized Turkey as a candidate country for the full membership. As indicated at the beginning of this chapter, Turkey's active economic and political role in the Black Sea region is seen by foreign policy makers as a contributing factor to the attainment of full EU membership.

Given the liberal regime for foreign direct investment, the large domestic market and its access to the European market for manufactured commodities, Turkey offers a favourable base for investors to have access to Black Sea markets. Despite the liberalization of the trade regime, direct foreign investment, which accounts for about 0.5 per cent of its GDP, remains low.

The slow inflow of foreign direct investment can also be attributed to macroeconomic instability. Despite improvements in the trade regime, macroeconomic instability continues to be a matter of concern. Over the past decade, Turkey has been unable to break the cycle of inflation, public spending deficits and currency depreciation. The structural causes of macroeceonomic instability need to be tackled by improving the efficiency of tax collection, restructuring and privatizing public sector enterprises, reforming the social security system and reviewing public expenditure. There is also a need to focus more on investment in infrastructure and human capital.[42] Although a new structural reform package particularly in social security, privatization and finance, was underway at the end of

1999, the effects of the massive earthquake which hit Turkey's industrial core in August are likely to slow down the reform process.

Since the collapse of the Soviet Union, Turkey's exports to the Black Sea countries in manufactured goods have been expanding rapidly. As the Commission's Regular Report on Turkey recorded; the total volume of exports to the Post-Soviet states was growing fast. This performance has demonstrated Turkish industry's capacity to take immediate advantage of new market openings in its regional environment. As the Report emphasized there has also been a major shift in exports since 1992. The share of the former Soviet countries rose from 6 per cent in 1993 to 12 per cent in 1997 at the expense of partners such as Middle East countries. The EU has also been affected as its share declined from 53 per cent in 1990 to 51 per cent in 1997.[43] These trends indicate the growing importance of the former Soviet countries in Turkey's post-Cold War foreign trade policies.

Apart from the formal economy, there has also been a rapid growth in the informal economic sector between Turkey and the other Black Sea countries. The so-called 'suitcase trade' between the Black Sea countries and Turkey reached $8.5 billion. This accounted for nearly 40 per cent of Turkey's overall exports in 1997.[44] The recent Russian financial crisis has also affected the Turkish economy badly, particularly the cross-border trade. However, this is expected to have only a short-term negative effect on the economy, as Turkey was recovering from the slow economic growth of the late 1990s.[45]

Apart from economic variables, political legitimacy, stability and cohesion are important factors to be taken into account if Turkey is to play an active role in the formation of a regional core in the Black Sea area. In general political terms Turkey has a democratically-elected government and parliament. However, its political stability is constantly threatened by the ethnic conflict in the south east and by the challenge of Islamic radicalism. The influence of the military in the decision-making process, through the National Security Council, is still an obstacle to the development of a proper and full democratic system. Despite the recognition by politicians of the need to improve human rights standards, political imprisonment and cases of torture and disappearances persist. All these shortcomings render Turkey less than a perfect role model in the regional democratization of the Black Sea.[46] As a result of the recognition of Turkey's candidacy by the EU for full membership at the end of 1999 in Helsinki there were some signs of a commitment to resolve these political issues in Turkey. It is still, however, too early to predict how and when such political reforms will be introduced and implemented. It is highly likely that economic growth followed by democratic and political consolidation will increase the chances of Turkey becoming a key regional player in the Black Sea.

As the instigator of the BSEC project, Turkey has the potential to play a key regional role in the Black Sea. However, as the experience of other regional cooperation projects demonstrates, the nucleus of regional cooperation and convergence tends to develop around a country or a group of countries. Of course, this regional core does not have to comprise of only one country. In fact, the formation of successful regional cooperation between two or more key regional actors can set a good precedent for the rest of the region and encourage cooperative habits. At present, Russia and Greece are the other two key regional actors. Thus, the success of the BSEC will be dependent upon the evolution of cooperation between these three key players: Greece is a full member of the EU with its advanced economy; Turkey is an emerging regional economy with its full customs union with the EU and Russia is an important Black Sea power. Therefore, it is worth examining the bilateral relationship developing between Turkey and these two key players in turn, with regard to regional cooperation in the Black Sea. This does not mean that the other Black Sea countries are excluded from the equation. These three key players constitute the main axis that will hold the Black Sea together. Therefore, the future of regional cooperation will be determined by the pattern of relationship between these three key players. In this context, it must be noted that Ukraine also plays an important balancing role in the equation. Ukraine's role in the Black Sea is discussed in another chapter in this volume.

Turkey and Russia

When it comes to Russian-Turkish relations it is common to point out the historical animosities between the two countries. It is true that the Russian and Ottoman Empires were competing powers in the Black Sea for centuries. The Black Sea and the Turkish Straits have always been an important passageway for Russia's access to the Mediterranean and the other warm seas. Despite historical mutual mistrust between Turkey and Russia, since the foundation of Turkish Republic, the competition over the control of the Black Sea has never led to a direct physical confrontation, nor has the relationship always been one of conflict. Indeed, during the formative years of the Republic the newly-established Soviet Regime had been a natural ally of Turkey against the European powers.[47] Following the Second World War, under Cold War circumstances, Turkish-Russian relationships were mainly determined by East-West ideological competition and military blocs. The peace between the Soviet Union and Turkey was contained within the east-west military balance. The Black Sea for the most part of this century remained a divided and closed sea.

The end of the Cold War has opened up a new chapter in Turkish-Russian relations. As was indicated at the beginning of this chapter the BSEC was initially conceived as a common economic space between Bulgaria, Romania, the Soviet Union and Turkey in 1990 and the idea was consistent with Gorbachev's concept of a 'Common European House'. After the disintegration of the Soviet Union, negotiations continued with the newly-independent states of the Soviet Union (Commonwealth of Independent States) and when the agreement establishing the BSEC process was eventually signed in Istanbul. The idea was well-received by Russian public opinion, for example *Izvestia* stressed the political significance of the Istanbul Summit and suggested that for Russia, Black Sea Economic Cooperation would 'ensure the security of its southern borders'. It was also emphasized that 'common association, even if it is an economic one, might become an important stabilizing factor, an additional mechanism to settle differences and conflicts'.[48] This initial optimism was not shared by everybody. Some Russian commentators exercised caution and emphasized the geopolitical rather than the economic implications of the initiation of the BSEC by Turkey. It was asserted that the Istanbul Summit was likely 'to legitimize both the economic and the political leadership of Turkey' in the Black Sea region. Russia was further concerned that the BSEC could be used by Turkey to reinforce its position in the region in order to achieve its main goal, that of joining the EU.[49]

Indeed, early optimism about the positive role of the BSEC has been replaced by the pessimist view that the BSEC was mainly Turkey's regional lever for exerting its regional influence and hegemony. This Russian perception persisted well into the 1990s. The Russian predicament, concerning Turkey's assertive policies, was enhanced by the recent political developments in the Black Sea area. First of all, the emergence of Ukrainian-Turkish collaboration in the early 1990s was a matter of concern and caused Russia to treat Turkish policies in the Black Sea with caution. There was also the suspicion that NATO could be extended to the Black Sea area through the admission of new members and partnership agreements and eventually directly threaten the Russian interests in the Black Sea. Turkey's active role in regional policies as assigned and endorsed by the US must also be closely monitored by the Russians. Moreover, Russians were suspicious that Turkey was actively seeking to promote Pan-Turkist policies in Transcaucasia and Central Asia; last but not least concerned by the competition over the exploitation, distribution and transportation of energy in the Caspian Sea area, particularly in Azerbaijan. Turkey's every move in this area is seen as an effort to bypass Russia in Transcaucasian energy projects and pipelines.

Some of these Russian concerns are well founded but others are not. Turkey's aspirations to establish strong links with the Central Asian states have been hampered by its own financial constraints and domestic problems. As a Turkish analyst has observed, 'Turkey's inroads into Azerbaijan and Central Asia have actually been very low-key and the Turks – despite their rhetoric that the twenty-first century would be a Turkic century – have done their utmost not to challenge Russia directly and to avoid provoking their northern neighbour.' Turkey is still interested in establishing economic and cultural links with the Central Asian countries. However, for Turkey Azerbaijan remains a strategically-important partner country.[50] On the other hand, NATO's unchecked expansion and military activities deep into the Black Sea inevitably undermine regional stability and make overall regional cooperation difficult.[51] In the long run, Nato's enlargement to the Black Sea countries is likely to alienate and antagonize Russia. In addition some circles in Turkey have expressed their fear that this would contribute to Russian perceptions of strategic containment by antagonistic western powers.[52]

Turning from Russian concerns about Turkey's growing role in the Black Sea, the most important issue between Russia and Turkey relates to the transportation of, and access to, energy resources in the Caspian Sea. As was observed by a leading analyst, 'Turkey's main goal across the CIS, therefore, is access to markets, particularly in energy, in order to play this prominent trading role abroad based on a flourishing domestic economy.'[53]

Energy is the most important single issue, one that will determine the course of Turkish-Russian relations. In energy issues, Turkey's policies towards Russia have been somewhat ambivalent. On the one hand, with American backing, Turkey has been trying to divert the transportation of oil and gas from the Caspian Sea and Central Asia to the Mediterranean through pipeline projects over Georgia and Azerbaijan thereby avoiding the Russian route.[54] On the other, bilateral interdependence and cooperation in energy issues between Russia and Turkey has been rapidly increasing. In the 1990s, Russia became Turkey's most important energy partner.[55] In April 1997 Turkey signed a $13.5 billion deal with the Russian natural gas company (Gasprom). Under the 25-year agreement, Russia will import natural gas to help meet Turkey's growing demand for energy. Export to Turkey is expected to increase by nearly 30 billion cubic meters a year by 2010. Nearly all Turkey's natural gas is at present transported through a single pipeline via the Balkans. Energy consumption in Turkey is also rising rapidly by nearly 10 per cent a year. According to the calculations of the Turkish Ministry of Energy, natural energy consumption is expected to rise 25 times to 60 billion cubic meters a year by 2010.[56]

Faced with increasing dependence on a single supplier, namely Russia, Turkey is still trying to diversify its energy suppliers and has concluded gas import agreements with Iran, Algeria, Turkmenistan and Yemen. Despite the new natural gas agreements Russia provides nearly 54 per cent of Turkey's natural gas demand in comparison to Iran's 20 per cent and Algeria's 9 per cent share.[57] Recently, Turkey sought to sign a natural gas deal with Turkmenistan. According to this Trans-Caspian project, nearly 16 billion cubic meters of natural gas is expected to flow from Turkmenistan to the growing Turkish market every year. To a certain extent this project aims to diversify the natural gas flow from the single major supplier, Russia, to Central Asia. It is expected to be ready by 2004.[58] In the meantime, Russia remains the main supplier of Turkey's natural gas. The recent plan to lay a gas pipeline across the Black Sea is designed by Russia to meet the increasing demands of the Turkish energy market. Negotiations are in progress to build a natural gas pipeline under the Black Sea. The Blue Stream pipeline project between Russia and Turkey is expected to transport 25 billion cubic meters of Russian natural gas to Ankara from Russia via the Black Sea.[59] Construction of the part of the pipeline through Turkish terri- tory is to start soon, under an agreement signed between Turkey and Russia. Russia is financing the part of the pipeline on its own territory. An agreement with a consortium, consisting of Italian, Russian, French and Japanese firms, to build the pipeline was signed in November 1999.

Turkish policy makers see security of supply in the volatile Black Sea region as one of the most important objectives of Turkey's energy policies in the twenty-first century. This takes into account the environmental implications of increasing energy flows in the region. Turkey's demand for natural gas, as an emerging competitive economy, will increase while the relative share of oil in energy consumption will decrease in relative terms.[60] The management of interdependence in energy issues will be the crucial determining factor in the future of Turkish-Russian relations.

On the economic front, Russia has become an important trade partner for Turkey. According to the Foreign Economic Relations Board in Istanbul, Turkey has become the second-largest trading partner of Russia after Germany. The trade volume between these two countries increased from $1.4 billion in 1992 to $3.3 billion dollars. The total value of construction projects carried out by Turkish firms in Russia also exceeded

$6 billion.[61] Apart from the registered trade flows, in 1997 the so-called cross-border 'suitcase trade' with the Black Sea countries reached nearly $11 billion. Nearly half of this unregistered trade has been with Russia.[62] In 1995, Russia was also Turkey's fourth largest trading partner. [63]

Since 1998, Russia has been in serious financial and economic crisis. This has naturally affected the trade between Turkey and Russia. However, it has not led to the immediate flight of Turkish investment and business from Russia. Unlike their European and American counterparts, Turkish businessmen are used to working in an unstable macroeconomic environment.[64] It seems that the Russian market is too lucrative and important for Turkish investors to abandon. In the long-term, the increasing energy dependence of Turkey on Russia will not allow trade diversion from the Russian market. On the contrary, despite political instabilities, economically Russia will remain an important partner for Turkey.[65] Given the above developments in the 1990s, Russia and Turkey possess all the objective factors needed to form the dynamic core of regional cooperation in the Black Sea area. The regional political circumstances and the direction of Russian internal politics as crucial intervening variables will affect the process of cooperation. In general, it would not be wrong to suggest that the way in which the relationship between Russia and Turkey develops will determine the future of the Black Sea Economic Cooperation process. The initial Russian perception of the BSEC as the lever of Turkish post-Cold War foreign policy to establish its hegemony in the Black Sea area seems to be no longer valid. BSEC is now seen by some official circles in Russia as an integral part of the new European architecture and a contributory factor in the European integration process.[66] In the long run, the BSEC constitutes a fertile institutional ground on which to manage the increasing interdependence between Russia and Turkey in a constructive and cooperative manner.

Greece and Turkey

Greece has no borders in the Black Sea, but for cultural, economic and historical reasons Greece is a Black Sea country.[67] At the beginning of the 1990s, Greece watched the inception of the BSEC with suspicion and initially, like Russia, regarded it as the lever by which Turkish foreign policy would seek to establish its hegemony in the region. Therefore, Greece's desire to participate in the BSEC as a founder member resulted from an intention to counterbalance Turkey's political influence in the Black Sea area. Greek attitudes towards the BSEC in its formative years can be characterized by the mistrust and suspicion of Turkish motivations.

On the other hand, Turkey did not raise any objections to Greece's participation in the BSEC as a founder member.[68] Despite the reservations of some Turkish diplomats that the BSEC could be turned into another political platform for competing national interests, Greece's accession to the BSEC occurred without any major Turkish objections. In fact, Turkey invited Greece to the Istanbul Summit as one of the founding members. Bulgaria and Russia were particularly in favour of Greece's full membership. It was anticipated that Greece's full membership of the EU would facilitate financial backing from the EU. It was also felt that Greece's participation would strengthen the cultural and political links between these three Orthodox countries. Between 1992 and 1996, Greece was reluctant to commit itself to the objectives and operations of the BSEC. In this period Greece treated the BSEC as another political platform where Turkish influence should be minimized. Greece and Turkey, for instance, have competed over the venue and the structure of the Black Sea Trade and Development Bank. This in turn has delayed its establishment and the generation of financial revenues for the Bank. Finally the Bank started its operations in 1998.

This was, in fact, a familiar pattern in the relationship between Turkey and Greece as is manifested by the frequent exercise of veto and the promotion of national interests within the EU and other European institutions.

Greece with its relatively strong economic base and stable macroeconomic structure is an important Balkan and Black Sea country. In fact, for the time being it is the only full EU member in the BSEC.[69] Therefore, potentially it has a central role to play in the regional cooperation process. This, however, is dependent upon how Greek-Turkish relations develop within the BSEC framework. There is always a risk of BSEC becoming another forum within which Greece and Turkey can use their veto power to maximize their national interests rather than to promote the objectives of regional cooperation. Genuine political cooperation is not foreseeable in the short-term. There are too many unresolved bilateral political problems between Greece and Turkey: the territorial disputes in the Aegean Sea, the Cyprus problem and minority issues still constitute important obstacles.[70] Bilateral problems often creep into the negotiation and cooperation process in other European institutions. For instance, Greece has so far vetoed the reactivation of financial protocols in Turkey's association process with the EU on the basis of issues in Cyprus and Aegean Sea. It would be ambitious to expect that Greece and Turkey should be committed to full cooperation within the BSEC structures unless they first resolve their conflicting interests within the EU framework. The BSEC is not high on the agenda for Greece's foreign policy and her priorities in the long run lie with European integration.

On the economic front, the level of trade interdependence between Greece and Turkey is comparatively low.[71] However, despite the existing tensions which sometimes verge on direct conflict, Turkish and Greek businessmen manage to meet to explore the possibilities of bilateral trade.[72] Meetings of Greek-Turkish Business Councils sometimes take place against the background of a strained political relationship.[73] The business and interest-oriented groups in Turkey and Greece are usually more enthusiastic about cooperation than their governments are. In this sense the BSEC, with its trade mandate, provides an encouraging, potential business environment for Turkish and Greek investors and businessmen for joint investments in the third countries.[74] More, importantly, the customs union agreement between Turkey and the EU is, in the long run, bound to accelerate the bilateral trade flows between Turkey and Greece. However, a favourable trade environment can only be created if both parties first resolve their political problems.

Since the new Simitis Government came to power in 1996, Greece has adopted more pragmatic regional policies and its attitude towards the BSEC has changed drastically. The Greek perception of the BSEC as providing Turkey with political leverage has been replaced by more pragmatic policies towards the Black Sea area where Greek trade and investments should be promoted.[75] Greece has been actively promoting the establishment of the Black Sea Trade and Development Bank. As a full EU member, Greece is in a position to attract EU financial resources for BSEC programmes. In addition Greece has cultural interests in the area because of the existence of Greek-speaking communities around the Black Sea. Greece has also realized that the stability of the region is crucial for its well-being. Like Turkey, Greece is also located at a strategic point where political instability can threaten political and economic interests.

Recently, the tragic earthquakes that hit Turkey and Greece in 1999 created a favourable environment between the two countries. Turkish and Greek civil society organizations provided assistance in kind and rescue teams from both countries arrived to help one another in emergency aid and operations. The societal interaction between both countries has triggered a new process of rapprochement between both countries. This positive development was reflected in the conclusions of the EU summit in Helsinki in which Greece finally lifted its veto against Turkey's prospective membership and Turkey's official candidacy for full membership was recognized. Since the Helsinki Summit, Greek and Turkish governments have been planning to pay official visits to each other to reach cooperation agreements in low issue areas such as trade, combating crime, tourism, and student exchanges, while avoiding the bilateral negotiations in high politics areas particularly on issues relating to Cyprus and the Aegean. Both governments are constrained by domestic political factors and seem reluctant to make concessions over sensitive national issues. However, as a result of the removal of Greek objections to Turkey's full membership, Greece and Turkey are expected to converge within the integrative framework of the EU policies and structures. In the Helsinki Summit, it was also implied that solving the bilateral problems between Greece and Turkey would facilitate Turkey's accession process to the EU. The level of cooperation and convergence between two countries within the EU is also likely to have a positive effect on the cooperation process within the BSEC. Although it is difficult to predict the direction of Turkish-Greek relations in the long run suffice it to say that developments at the end of 1999 point in the direction of cooperation rather than conflict. This, however, cannot be taken for granted as different domestic, regional and geopolitical variables may intervene in the process. The main context of their relationship remains the EU. This is not to suggest that the cooperation process between Greece and Turkey in the Black Sea will become less important in their foreign policy agendas. On the contrary, as the EU enlarges towards the Black Sea, the BSEC as an organization will gain in significance. Thus, the EU's role in the Black Sea area deserves a separate section.

The EU and the Black Sea

Since the collapse of the Cold War the EU has emerged as an important actor in the Black Sea region. The EU has been developing bilateral relationships with the Black Sea countries through cooperation and association agreements. European Agreements were already in force with Bulgaria and Romania. Partnership and Cooperation Agreements have been signed with Russia, Ukraine and Moldova and the three Caucasian Republics: Armenia, Georgia and Azerbaijan.[76] The Conclusions of the Helsinki Summit in December 1999 also confirmed the importance of the enlargement process for stability and prosperity for the entire European continent. In this direction, the Council of the EU decided to convene bilateral conferences in early 2000 to begin negotiations for membership with Bulgaria and Romania as well as Turkey which are three Black Sea countries. The Conclusions of the Summit at Helsinki indicated that each candidate will be judged on its own merits. It also stated that 'Turkey, like other candidates, will benefit from pre-accession strategy to stimulate and support its reforms'. Given that these Black Sea countries are included in the orbit of the widening process and Greece is already a full member, it is easy to predict that enlargement will shift the boundaries of the EU eastward to the shores of the Black Sea.

The EU's presence in the Black Sea region in the early 1990s was characterized as bilateralism. This initially imposed certain constraints on the EU's relations with the Black Sea as a whole in the early 1990s. The need for greater engagement was not recognized until the late 1990s. As 'Agenda 2000' stated 'the importance of regional cooperation will increase as the Union enlarges, as its development will promote the openness of the enlarged Union towards its neighbours, so that no dividing lines are drawn on the European continent'.[77] In this context, the EU has come to realize that the Black Sea has a specific role in overcoming the divisions of the Cold War. Indeed, in 1997, the European Commission in its report to the Council affirmed that 'Enlargement will further increase the Black Sea region's significance to the European Union. The EU has a major interest in promoting political stability and economic prosperity in the Black Sea region and stimulating the development links both within the region and with the EU.' The same report also stated that the Black Sea region constitutes an area of increasing strategic importance for the European Union. With a population of 190 million, the region provides a potentially important market for EU goods. Furthermore, it is a vital transit route for energy resources to Europe.[78] In the late 1990s the BSEC has been closely observed by the EU as a stabilizing factor in a volatile region as its significance for access to Caspian and Central Asian energy resources has increased.[79] Therefore, modernization of the regional infrastructure in energy and transportation facilities has taken priority in the EU's emerging strategy towards the Black Sea region.[80] Apart from the energy, transport and communication facilities connecting the Black Sea to Europe, regional commercial cooperation and the creation of favourable conditions to attract EU and foreign investment; sustainable development, environmental protection and nuclear safety areas have been emphasized as priorities.

The EU has also been active in providing financial assistance to the Black Sea region. As the Commission communication reported between 1991 and 1996, an estimated 490 million ECU (European Currency Unit) has been granted to the regional development and cooperation projects. These include the modernization of oil and energy transportation facilities, the establishment and the coordination of the activities of the Black Sea Energy Centre, and the Black Sea environmental action programmes. The EU also contributed to the Black Sea Trade and Development

Bank's business activities. Technical assistance is provided exclusively through existing instruments, mainly Tacis, Phare and Meda external aid programmes. The EU has been developing 'Black Sea synergies' in the framework of current Community assistance programmes to stimulate regional cooperation and development. Since 1997, EU representatives have also been participating in meetings of the BSEC as observers.

Primarily, the long-term interests of the BSEC countries lie with the EU, for the majority of BSEC members joining the EU remains the final objective. In this sense, the promotion of regional cooperation is seen not as an alternative but as part of a transition strategy towards the European integration. In this sense, the EU's role in the promotion of the Black Sea cooperation cannot be underestimated. In fact, the BSEC countries welcomed the conclusions of the EU Council of Ministers in 1997 as a first step towards a comprehensive strategy in its policies in the Black Sea region.[81] In the same way, the BSEC has also been seeking the EU's support for its long-term objective : integration into Europe. The adoption of the Platform for Cooperation between the BSEC and the EU by the Council of Ministers of the BSEC confirmed that 'The BSEC attaches particular importance to its cooperation with the EU, with the ultimate aim to progressively shape the EU-BSEC economic area' and thereby integrate the BSEC into European economic space. In this sense, the BSEC is, and will be, increasingly, seen by both parties as a preliminary and complementary cooperation process for joining the European integration as part of an overall Pan-European strategy.

Conclusions

Before drawing any conclusions with regard to regional cooperation in the Black Sea, I have to distinguish between regionalism and regionalization. The former refers to political desire or voluntarism on the part of elites to promote regional cooperation and institutions within defined geographical boundaries or rather around regional ecological, economic and social concerns. Thus, regionalism refers to a project or attitude as an organizing political principle. On the other hand, regionalization refers to the actual or perceived interdependence in salient regional issues and intensifying regional flows of energy, population and economic transactions.

As was stated at the beginning of this chapter, the initiation of the BSEC was due to the regionalist attempts of Turkish policy-makers and elites to build a regional identity in order to relate to the overall Pan-Europeanization process in the post-Cold War era. Initially this regionalist attempt was treated by other key regional actors with caution, on the grounds that Turkey was trying to exert its political influence through BSEC. In this sense, regionalism in the Black Sea area could initially be regarded as weak regionalism. However, regional organizations have their own momentum and once they are installed they have unintended consequences for the regional states. Once it was established, the regional countries gradually came to realize that the BSEC could be utilized as a framework for cooperation within which regional interdependence can be managed. Towards the end of 1990s as the regionalization of the Black Sea has increased, in salient regional issues such as energy and trade, the other countries' attitude towards the BSEC has accordingly changed. The recognition of the BSEC by the EU as a complementary cooperation framework to the European integration has also reinforced its status and legitimacy in other countries' quest to join Europe. For the newly-independent states of the Soviet Union, the BSEC also provided a platform outside Russia's influence and hegemony. The BSEC enables these countries to have an equal voice with Russia.

The BSEC is not a regional security organization. However, it offers an external regional environment within which the smooth transition to democracy and market economy can be accelerated. Its functionalist style and piecemeal approach to regional issues, in the long run, may generate a regional sense of common interest and the establishment of regional economic infrastructure may create incentives for further regional economic cooperation. In this sense, the BSEC provides a safeguard in the enlargement of the EU to the Black Sea region. Moreover, it also acts as an intellectual lifeboat in which to cross the choppy political waters of the Black Sea, giving a sense of direction to diplomats, business circles and politicians in the twenty-first century.

Notes

1   Permanent International Secretariat, BSEC, Inauguration of the Organization of the Black Sea Economic Cooperation, *Press Release*, No:52 Istanbul, May 1999.
2   *Newspot*, 20 December 1990.
3   *Monthly Summary and News Analysis of the CIS and East European Press* V.XVII, No. 61992. pp 14–15.
4   The final document consists of the Summit Declaration on the Black Sea Economic Cooperation and the Bosphorus Statement. Permanent International Secretariat, Black Sea Economic Cooperation, *Handbook of Documents, BSEC*, Volume 1, Istanbul, July 1995.
5   Oktay Ozuye, 'Black Sea Economic Cooperation', *Mediterranean Quarterly*, V.3 (3) pp. 48–54.
6   *Handbook of Documents, V.1*, p 3.

7   Official Journal of the European Communities, No.C 337/225, 1992.

8   Permanent International Secretariat, Inauguration of the Organization of the Black Sea Economic Cooperation, *Press Release*, No. 52 Istanbul, May 1999.

9   Rules of Procedure of the Black Sea Economic Cooperation, in *Handbook of Documents*, V I, July 1995 p 515.

10 Ines Hartwig, The Black Sea Economic Cooperation Process, *European Institute of Public Administration*, No.1 1997 p 4.

11 Interviews with the Deputy General Secretary of the BSEC, Ambassador Nurver Nures.

12 Interviews with the BSEC officials.

13 The ten members of the PABSEC are: Albania, Armenia, Azerbaijan, Georgia, Greece, Moldova, Romania, Russia, Turkey and Ukraine.

14 These are the Russian-Turkish Business Council, Ukrainian-Turkish and Greek-Turkish Business Councils.

15 Ercan Ozer, Black Sea: A Test Case, Unpublished conference paper, *Economic Developments and Reforms in Cooperation Partner Countries: External Economic Relations with Particular Focus on Regional Cooperation*, NATO, Brussels, 1997.

16 BSEC: New Architecture and New Visions, p 26.

17 J. Fitzmaurice 'Regional Cooperation in Central Europe' *West European Politics*, V.16 (3) pp 389–399.

18 General Secretariat of the BSEC, *Draft Report* adopted at Special by the Ministers Responsible for Economic Affairs (BS/SFM/R 97).

19 See an optimistic assessment by Assistant Secretary General of the Black Sea Economic Cooperation on the possibility of establishment of a free trade zone in the Black Sea, Evgenii Borisenko, 'Black Sea Free-Trade Zone', *International Affairs*, V 45 (2) 1999, pp 110–117.

20 Commission of the European Union: 'Regional Cooperation in The Black Sea', p 7.

21 Permanent International Secretariat of the BSEC, Meeting of the Ministers of Foreign Affairs Tbilisi, 30 April, 1999, Annex V BS/FM/R(99)1.

22 BSEC-European Commission Workshop on Border Crossing Improvement and Trade Facilitation in the Black Sea Region, University of Trakya, Edirne, 11–13 November 1996, Summary of Proceedings, Black Sea Economic Cooperation, *Handbook of Documents*, V 3, Istanbul, January 1998, pp 229–233.

23 Summary Proceedings of the Workshop on Small and Medium-Sized Enterprises in Foreign Trade, Ibid.

24 Marcelo Selowsky, Background Paper, the World Bank Group, Views from Entrepreneurs and World Bank Country Economists, Improving Environment and Investment in the CIS and Baltic Countries, London, April 1997.

25 In 1995 direct foreign investment is estimated to stand at \$4.874 million compared to 2.915 million in 1994 and \$2.034 million in 1993.

26 C. Papazoglu and P. Liargovas, An Assessment of Foreign Direct Investment towards the BSEC Transition Economies, *Economia Internazionale*, V.50 August, 1997, pp 475–487.

27   Interviews with Businessmen, 'Opportunities in the Black Sea Region' Organized by Turkish-British Chamber of Commerce and Industry, Department of Trade and Industry and Middle East Association in London, 14 July 1997.

28   Information provided by BSEC officials.

29   SDRs are a composite of several state currencies and fluctuate in value along with them. Greece, Turkey and Russia are the largest contributors in the bank at 16.5 per cent each. Bulgaria, Romania and Ukraine will each contribute 13.5 per cent and Albania, Armenia, Azerbaijan, Georgia will have a 2 per cent stake. Daniel A. Connely, 'Black Sea Economic Cooperation' RFE/RL Research Report, V3 no. 26 July 1994. p 35.

30   For the political aspect of the energy issues in the Black Sea see Bülent Gökay's chapter in this volume.

31   Bernard Laponche and Dominique Campana, Analysis and projection of the future of the energy consumption in the countries of the Black Sea Economic Cooperation, *Perspectives in Energy*, 1994, Volume 3, pp 193–206.

32   As the Black Sea is in the process of becoming an energy super-highway, issues of energy distribution and transportation are increasingly linked to issues of the environment. Environment is another salient regional issue in the Black Sea region which is dealt with in another chapter in this book see Laurence David Mee's chapter in this volume.

33   'EU-Black Sea Region: Extending Cooperation between two key players in the World Energy market, Bucharest', 28 November 1997.

34   Interview with the BSEC Officials, June 1999.

35   Rules of Procedure of the Black Sea Economic Cooperation, Istanbul 17 June 1993, Permanent International Secretariat, Handbook of Documents, Volume 1, July 1995 p 515.

36   BSEC Permanent International Secretariat, *BSEC: New Architecture*, New Vision, (Third Edition) Istanbul, Turkey, 1998.

37   William Wallace, Introduction: The Dynamics of European Integration, in William Wallace (Ed), *The Dynamics of European Integration*, (London, 1990) pp 15–18

38   Oral Sander, Turkey's Role in NATO: A Time for New Perspectives, *NATO Review*, June 1990, pp 24–28.

39   Graham E. Fuller, *Turkey's New Geopolitics, From Balkans to Western China* (Oxford: 1993).

40   Mina Toksoz, The Turkey-EU customs union, Economic Intelligence Unit (EIU) *European Trends 1st Quarter* 1996, pp 71–75.

41   Communications of the Commission, Doc 97/6, Strasbourg, 15 July 1997.

42   Commission of the European Union, *Regular Report on Turkey's Progress Towards Accession*, Brussels, November, 1998.

43   Ibid.

44   Information given by Deputy Secretary of the BSEC, Ambassador Nurver Nures, Middle East Association, London in June 1997.

45   Commission of the European Union, *Regular Report on Turkey's Progress Towards Accession*, 13 October 1999.

46 Ibid.

47 The Cooperation Agreement of 1921 between the Soviet Union and Turkey was followed by the Treaty of Friendship and Neutrality in 1925 by which Turkey and Russia agreed to abstain from any aggression against each other. With the end of the war Turkish-Soviet Union Relations deteriorated; on 20 March 1945, the USSR abrogated the Treaty of Neutrality and Friendship and demanded some territorial concessions in the Straits and Eastern Borders.

48 Commonwealth of Independent States and the Middle East, Monthly Summary and News Analysis of the CIS and East European Press, V.XVII, No.6, 1992 p 11.

49 Ibid, p 12.

50 Suha Bolukbasi, Ankara's Baku-Centreed Transcaucasia Policy: Has it Failed? *Middle East Journal*, V. 51 No. 1, Winter 1997 pp 81–94.

51 See Kovalsky's chapter in this volume.

52 For Turkey's cautious approach to the NATO enlargement, Ali L. Karaosmanoglu, NATO Enlargement and the South: A Turkish Perspective, *Security Dialogue*, V. 30 (2), pp 213–224.

53 Stephen J. Blank, The Eastern Question Revived: Turkey and Russia Contend for Eurasia in David Menashri (ed) *Central Asia Meets the Middle East*, Frank Cass, 1998 pp 168–188.

54 For a detailed analysis of the geopolitics of Caspian Oil, see Bülent Gökay's chapter in this volume.

55 The Voice of Turkey, 16 March 1998.

56 These figures and the details of Russian-Turkish trade in natural gas are reported in *Financial Times*, 29 April 1997, Turkey signs £8bn deal to import gas from Russia.

57 Energy balance data has been obtained from Black Sea Regional Energy Centre, Black Sea Energy Review-Turkey, Sofia, 1999.

58 *The Independent*, 19 November 1999.

59 *Anatolian Agency*, 8 January 1999.

60 According to the energy data review on Turkey obtained from the Black Sea Energy Centre, oil's share of energy demand will drop from 52 per cent in 1995 to about 36 per cent in 2020, it will still be main energy source.

61 The number of Turkish firms operating in Russia exceeded 300 which excludes Russian-Turkish joint ventures. Apart from construction, the extent of business ranges from banks to tourism ventures, retail stores, from the production of construction material to housing complexes, business centres to food-processing. Interview with Ambassador Nurver Nures, June 1999.

62 There are no reliable statistics, the estimated total value of the suitcase trade varies between 8 and 11 billion dollars.

63 Bulletin of Foreign Economic Relations, Turkey and BSEC Countries, figures were cited by Ali L. Karaosmanoglu, *Security Dialogue*. See also Commonwealth of Independent States and The Middle East, *Monthly Summary and News Analysis of the CIS Press*, V XX No.6–7 1995.

64   Interview with the Businessmen in the Russian-Turkish Business Council, 25 June 1999, Istanbul.

65   Se Ali L. Karaosmanoglu, Security Dialogue, p 219.

66   See Evgenii Borisenko and Igor Semenenko, Black Sea Economic Cooperation.

67   Neal Ascherson, *Black Sea*, London, 1995.

68   Sukru Elekdag, 'Black Sea Economic Cooperation', *Milliyet* (Daily In Turkish), 25 November 1996.

69   Greece has the highest per capita income in the BSEC above 7000 US dollars.

70   For the discussion of the problems between Greece and Turkey, see Sükrü S. Gürel Turkey and Greece: A Difficult Aegean Relationship, in Canan Balkir, *Turkey and Europe*, London, 1993 pp 162–190.

71   The trade volume between Greece and Turkey at the end of 1999 stands just over 800 million US Dollars, in comparison with Turkey's other trade partners in the Black Sea such as Russia this remains insignificant.

72   Tunç Aybak, 'Dynamics of Association, Turkey and European Integration', *Cambridge Review of International Affairs*, V.X No.1 1996 pp 69–70.

73   For instance, despite the political tension between Greece and Turkey over the territorial status of the islet Imia, the Turkish-Greek Business Council met in Athens to explore business opportunities in joint investments, trade, tourism and environment in the Balkans and the Black Sea area. They also decided to meet at least twice a year to review their business agenda, See 'The Common Interests of Turks and Greeks' by Gulden Ayman, *Radikal*, 11 December 1996.

74   A multimillion joint investment project between Greek, Romanian and Turkish companies was signed in Romania recently, information provided by the BSEC in Istanbul.

75   The Establishment of the International Centre for Black Sea Studies in Athens indicates this change of perception with regard to the BSEC. The aim of the Centre is to promote research in regional economic and social problems and investment opportunities and propose solutions to the issues in the Black Sea area

76   Christopher Hillion, Partnership and Cooperation Agreements between the European Union and the New Independent States of the Ex-Soviet Union' *European Affairs Review*, 3, 1998, pp 399–420.

77   Communication from Commission to the Council *Regional Cooperation in the Black Sea area: State of play. perspectives for EU action encouraging its further development* CB-CO-97-612-EN-C/COM/97/0597,1997.

78   Ibid, p1.

79   Graham Avery and Fraser Cameron, *The Enlargement of The European Union*, Reprinted, Sheffield, 1999.

80   See suggested priority objectives, European Commission's Report to the Council, Regional Cooperation in the Black Sea, p 8.

81   As *The Economist* reported for instance, the EU has told the Visegard regional group that regional cooperation is almost 'a precondition for joining the EU.' 22 May 1999 p 52.

CHAPTER FOUR

The Black Sea World as a Unit of Analysis

Eyüp Özveren

The recent dismemberment of the Soviet Empire has stimulated a renewed interest, academic or otherwise, in the Black Sea region. This is a radical change since the Black Sea, under the shadow of the Soviet Union, had remained in virtual obscurity after the Second World War and indeed for much of the second half of the twentieth century. As will become obvious below, it is no coincidence that the last time the Black Sea was approached as a region that could legitimately constitute the subject-matter of academic inquiry was during the geostrategic high tide of the Second World War.

In this work the various historiographical treatments of the Black Sea world will be considered in turn. Of these the most commonplace approach is one which concentrates on national cases, which misses the salient point that national histories unfold against a backdrop of wider historical structures and patterns. Moreover, according to this approach, the region becomes the simple arithmetic summation of the various national histories. At best, this tradition refers to the Black Sea as a passive geography, the stage on which national histories interact with one another by way of cultural exchanges, trade, diplomacy, and warfare only to mature towards their particular destinies.

In juxtaposition to this inductivist perspective – in which the whole is the simple sum of independently existing individual units – exists an opposite tendency that underrates the Black Sea as the periphery of larger units of analysis. Among the latter, we could cite approaches that see this geography as a mere extension of the greater Russian zone of influence, or the backyard of the Ottoman Empire, or the frontier of Europe, and finally as an extension of the Mediterranean world. What these approaches have in common is the placement of the Black Sea in the margins of other, allegedly, more historically important geographical units. Subsequently, the

Black Sea remains in obscurity, irrespective of which unit of analysis is in question.

However, of the various formulations referred to above, one alone has important implications for the study of the Black Sea world. This is the, now, classic study of the sixteenth-century Mediterranean by eminent French historian Fernand Braudel although this study only pays lip service to the Black Sea as a backyard of the Mediterranean. However Braudel develops a conception of unit of analysis that puts emphasis on the active participation of the geography in the constitution of the Mediterranean as a "world", distinguished by the interaction of a multitude of agencies, namely empires, states, cities, and peoples, by way of participating in a single division of labour. This approach to the historical constitution of a unit of analysis has been taken up and applied to the Balkans by the leading historian of former Yugoslav origin, Traian Stoianovich. It will be argued that this shift has been far from entirely satisfactory as the true subject-matter of inquiry (in the sense of Braudel) ought not to have been the Balkans, as Stoianovich thought, but the Black Sea world of which the greater area of the Balkans form a part.

Finally, a discussion of a much neglected critique will be presented, that of Bratianu. Bratianu was a Romanian historian of the interwar period and hence a contemporary of Braudel. George I. Bratianu attempted to produce a history of the Black Sea that would do justice to it as a proper unit of analysis. Originally planned as a two-volume study of the Black Sea and the Eastern Question, it was originally titled *La Mer Noire et la Question d'Orient*, unfortunately the second volume dealing with the later period was lost during the war in Romania and only the first volume in manuscript form, which covers the period up to the conquest of Istanbul by the Ottomans, has survived the Second World War. The work's final title was *La Mer Noire des Origines à la conquete ottomane*.

That Bratianu chose to write such a work during the Second World War provides sufficient guidelines as to what his motive in writing it may have been. It remains to us to reconstruct in the light of what remains, what the envisaged work could have accomplished. It will be argued that an intellectual transposition of Bratianu's perspective as manifested in this first volume, in synthesis with Braudel's approach cited above, could provide us with the fundamentals of a proper conception of the Black Sea as a unit of analysis. Only a solid historical and analytical foundation of this kind can equip us with the urgently-needed transdisciplinary tools with which to address the prospects of the Black Sea economic cooperation, its relationship to European unification, as well as to the Eurasian geostrategic fault lines.

The Black Sea as Backyard of the Mediterranean

Braudel approached the Black Sea as an extension of the Mediterranean, in his two-volume history of the Mediterranean, during the "long sixteenth century", he devoted a subsection to "The Black Sea, preserve of Constantinople". This subsection, albeit only three pages in a text of some 1200, is nevertheless strong in its interpretive scheme as well as rich in detail. It is discussed in the fourth section of the first part of the book which explores the "Role of the Environment", in the chapter "The Heart of the Mediterranean: Seas and Coasts".

I have chosen to deal with the precise coordinates of Braudel's treatment of the Black Sea because his study of the Mediterranean is a sophisticated exercise in the taxonomic organization of his subject-matter of inquiry. Nevertheless, the fact that the discussion of the Black Sea comes first among his geographical specifications does not attest to its relative importance. Far from it, rather Braudel chose to approach the Mediterranean in a clockwise movement starting from the outskirts. In fact, earlier in the history, Braudel had characterized the Black Sea as "only partly Mediterranean" (Braudel, I, 1976: 109). What this latter phrase meant required further explanation and Braudel began his subsection on the Black Sea with a characterization to that effect:

> *The far-off Black Sea, limit of Mediterranean shipping,* was ringed round by wild lands, with a few exceptions, both uncivilized and de-civilized. Great mountains bordered it to the south and east, hostile mountains through which the roads made their difficult way from Persia, Armenia, and Mesopotamia to the great centre of Trebizond. To the north by contrast rolled the great Russian plains, a land of passage and nomadism, over which a jealous guard was still maintained by the Crimean Tartars in the sixteenth century. It was only in the following century that the Russian outlaws, the Cossacks, were to reach the shore of the sea and begin their piracy at the expense of the Turks. Already in the sixteenth century, the Muscovites were taking advantage of the winter to make 'courreries' towards its shores. (Braudel, I, 1976: 110; emphasis mine).

It should be noted here that Braudel's above description of this geography mirrors on a small-scale his definition of the greater Mediterranean world as a geographical unit. Nevertheless Braudel chose to treat the Mediterranean world as a distinct unit of analysis whereas he hesitated to do this for the Black Sea. This can be explained by the fact that geographies are animated by the historical configuration of dynamic processes. In other words, seemingly geographical units of analysis are as historically constituted as the processes they purport to explain. Paraphrasing Braudel on the effect of the Mediterranean on Europe in general, we can say that the Mediterranean influenced deeply and "has contributed in no small measure to prevent the unity of that [Black Sea world], which it has attracted towards its shores and then divided to its own advantage." (Braudel, I, 1976: 188).

In spite of everything the question of boundaries remains a salient point for the characterization of the unit of analysis. In fact in chapter three of the first part of his book, Braudel sought to deal with this question of delineating boundaries. He chose to approach the boundary from the other side, under the heading "The Russian isthmus: leading to the Black and Caspian Sea." He made it clear where the 'pulling-effect' of the Mediterranean came to a halt. This was the dividing line. Furthermore, if anything, this line not only separated the Mediterranean from Europe but also divided into two the potential Black Sea world, part of which was brought into the orbit of the Mediterranean:

> It would be easy to say, and almost to prove, that in the sixteenth century there was no Russian isthmus, no isthmus, that is, playing a connecting role and bringing large exchange movements to the Mediterranean. The whole of southern Russia was a deserted land, crossed only by the bands of Tartar nomads, whose swift horses carried them to the northern edge of the Caucasus or to the shores of the Caspian Sea, as well as towards Moscow – which they burnt in 1571 – or into the lands of Danube, which they ravaged unmercifully. At the end of the eighteenth century Russian settlers were again to find an immense waste land, empty except for a few nomadic brigands raising their camels and horses. (Braudel, I, 1976: 191)

The fact that the Russians were not oriented toward the Black Sea at this point in time is largely to be explained by the 'pulling-effect' the economic expansion of the Baltic exerted upon the Russian lands, as well as by their focus on the Caspian Sea *en route* to Persian trade. It is no coincidence that the English entertained a scheme during the third quarter of the sixteenth century to circumvent the Mediterranean *pace* the Portuguese (1498), as well as to avoid the Black Sea – which had by then become "a Turkish lake and a well-guarded one" – by a combination of land and sea routes that proceeded by way of the Caspian Sea and the Russian isthmus (Braudel, I, 1976: 193-94).

During the sixteenth century the Black Sea was, increasingly, reduced to the status of an Ottoman lake. Istanbul played a critical role in this transformation. Istanbul, "an urban monster, a composite metropolis" (Braudel, I, 1976: 348) by all demographic standards of the time, relied heavily on the Black Sea for the daily provisioning of its vast populace. The fortunes of the Black Sea as a closed lake and of Istanbul as a self-consolidating capital city were inextricably linked. Just as the Black Sea played a significant role in the growth of Istanbul as a major city, the policy of the imperial state was consciously directed towards the restructuring of the Black Sea into a "unit" relatively insulated from the rest of the world. Braudel's cautious characterization of the Black Sea confirms this view:

> One has the impression that Constantinople *monopolized* the long-distance trade as well as the domestic trade of the Black Sea; *acting as a screen* between this Mediterranean extremity and the rest of the sea. Almost on its doorstep, the Black Sea was the *supplying region* without which the mighty capital could not survive, for it was only inadequately provided for by the tribute of the Balkans (mostly sheep) and the wheat, rice and beans brought in by fleets of Alexandria, along with spices and drugs. (Braudel, I, 1976: 110-11; emphases mine)

Furthermore, Istanbul sought, rather jealously, to elaborate and guard its monopoly over the Black Sea for the centuries to come.[1] Consequently, the Black Sea was reconstituted into an economic unit cut off from the rest of the Mediterranean by virtue of the specific Ottoman policy. It should be noted that this economic unit was not formed as a result of the natural tendency inherent in a converging process of market formation. Instead, Istanbul imposed upon the Black Sea a certain division of labour geared towards its massive provisioning requirements.[2] The forceful institution of this monopoly set the stage for whatever market-like convergence could follow within the given parameters. As such, it was not so much the deepening of a division of labour that followed the expansion of the market, but rather the imposition of a certain division of labour, within the context of which the carefully-orchestrated exchanges converging in Istanbul could take on the appearance of a market process:

> Without doubt, Constantinople drew continually on the inexhaustible riches of the empire, under *a system organized by a meticulous, authoritarian and **dirigiste** government. The supply zones were chosen to suit the convenience of methods of transport, prices were fixed, and if necessary requisitioning was enforced. Strict regulations* fixed the points where merchandise could be unloaded on the quays of the port of Constantinople. It was at Un Kapani, for instance, that grain from the Black Sea was unloaded. (Braudel, I, 1976: 351; emphasis mine except for the bold characterization)

Once the above truth, concerning the nature of the monopoly Istanbul exerted over the Black Sea as a "command economy", is acknowledged, it is no longer possible to refer to the Black Sea as a simple extension of the Mediterranean, except by virtue of the fact that the Ottoman Empire that cut it off from the Mediterranean was in fact a major "actor" on the Mediterranean scene during the period of Braudel's study.

Braudel himself never elaborated on the implications of this historiographical procedure. The more the Black Sea became a quasi-autonomous unit like the Mediterranean world that constituted the subject-matter of Braudel's inquiry, the sharper the difference between the two processes that helped consolidate the two units. The reconstruction of the Black Sea world as a "unit" followed in the footsteps of the Ottoman conquest of the region and the imposition of a singular political structure of governance over the entire economic space. In juxtaposition, the Mediterranean world emerged as a unit precisely because its underlying civilizational and economic processes tended to converge against the backdrop of a self-consolidating, multipolar structure of governance, within which empires and city-states interacted with nascent nation-state projects in a constant state of rivalry. In other words, the Black Sea became as much a unit – albeit a much smaller one – as the Mediterranean, as it came to represent the opposite of the process responsible for the formation of the Mediterranean world in the first place.[3]

The contradictory logics apparent in the Black Sea world and the Mediterranean world of the "long sixteenth century" should not mislead us into overlooking the important point that the texture of reality always displays a richer grain. No matter how well-administered, a provisioning-centred command economy cultivates in its very shadow a distorted market ranging from the illegal phenomenon of the black market that survives against all intent to suppress it, all the way to the subsidiary processes of trade that are tolerated as a second-best solution for the sake of lesser provisioning needs. The co-existence of these two tendencies holds the key to the historical transition from one logic to the other at critical conjunctures. The origins of the nineteenth-century transformation in the Black Sea world are traceable to the shadowy zone of the command economy in question:

> But of course all trade did not flow along these official channels. By its very size the city exercised an enormous power of attraction. We should note the role played in the grain trade by the big merchants who exploited the small transporters of the Black Sea, and that played by the Greek and Turkish captains of Yeni Koy, on the European shore of the Bosphorus, or of the Top Hane, near the quays of Galata, who amassed huge personal fortunes, acted as intermediaries and transporters, and were involved on more than one occasion in the contraband

passage of grain to the West from the islands of the Archipelago. (Braudel, I, 1976: 351; emphasis mine)

Such opaque zones, that remain in the penumbra of a centrally-administered economy, contain the micro-foundations of accumulation which lead to qualitative transformations of the historical system in question, provided macro-level shifts in the global environment obtain. This was precisely what happened in the nineteenth century. Given a new international division of labour brought about by the so-called Industrial Revolution and a concomitant configuration of global forces around the novel form of the nation-state as propagated as a direct consequence of the French Revolution, these loci of micro-level accumulation could gain a renewed vigour and come to prominence. The replacement of the sixteenth-century order by that of the nineteenth century was therefore a very significant transformation as far as the structures of the *longue durée* were concerned.

Braudel through Stoianovich, Balkans through the Mediterranean

The *Annales* school of historiography, of which Braudel was a prominent second-generation member, has radically altered the parameters of transdisciplinary historical research. As such, it has attracted much scholarly attention. Not only was it the first consistent and comprehensive academic alternative to the Rankean approach characteristic of nineteenth-century historiography, but also it has proven successful in spreading across national and cultural barriers, particularly in the Mediterranean countries and in Eastern Europe, thereby demonstrating its strength as an international movement (Aymard, 1978; Pomian, 1978). Fernand Braudel has occupied a central position in the spread of the *Annales* approach especially in Mediterranean Europe, Poland and in Latin America. Rather than, as in the Rankean approach, placing the emphasis on events as building-blocks of history out of which the past can allegedly be reconstituted as it actually was, Braudel represented events as the dust of history and put in their stead conjunctures and structures of the *longue durée* (Braudel, 1958). Whereas the Rankean narrative foregrounds the erratic movement of events that are primarily of political singularity and significance, Braudel's version of the *Annales* approach shifted the spotlight to the more repetitive and enduring aspects of social reality. Working within the *Annales* tradition, while branching out from it, Braudel offers a distinct alternative to historiographical convention. Unfortunately,

Braudel's scheme was only made explicit in the later part of his career, though much of it is present in a subtle form in his work on the Mediterranean. First and foremost among the several scholars who have been attracted by the originality of the *Annales* approach is Traian Stoianovich – although one who has missed the special status of Braudel's work in it.

Stoianovich is the author of a major study on the *Annales* school (1976) as well as a leading historian of South-East Europe. As such, it is no surprise that he has sought to apply the *Annales* approach to his actual work on the history of South-East Europe. Stoianovich had already noted with admiration how Braudel had immersed himself within the Mediterranean world like a picaresque wanderer (Stoianovich, 1976: 66). One gets the same impression when one reads Stoianovich's writings in history on his part of the world. However, his interpretation of the *Annales* approach puts the emphasis on a number of factors. First among these is the placement of the historian vis-à-vis the subject-matter treated. The idea of an "economic structure" borrowed from the French heterodox economists of the inter-war period (Stoianovich, 1976: 106) comes next. Thirdly, the notion of "mentalities" that govern the self-perception of a society at a given point in time, and provide it with the infrastructure within which the economy and daily life continue to function is afforded special attention. Fourthly is history written from the vantage point "of the ignored, down-trodden, proscript, vanquished, and nonconsensual", this perspective is notable given its affinity with the goals of the now fashionable so-called Subaltern Studies literature. Last but not least, the notion of a simultaneity of otherwise different durations has attracted Stoianovich's attention. This last point follows specifically from Braudel, whereas the others were more general characteristics of the *Annales* approach. Stoianovich rightly summarizes Braudel's tri-partite model of temporality as follows:

> ... duration at a quasi-immobile level of structures and traditions, with the ponderous action of the cosmos, geography, biology, collective psychology, and sociology; a level of middle-range duration of conjunctures or periodic cycles of varying length but rarely exceeding several generations; a level of short duration of events, at which almost every action is boom, bang, flash, gnash, news, and noise, but often exerts only a temporary impact. (Stoianovich, 1976: 109)

Stoianovich has a tendency to read Braudel, more specifically his work on the Mediterranean, in the light of the *Annales* paradigm, just as he over-reads the *Annales* paradigm in the light of the then state-of-the-art social sciences, French or otherwise (Stoianovich, 1978). It is my contention that the later works of Braudel provide us with a more crystallized version of his specific approach within the *Annales* tradition. A retrospective reading of early works in the light of the later works would bring to light the dormant elements of distinction in the former. It is no coincidence that the second edition of *The Mediterranean* has a new section "Can a Model be Made of the Mediterranean Economy?" This exercise on the interrelationships of the classical categories of production, consumption, exchange, and distribution in the manner of the French Physiocrat François Quesnay, as noted by Stoianovich himself (Stoianovich, 1976: 68), was an attempt to solidify the conception of the economy in terms of a unit of division of labour that determined the boundaries of the historical system in question.

It is possible to interpret Braudel's Mediterranean in two ways. One interpretation would emphasize that the Mediterranean world is the spatial expression of a single division of labour, that is a "world-economy" (*économie-monde* as Braudel re-named it after the *Weltwirtschaft* conception of the German historians, Braudel, 1985: 85), whereas the other would insist on characterizing it as a distinct civilizational space. This second interpretation would require a further characterization of what the term "civilization" would mean in Braudel's scheme of analysis. Unfortunately, the term "civilization" has been so overused in nineteenth and twentieth-century scholarship (Wallerstein, 1991b) that it has developed a multiplicity of connotations. Braudel himself must have felt rather uncomfortable with this fact as he felt obliged to emphasize in his later trilogy that his analytical scheme involves *material* civilization (Braudel, 1981: 23-24). When approached under this definition of the word, the Mediterranean was in fact a single civilizational space. However, when one has in mind the commonplace conception of the term as understood by many historians, the Mediterranean world was a terrain of contesting civilizations. Therefore, in this latter case, its unity could not be attributed to the civilizational common denominator. The sixteenth-century Mediterranean world was, in Braudel's view, distinguished insofar as it displayed a single material civilization that dictated the common parameters of everyday life while simultaneously being identified with a centripetal division of labour. This was a specific feature of the sixteenth-century Mediterranean world.

As is further elaborated in his trilogy, Braudel works with what can be best understood as a pyramid metaphor – even though he gives the example of a three-storey house – its bottom and widest layer consists of material civilization or life, the middle layer of the market economy, and the tip refers to capitalism (Braudel, 1981: 23-24; 1982: 21-22). The Mediterranean world, when approached in relation to this pyramid, was characterized by the lower two layers, which almost overlapped in scope. Where they differed from one another was the rate of change, as the market was the dynamic domain and material life the slow-changing realm.

Stoianovich's dedication to *A Study in Balkan Civilization* (1967)[4] refers to Braudel as his mentor. The book's brief Preface displays the strong influence of Braudel and the *Annales*. The intent of this book was a history that moved beyond events, a "total history" moreover a "problem history". Stoianovich's methodological preference was that of an interdisciplinary pursuit covering a wide range of questions associated with anthropological and sociological theories and economic change. In addition Stoianovich felt obliged to further specify the large-scale, long-term orientation of his scope of inquiry:

> The book differs from anthropological studies in that it deals with large regional subcultures – Balkan civilization in the plural – instead of confining itself to "little communities". It is also historical or diachronic, a study of social space-time relationships. It differs no less from historical studies of the traditional type; for example, it is not limited to the usual short period of historians – a decade or a century – but embraces eight or nine millenia. It is, moreover, not a history of empires, kingdoms, republics, or city-states, but a history of peoples. (Stoianovich, 1967: viii).

Inspired by Braudel's *Mediterranean*, noted not so much for its pyramidal metaphor which wasn't explicitly stated until the later trilogy, Stoianovich nevertheless developed a conceptual organization of his subject-matter that closely resembled a pyramid:

> Each chapter is an entity in itself, but the chapters should in fact be read consecutively, for each is a view into a particular system of coherences, notably of the structure that must exist before the next structure can arise. The deepest structure relates to the earth and cosmos, above it is a biological layer, above the biological a technological, above the technological a social, above the social an economic stratum. The geographical and biological structures change most slowly, and only after the rise of an economic or pure-economic structure can there be human individuality or a personality culture. (Stoianovich, 1967: 5)

In spite of his novel orientation *pace* Braudel, Stoianovich succumbed to an approach where the civilizational infrastructure of the edifice took on exaggerated proportions, with an unfortunate emphasis on plurality rather than singularity, whereas the implications of an "economic division of labour" in terms of the unit of analysis were overlooked. In fact, the entire chapter on the "Economy" includes no single good reason as to why the Balkans should be treated as a "unit of analysis" (Stoianovich, 1967: 155-

168). As a consequence, after some 200 pages, the Balkans as a unit of analysis, as well as the case for a Balkan civilization, remains to be justified despite Stoianovich's remarkable achievements by other standards. Unsurprisingly Stoianovich once more deployed his preferred version of Braudel's framework in *Balkan Worlds: The First and Last Europe* (1994).[5] Whatever this study's merits, it did not overcome the inherent problems of the earlier work as far as the legitimization of the "unit of analysis" is concerned. In retrospect, it seems that Stoianovich, a notable historian having already specialized in his native Balkans, searched for a more productive scheme of analysis. Having found in Braudel the ingredients necessary for a novel re-interpretation of Balkan history, he went on to demonstrate successfully what new and more could be said about his subject-matter.[6] Stoianovich's Balkans was a land mass divided in important ways. As he himself noted, each part turned to a different sea, be that the Adriatic, or the Ionian, or the Aegean, or the Black Sea (Stoianovich, 1994: 1). These parts traded with one another by way of sea to the extent that they could not do so by way of land. If anything, the landscape of the Balkans divided rather than united the geography, in sharp contrast to the Mediterranean where the sea undertook a centripetal function by way of which distant land masses were brought into contact.[7]

Bratianu as the Obscure Braudel of the Black Sea

More often than not, scholarship has tended to see the Balkans as an extension of the greater Mediterranean area.[8] In this respect, the fate of the Balkans has been no different from that of the Black Sea. Despite this fact, however, it makes much more sense to take the Black Sea rather than the Balkans as the unit of analysis. It is my contention that the Balkans constitute a zone within the Black Sea world, rather than being a meaningful unit of analysis in itself (Özveren, 1997: 86n). As for the study of the Black Sea, Braudel's previously-cited characterization seems to indicate that the Black Sea was what the Mediterranean was not, at least for "the long sixteenth century". This was largely because the Black Sea became an Ottoman preserve, thereby paving the way to the containment of an economic space under the jurisdiction of a single political structure. As a consequence, the market had become subservient to the tightly designed division of labour imposed from the centre with an eye to the provisioning principle. In juxtaposition, the Mediterranean was characterized by the overlapping of multiple state structures with a single economic space where the logic of the economy was based on the market principle operating through the division of labour.[9]

The Black Sea of the sixteenth century was substantially different from the Black Sea of previous centuries. What made the critical difference was the enforcement of Ottoman control that could swiftly be expanded all the way to its limits after the conquest of Istanbul in 1453. So, in order to comprehend the pre-sixteenth century structure of the Black Sea world, one has to return to Bratianu's much neglected[10] yet invaluable study of the Black Sea *La mer Noire des origines à la conquete ottomane* (1969). The endpoint of Bratianu's study coincides with the beginning of Braudel's narrative of the Black Sea as an Ottoman preserve. After extensive research in the highly relevant Venetian and Genovese archives the importance of the subject tempted Bratianu to expand the scope of his intended study and aimed to cover, in a comprehensive singular work Black Sea trade, from its origins in remote antiquity through to modern times. It was with this in mind that he addressed a course he gave at the University of Bucharest during 1942-43, to the evolution of the "*Question de la mer Noire*" (The Black Sea Question, Bratianu, 1969:38).

As noted Bratianu's work on the Black Sea is clearly the contemporary of Braudel's Mediterranean study. In fact Braudel cited one work of Bratianu (Bratianu, 1938) in his discussion of the Black Sea, as the supporting source for the opening up of the Black Sea to the Italians in the thirteenth century as a direct consequence of the political decline of the Byzantine Empire (Braudel, 1976, I: 111).[11] More importantly, Braudel cited an article of Bratianu that characterized the Black Sea, in a holistic fashion, as the *plaque tournante* (turntable) of international trade at the end of the Middle Ages (Braudel, 1976, I: 112). This article was published during the war (Bratianu, 1944), and reappears as a chapter in his (posthumously) published book. It is well established that one major historiographical innovation associated with Braudel was the shift of focus to the study of structures.[12] It remains to be seen whether Bratianu's study of the Black Sea renders itself readily to the identification of another structure of the *longue durée*. If it does, then the long-term history of the Black Sea world can, in fact, be conceived as a pendular motion between the two structures, of which one has already been identified above in the work of Braudel.

Just like Braudel on the Mediterranean, Bratianu's starting-point was the geographical characterization of the Black Sea question. It was a sea that was almost closed, a sea that did not communicate with the Mediterranean except for the narrow Straits, and yet nevertheless had access to the Asian Steppes and the land mass of Central Europe by way of major rivers and multiple continental routes that tended towards its ports. Furthermore, because it is situated at the crossroads of Europe and Asia, the Black Sea possessed the attributes of a permanent zone of transition, which it imprinted upon the peoples and states that occupied its coastlines. Unlike the Mediterranean, the Black Sea was an inhospitable sea that was virtually closed to navigation during much of the long winters stretching at least from November to March. At best, it permitted coastline navigation during a few months of the year. These geographical attributes dictated the constant parameters of the Black Sea world – except for minor changes that improved access to navigable rivers such as the Danube – as reflected in the structures of the *longue durée* and the everyday life of the inhabitants.

In Bratianu's depiction of the Black Sea world it is possible to identify two alternating structures. If there is a pattern to the history of the Black Sea built upon the foundations provided by geography discussed above, it consists of the succession of these structures. While placing the Black Sea at the civilizational crossroads between the East and West in general terms, Bratianu's account singles out the North-South axis as the backbone of the Black Sea world. Irrespective of which of the two structures obtains, this axis remains dominant. At most, the actual degree of dominance of this axis increases or decreases in relation to the particular structure in effect.

Long before the ultimate hegemony of Athens, the Black Sea was colonized by the Ionian cities led by Miletus in antiquity. A particular division of labour was imposed that derived its logic from the requisites of geography. The demand for the grain, slaves, fish, and wax of the Black Sea was matched by the exports of manufacturers arriving from the numerous cities of the Greek and Italian peninsulas. Given the commodity structure of trade, the nature of the Black Sea world's role in these exchanges can be defined as peripheral from the very beginning. As early as this, there developed a *modus vivendi* among the Greek colonizers on the one side and on the other the Persian and Scythian Empires. Whereas the former brought in trade, the latter established the minimal conditions of law and order, namely security, essential for the continuation of trade.[13] On the one hand, we observe a continuity over time in the civilization of the once-colonized ports. On the other side, we observe another continuity despite periodic disruptions: the Persian and Scythian empires were succeeded by the brief epoch of Hellenistic monarchies, only to yield their place to the Roman Empire (Bratianu, 1969: 49). In the course of time, the Roman Empire paved the way to the Byzantine Empire during the Middle Ages, only to be succeeded by the Ottoman Empire. Along this line of succession, Istanbul emerged naturally as the pivotal point of concentration in the Southern pole of the North-South axis.[14] Given the North-South axis, Bratianu rightly insisted that it was always from the

South that the impulse for change came, and that the North reacted to this. In this sense, the Ottoman Empire was the natural inheritor of a set of policies that had long been consolidated in the southern pole (Bratianu, 1969: 50).[15] The line of succession in the South was matched by a chain of empires of the steppes in the North. Irrespective of the brief, yet violence-ridden, chaotic breakdowns of law and order in-between, a kind of complementary logic persisted in the North. So much so, that Genghiz Khan's Mongol Empire resembled its Persian precursor in antiquity in practice. Just as the Persian Empire had attracted commercially-minded Greek settlers, the Mongol Empire offered protection and privileges to Italian merchants in order to settle them in its territories thereby inaugurating a new era of prosperity (Bratianu, 1969: 50).[16]

The one structure of the Black Sea world acquired its first crystallized form under the Byzantines. The Byzantine rule, stemming from Istanbul, functioned as a locus responsible for the perpetuation and eventual transfer to the Ottomans of the heritage of antiquity concentrated along the coastline. Istanbul relied increasingly on the grain and fish of the region whereas the populace provided the imperial army with potential recruits (Bratianu, 1969: 118). When the political decline of the centre became apparent, Byzantine control retreated to the carefully selected number of strategic outposts along the littoral. As a second best to direct imperial rule of the entire Black Sea world which proved too costly to maintain, Byzantines sought to make working arrangements with the nomadic powers periodically installed in the North such as the soon-urban Khazars and the more mobile Petcheneks (Bratianu, 1969: 133-141).

The Byzantines converted the Black Sea into a closed lake the produce of which was destined for the provisioning of the capital city, as was the case before the crisis of invasions in the eleventh century (Bratianu, 1969: 154). When the Byzantines yielded to pressure from Italy to open up their territories to foreign trade, they still insisted on preserving their monopoly over the Black Sea as a hinterland closed to outsiders' traffic (Bratianu, 1969: 173-175). As the natural produce of the Black Sea coasts was destined to provisioning the populace of Istanbul, the Byzantine authorities did not see any advantage in allowing foreign competition into this "well-guarded hunting ground", reminiscent of – in Bratianu's words "identical" to – the Ottoman policy of the future (Bratianu, 1969: 175, 247, 327). Therefore, the one structure of the Black Sea world was manifested when the Byzantine domination was at its extreme and virtually exclusive.[17] The Byzantines had rehearsed this extreme case and the Ottomans were going to repeat it in a perfected and more enduring sense.

This structure was what Braudel had depicted in his study of "the long sixteenth century".

What's more the rule for the Ottoman period and less the exception, remained less the rule during the late Byzantine era and more the exception. This paves the way for the specification of the second structure characteristic of the Black Sea world. When the preconditions for full Byzantine hegemony did not obtain, as often they did not, the Black Sea world was politically fragmented and economically opened up to the exploitation of the outsiders. Bratianu cites 1204 as a turning-point for Italian intrusion into the Black Sea (Bratianu, 1969: 177). In addition, while some balance-of-power stimulated freedom of trade, the occasional excessive fragmentation of political power led to the relative insecurity of travel, a must for long-distance trade (Bratianu, 1969: 183). In this sense, the Mongol conquest should be seen as the reversal of the trend towards the eventual break-up of the region into many states, the disharmonies and ineffectiveness of which would jeopardize the prospects of the Black Sea as a single terrain. The Mongol rule brought back the minimal conditions of law and security for the conduct of trade in the North[18] at a time when Byzantine power was restricted to the South. This bi-polar configuration of power was characteristic of the second structure of the Black Sea world. It was then that free trade of some kind could flourish within the Black Sea world. Under this alternative structural arrangement, it was no coincidence that foreign merchants, supported by foreign finance and capital, led the way to the development of an early capitalist accumulation process within the context of an economic realm, the logic of which was no longer subservient to the provisioning mentality of a single politically-charged administration.

The Mongols put the North back in order thereby enabling the extension of long-distance trade towards Central Asia. Nomadic as they were, their encampment resembled a "city on the move" (*une ville en marche*), as a contemporary observer described it (Bratianu, 1969: 209). The combined effect of Mongol and subsequent Golden Horde consolidation in the North, and the restoration after the Latin *interregnum* of Byzantine rule in the South was to create a conjuncture favourable to the economic penetration of European traders – originally the Genovese (Bratianu, 1929) – on a large scale in order not only to take over *en masse* the trade of Byzantium but also to exploit the riches of the Black Sea region (Bratianu, 1969: 219). At this point the expansionary momentum of the Black Sea economic networks gained a new global meaning. The Asian routes by way of the Black Sea could rival the monopoly of the Mediterranean port of Alexandria in the eastern trade of Europe. At the dawn of early modern times, the historic encounter in the Black Sea basin of Mongols and Italians was one important factor that contributed to the development of European commercial and financial capitalism (Bratianu, 1969: 223). The retreat of Byzantine domination of regional trade went hand in hand with the devaluation of Byzantine currency which suffered severe setbacks as the generally accepted medium of exchange. In its place the Italian merchants promoted their own monetary and financial instruments and thereby gained access to additional profits and consolidated their position in the economic networks (Bratianu, 1969: 229). Born masters of monetary games, the Italian merchants came to occupy exclusively the commanding heights of the economic realm, the privileged domain which Braudel sparingly named as "capitalism" in order to counterpoise it with the market as the "anti-market" (*contre-marché*) (Braudel, 1985: 56, Wallerstein, 1991a).

Bratianu places a strong emphasis on the formative influence of the Black Sea on the fortunes of European capitalism in its earliest stage.[19] In fact Bratianu's account of the advantages to the Black Sea in assuming this role brings to the foreground the relative institutional flexibility and administrative innovativeness that prevailed in the region.[20] Freed from the fetters of the European past, the Black Sea became a laboratory for capitalist experimentation at a time when the characteristic institutions of capitalism had not yet taken their definitive shape. Bratianu looks back upon the peculiar formations of the Black Sea in the light of early modern Europe only to identify there the embryonic forms of capitalist organization.[21] First and foremost, in return for the law and order it provided, sustaining the Mongol rule was much less costly than that of its overburdened and paralysed Byzantine counterpart. The Mongol rule that developed, in zones that were once Byzantine, brought with it not only stability in the place of chaos, but more importantly shifted priorities of economic policy. Whereas the Byzantines had been rather conservative insofar as they placed high the objectives of provisioning and bureaucratic regulation of regional trade in conformity with the needs of the administration, the Mongols sought instead to encourage the freer flow of long-distance trade across their territories in order to expand their revenue base (Bratianu, 1969: 230). Consequently, by the end of the thirteenth century, the Black Sea had become a centre of primary economic importance with global repercussions (Bratianu, 1969: 232). One major strength of Bratianu's work lay in its treatment of the Black Sea in relation to Europe as well as Asia. This amounted to no less than "a perspective of the world" in Braudel's terminology (Braudel, 1984). In juxtaposition to the slow changing structures of the long-term Braudel identified, Bratianu hereby placed the highly dynamic and volatile processes of conjuncture that indicated the fortunes of the market process and capitalist accumulation.

Whereas thirteenth-century prosperity in the Black sea basin had come about under Genovese hegemony, the mid-fourteenth-century upswing coincided with the Genovese-Venetian rivalry (Bratianu, 1969: 239). This process culminated in the mature phase of the so-called second structure of Black Sea political economy. The Italians bitterly contested one another over the right for free and safe passage through the Straits, thereby inaugurating the strategic centrality of the Straits as the gateway to the Black Sea. The Straits Question thus became a permanent feature of Black Sea political economy. If the influx of the Italians was one sign of the opening-up of the Black Sea as the logic of administrative provisioning receded, the economic formation of the Wallachian and Moldovian principalities with the prospects of a passageway to the Great Hungarian Plain placed for the first time the reality of the Danube on the political economic map of the region.[22] It was as of then that the Danubian Question became a permanent corollary of the Black Sea question (Bratianu, 1969: 275). At this point the Danubian Question became a second permanent feature of the Black Sea political economy. It is no surprise that, since then, the Danubian Question accompanies the Straits Question into virtually every balance-of-power equation that seals the fate of the Black Sea world.

Casting the Future against the Pattern of History

Having learned the lessons of the First World War all too well, Bratianu drew a parallel between the provisioning-oriented policies of Byzantine Empire and the Ottoman Empire during their heyday and the provisioning concerns of the war economies in the early twentieth century. Citing how the defective organization of the distribution of bread in Petrograd contributed to the outbreak of the 1917 Revolution, he sought to justify the logic of a provisioning concern that could help install a command economy. The parallel between the thirteenth-century Byzantine Empire and the nineteenth-century Ottoman Empire that had yielded to the pressure of opening-up to a system of "free-trade" instituted under a regime of capitulations was equally clear to Bratianu. As such, he had discovered a pattern of Black Sea history as an alteration between two structures of political economy. In this sense, Bratianu's work bore the heavy imprint of theoretical debates concerning the relative merits and feasibility of market economy and planning.[23] What Bratianu could not foresee was how the line from provisioning to the command economy of war could so easily extend further into supposedly socialist, central planning and that the Black Sea world could fall prey to a full-fledged effort in economic planning stemming from the Soviet Union.

The nineteenth-century transformation of the world economy brought with it the swing of the pendulum once more from a politically-administrated, self-enclosed economy to a multi-centred, market-oriented economic orientation in the Black Sea. The opening up of the Black Sea to foreigners further approximated the picture to that of the period between the Byzantine and Ottoman supremacies. The *dramatis personae* changed as this time the Ottomans and Russians competed for regional political hegemony among themselves as well as with the Austrians, amidst a scene characterized by further potential fragmentation of political governance in tune with the demands of nation-state projects in the making. Furthermore, the British and French, later to be accompanied by the Germans, took the place of Italians as the outsiders willing to intrude.

During the Second World War Bratianu had referred to the Turks and Russians at the end of the Byzantine era as the forces of the future (Bratianu, 1969: 305). The nineteenth century witnessed a contest between these two the long-term loser of which turned out to be, in the twentieth century, none other than the Black Sea itself. Russian advances at the expense of the Ottomans reached a critical threshold in the wake of the twentieth century. For the first time in history, the balance along the North-South axis changed in favour of the North when the Ottoman Empire collapsed while the Russian Empire reconstituted itself as a Soviet Empire that played the superpower role in the international order. Much of the second half of the twentieth century that came to be identified with the Iron Curtain and the Cold War meant for the Black Sea a historic moment of freeze. With the exception of Turkey that continued to exercise sovereignty over the Straits, the Black Sea fell prey to the Soviet sphere of influence, while the Danube was practically inactivated by the East-West divide and the inward-looking developmental strategies of the so-called socialist states. Hence, for the first time, a power in the North, assisted by the minor satellite regimes, attempted to reproduce the economic logic of the Byzantine and Ottoman Empires *vis-à-vis* the Black Sea. Yet it failed in scope and brought about a fracturing of the Black Sea that made it dysfunctional economically. In retrospect, the Soviet *interregnum* was an anomaly, it was a structural inversion of the North-South axis, as well as being an anachronism as far as its economic logic was concerned. The world economy had changed so much as not to tolerate as normal a regional difference, as had been the case in the heyday of the

Byzantine and Ottoman Empires. As such, the seeming Soviet success came with a heavy economic price. The Black Sea remained fractured, paralysed and defunct as a zone of capital accumulation until the dismemberment of the Soviet Empire.

With the fall of the Soviet Empire has arrived a new era. Present trends in the region reveal a momentum for the Black Sea to recuperate its losses and assume an important role with respect to both the states and peoples of the region as well as in relation with the global political economy in-the-making by way of blocs along the Eurasian axis. What the future has in store can only be estimated by looking at present trends. However, the Black Sea of the twenty-first century is more likely to replicate the politically polycentric, economically market-integrated model of the nineteenth century which was itself prefigured by the circumstances that obtained with the waning of Byzantine power before the installation of Ottoman rule. Given the pattern of history that has prevailed over the past thousand years, the evidence supports the likelihood of this as an option. It should be recalled that this option was rather weak at the beginning only to gain strength in the course of time and to make a stronger comeback each time it suffered a serious setback. While this polycentric, economically-flexible mode is highly desirable as far as the economic exigencies of the international system are concerned, to survive and deliver its promise, it requires the effective – and hopefully this time voluntary – constitution of law and order within the Black Sea world.

Notes

1   There exists consensus over this characterization *pace* Braudel. Diverse historians of the Ottoman Empire approximate to this view (McGowan, 1981; Mantran, 1983; Faroqhi, 1994). As such, it has stood the test of time.

2   Nevertheless, the rich and diverse resources as well as the geographical division of labour that existed in the first place was conducive to further consolidation under Ottoman rule: "In the first place there was the produce of its own shores: dried fish, the botargo and caviar of the 'Russian' rivers, the wood indispensable to the Turkish fleet, iron from Mingrelia, grain, and wool; the latter was collected at Varna and loaded along with hides on to the great Ragusan vessels; the grain was cornered by Constantinople." (Braudel, I, 1976: 110).

3   Only in the nineteenth century, with the dismemberment of the Ottoman sovereignty over the region and the creation of multiple states, this process would be reversed. As of then a multipolar structure of governance would emerge. However, by then the Black Sea could only become an economically meaningful unit of analysis within the parameters of a broader world economy.

This would make it a candidate for regionality, whereas the Mediterranean world which Braudel identified was not a region within the world economy, but a precursor of it. To put it differently, the concept of a world economy as identified with a single division of labour was first realized historically in the Mediterranean. Once it was realized at a greater scale in the European world economy that also encompassed Latin America as a periphery, the Mediterranean world was transformed into a region and then forced to lose its meaning as an independent economic unit.

4   Furthermore, in the Acknowledgements of the same book Stoianovich wrote: "My greatest intellectual debt – is to my friend and mentor, Fernand Braudel. In a less personal way, I am under deep obligation to the searching, probing, experimental method of *Annales (Economies, Sociétés, Civilisations)*." (Stoianovich, 1967).

5   Stoianovich's many articles have been reassembled into a two-part, four-volume collection (Stoianovich, 1992, 1994). The headings used in their reclassification bear the heavy mark of the *Annales* school in general, and of Braudel in particular. However, the fact that these articles could so easily be placed under these categories attests to the close affinity between the historical interests of Braudel the mentor, and Stoianovich, the disciple.

6   Nor is Stoianovich alone in this task. Maria Todorova, a Bulgarian historian who subscribes equally to the category of the Balkans, displays symptoms of the French historiographical influence. Not only does she acknowledge the role of the *longue durée* in the macrohistorical domain, but also she elaborates the possibilities of delineating a Balkan *mentalité* (Todorova, 1997: 165, 180).

7   By contrast, K. N. Chaudhuri, inspired by, and in constant dialogue with, the work of Braudel, chose the Indian Ocean as a unit of analysis, thereby preserving the primacy of the sea as constitutive of historical space the effects of which exerted a determining influence on the economic and civilizational realities (Chaudhuri, 1985: 1; 1990). In a similar vein, the same framework of analysis has been applied to South-East Asia in a thought-provoking lecture (Lombard, 1996).

8   The same conclusion has been affirmed by a contemporary specialist of the Balkans: "Methodological and semantic paucity notwithstanding, there is no doubt that the Balkans represent a cultural region, possibly a subregion of the larger Mediterranean area." (Todorova, 1997: 181).

9   In addition to the implicit characterization of the Mediterranean world discussed above at length, in the brief concluding section of his study, Braudel cites Labrousse in support of his emphasis on the market principle: "The Mediterranean as a unit, with its creative space, the amazing freedom of its sea-routes *(its automatic free trade as Ernest Labrousse called it)* with its many regions, so different yet so alike, its cities born of movement, its complementary populations, its congenial enmities, is the unceasing work of human hands, but those hands have had to build with unpromising material, a natural environment far from fertile and often cruel, one that has imposed its

own long lasting limitations and obstacles." (Braudel, 1976, II: 1239; emphasis mine).

10 As far as this commonplace neglect is concerned, one of the latest attempts to redress the Euro-centric conception of macro history is a telling example. Its extensive bibliography does not include Bratianu's book, in spite of its common timespan with the critical period in Black Sea history and the overall parallelism of their themes, not to mention the author's interest in Fernand Braudel (Abu-Lughod, 1989).

11 I have been fortunate enough to find a rather rare copy of Bratianu's work in the Library of the Maison des Sciences de l'Homme, Paris, a renowned institution of research and learning founded by Fernand Braudel. Not surprisingly, this copy had found its way to the library by way of Braudel whose name was handwritten in the book. Hence, Braudel knew not only Bratianu's early article but also his *opus magnum*, the publication in 1969 of which, however, postdated the revised second and last edition of his *Mediterranean* in 1966.

12 "In historical analysis as I see it, rightly or wrongly, the long run always wins in the end. Annihilating innumerable events − all those which cannot be accommodated in the main ongoing current and which are therefore ruthlessly swept to one side − it indubitably limits both the freedom of the individual and even the role of chance. I am by temperament a 'structuralist', little tempted by the event, or even by the short-term conjuncture which is after all merely a grouping of events in the same area." (Braudel, 1976, II: 1242–1244).

13 The institution of law and order went hand in hand with protection extended to the mercantile interests. From the viewpoint of the state, this function was costly. The costs were covered by the revenue stimulating direct (taxes and customs) and indirect effects (expansion of the tax base) of prospective trade. From the viewpoint of the commercial enterprises, there was a price to be paid in the form of taxes for these otherwise highly desirable services. Nevertheless, there incurred "protection rents" for these enterprises that chose to work with the more powerful and efficient states. Bratianu's emphasis on the importance of political governance for the continuity of trade networks, but especially the protection-versus-enterprise interpretation of the symbiosis along the North-South axis, lends itself to an interpretation along the lines of the "protection rents" thesis (Lane, 1979).

14 The routes of Asia Minor had already converged on the Straits long before Istanbul was established. The founding of the New Rome in 330 AD was the logical culmination of this natural process. The region's strategic importance at a communication *nexus* reinforced its hegemony and led to Istanbul's consolidation (Bratianu, 1969: 108).

15 First and foremost among these policies was the principle of provisioning (Bratianu, 1938).

16   By speaking of a "significant parallelism" between the Greek-Persian symbiosis, and the Mongol-Italian one, Bratianu displays his deep sense of persistence and change by way of structural continuity in history (Bratianu, 1969: 171).

17   This characterization of the relationship of Byzantine Empire to the Black Sea at the height of its power is confirmed by a notable historian of Byzantium's privileged relation to the sea, at a time when the unity and coordination of the Empire in question was maintained by way of the sea routes (Ahrweiler, 1966: 166, 225n, 390).

18   In discussing the balance sheet of the Mongol Empire, a contemporary work reaches much the same conclusion: "In itself, unification does not necessarily reduce the overall costs of transit, but it has the potential to do so, depending upon policy choices. The chief contribution made by an administration based on 'law and order' is a reduction in unpredictable protection rent. By eliminating competing tribute gatherers and by regularizing tolls, unification makes transport costs calculable. Furthermore, although it can scarcely eliminate natural disasters, such as droughts that dry up watering holes, it can reduce overall risk by virtually eliminating human predators. As long as these advantages can be assured, trade will flourish." (Abu-Lughod, 1989: 182).

19   The former question of the origins of (European) capitalism has in the course of time yielded its place to the broader question of the European-*versus*-non European origins of European capitalism, which then paved the way to world-systemic formulations of the question of capitalist specificity (Frank & Gills, 1996). Bratianu's discussion of the Black Sea basin preserves its meaning irrespective of these shifts in historiography.

20   Bratianu insisted that the world-historic significance of the Black Sea was by no means reducible to the volume of its trade at the end of the Middle Ages. What counted more was the methods of doing things that were perfected there by way of trial and error in the relatively liberal atmosphere of a colonial zone that remained free from the heavy traditions and the corporatist order of the guild system characteristic of the European Middle Ages (Bratianu, 1969: 249).

21   The discussion of the temporary institution of the direct rule of the banking house of St. Georges (*La Casa di S. Georgio*) over the Genovese colonies of Crimea is a case in point. Bratianu makes the comparison with the India Companies of the eighteenth century that lay the foundations of colonial empires (Bratianu, 1969: 317).

22   The settlement of colonies in the mouth of the Danube first intensified after the Genovese inroads to the region during the thirteenth century. Vicina was one such settlement that developed spectacularly and then collapsed suddenly as a consequence of the fortunes of long-distance trade (Bratianu, 1935: 93).

23   Bratianu noted that at moments of crises of the world economy a certain antagonism came to the foreground. On the one side of this antagonism was the *etatiste* administrative tradition led by the principle of interventionism in economic matters, while on the other side, the novel principle of the liberty of

navigation and commerce – an essential factor for the formation and development of modern capitalism, – rested (Bratianu, 1938: 181).

References

Abu-Lughod, Janet L. (1989) *Before European Hegemony: The World System AD 1250–1350*. New York: Oxford University Press.

Ahrweiler, Hélene (1966) *Byzance et la mer: La Marine de guerre, la politique et les institutions maritimes de Byzance aux VIIe–XVe siecles*. Paris: Presses Universitaires de France.

Aymard, Maurice (1978) "Impact of the *Annales* School in Mediterranean Countries," *Review, of the Fernand Braudel Center*, I, 3/4, 53–64.

Bratianu, Georges I (1938) "Etudes sur l'Approvisonnement de Constantinople et le Monopole du Blé a l'époque Byzantine et Ottomane," *Etudes Byzantines d'Histoire Economique et Sociale*. Paris: Librairie Orientaliste Paul Geuthner, 128–181.

Bratianu, Georges I. (1969) *La Mer Noire des origines à la conquete ottomane*. Rome & Munich: Societas Academica Dacoromana.

Bratianu, Georges I. (1944) "La Mer Noire, plaque tournante du trafic international à la fin du Moyen Age," *Revue Historique du Sud-Est Européen*, XXI, 36–69.

Bratianu, Georges I. (1929) *Recherches sur le commerce Génois dans la Mer Noire au XVII siecle*. Paris: Paul Geuthner.

Bratianu, Georges I. (1935) *Recherches sur Vicina et Cetatea Alba: Contributions à l'histoire de la Domination Byzantine et Tatare et du Commerce Génois sur le Littoral Roumain de la Mer Noire*. Bucarest: 1935.

Braudel, Fernand (1981) *Civilization & Capitalism, 15th-18th Century*, vol I: *The Structures of Everyday Life*. New York: Harper & Row.

Braudel, Fernand (1982) *Civilization & Capitalism, 15th-18th Century*, vol II: *The Wheels of Commerce*. New York: Harper & Row.

Braudel, Fernand (1984) *Civilization & Capitalism, 15th-18th Century*, vol III: *The Perspective of the World*. New York: Harper & Row.

Braudel, Fernand (1985) *La dynamique du capitalisme*. Paris: Flammarion.

Braudel, Fernand (1958) "Histoire et Sciences sociales: La Longue dureé," *Annales: Economies, Societés, Civilisations*, 4: 725–753.

Braudel, Fernand (1976) *The Mediterranean and the Mediterranean World in the Age of Philip II*. London: Fontana/Collins [1949, 1966].

Chaudhuri, K. N. (1990) *Asia Before Europe: Economy and Civilization of the Indian Ocean from the Rise of Islam to 1750*. Cambridge: Cambridge University Press.

Chaudhuri, K. N. (1985) *Trade and Civilisation in the Indian Ocean: An Economic History from the Rise of Islam to 1750*. Cambridge: Cambridge University Press.

Faroqhi, Suraiya (1994) "Crisis and Change, 1590–1699," in H. Inalcik, ed., *An Economic and Social History of the Ottoman Empire, 1300–1914*. Cambridge: Cambridge University Press, 411–636.

Frank, André Gunder and Bary K. Gills, eds. (1996) *The World System: Five Hundred Years or Five Thousand?* London: Routledge.

Lane, Frederic C. (1979) *Profits from Power: Readings in Protection Rent and Violence-Controlling Enterprises.* Albany, New York: State University of New York Press.

Lombard, Denys (1996) "Une autre Méditerranée, l'Asie du sud-est," lecture given at the workshop on "Fernand Braudel aujourd'hui", organized by Centre de Recherches Historiques de l'E.H.E.S.S., June 12, 1996.

Mantran, Robert (1983) "Commerce maritime et économie dans l'Empire ottoman au XVIIIe siecle," in J. Bacqué-Grammont & P. Dumont, eds, *Economies et Sociétes dans l'Empire ottoman (fin du XVIIIe-debut du Xxe siecle).* Paris: Centre Nationale de la Recherche Scientifique, 289–96.

McGowan, Bruce (1981) *Economic Life in the Ottoman Europe: Taxation, Trade and the Struggle for Land, 1600–1800.* Cambridge: Cambridge University Press.

Özveren, Eyüp (1997) "A Framework for the Study of the Black Sea World, 1789–1915," *Review, of the Fernand Braudel Center,* XX, 1: 77–113.

Pomian, Krysztof (1978) "Impact of the *Annales* School in Eastern Europe," *Review, of the Fernand Braudel Center,* I, 3/4: 101–118.

Stoianovich, Traian (1967) *A Study in Balkan Civilization.* New York: Alfred A. Knopf.

Stoianovich, Traian (1994) *Balkan Worlds: The First and Last Europe.* Armonk: M. E. Sharpe.

Stoianovich, Traian (1976) *French Historical Method: The Annales Paradigm.* Ithaca & London: Cornell University Press.

Stoianovich, Traian (1992) *Between East and West: The Balkan and Mediterranean Worlds,* I & II: *Economies and Societies.* New Rochelle: Aristide D. Caratsas, Publisher.

Stoianovich, Traian (1994) *Between East and West: The Balkan and Mediterranean Worlds,* III & IV: *Material Culture and Mentalités.* New Rochelle: Aristide D. Caratsas.

Stoianovich, Traian (1978) "Social History: Perspective of the *Annales* Paradigm," *Review, of the Fernand Braudel Center,* I, 3/4: 19–48.

Todorova, Maria (1997) *Imagining the Balkans.* New York: Oxford University Press.

Wallerstein, Immanuel (1991a) "Braudel on Capitalism, or Everything Upside Down," in his *Unthinking Social Science: The Limits of Nineteenth-Century Paradigms.* Cambridge: Polity Press.

Wallerstein, Immanuel (1991b) "The Modern World System as a Civilization," in his *Geopolitics and Geoculture: Essays on the Changing World-System.* Cambridge: Cambridge University Press, 215–230.

CHAPTER FIVE

Ukraine and the
Black Sea Region*

Tor Bukkvoll

'Without the northern shores of the Black Sea
it will be impossible for Ukraine
to be a cultured country'
Mykhailo Drahomanov
Ukrainian philosopher
(1841-1895)[1]

Ukrainian politicians and foreign policy analysts often speak of the Black Sea region as the "third vector" of Ukrainian foreign policy. The "first vector" is the Eurasian one (Russia and other former Soviet republics) – foremost of which is Russia. It is a goal of Ukrainian foreign policy to reduce the importance of this vector. The "second vector" is the EuroAtlantic one (USA, Western and Central Europe). Ukraine is attempting to increase the importance of this particular vector.

The bulk of analyses of Ukrainian foreign policy have concentrated on Ukraine's attempts to find its place within the East–West divide.[2] So far there are few scholarly publications which have been specifically devoted to an analysis of Ukraine's position in the Black Sea region.[3] The analysis presented in this chapter will attempt to remedy that imbalance.

I will begin with some general remarks on the place of the Black Sea region in Ukrainian foreign policy since the time of independence, and then continue by analysing Ukraine perceptions of the Black Sea region specifying four dimensions: the strategic dimension, the economic dimension, the ethnic minority dimension, and the civil society dimension. For each dimension I will analyse Ukrainian perspectives regarding the possibilities for cooperation and for conflict. In the concluding sections of the analysis I will combine findings from each of these different dimensions, in order to reach a general assessment of Ukrainian perceptions of the Black Sea region.

When discussing Ukraine's relations with specific countries in the region, I will limit my analysis to those that Ukraine seems to consider most important for her foreign policy: these are Russia, Turkey, Romania, and Georgia.

The Black Sea Region in Ukrainian Foreign Policy since Independence

Even though the Black Sea region is not considered the most important one for Ukrainian foreign policy, Ukraine has been very conscious of itself as a Black Sea power ever since the country became independent in 1991. As early as May 1992 a Treaty of Friendship and Good Neighbourly Relations was signed with Turkey. Later Ukraine signed similar treaties with most Black Sea states. Fairly early on Ukraine adopted an understanding of the Black Sea area as a regional entity with political processes of its own, and the country was one of the initial signatories to the Bosphorus Declaration in February 1992, which marked the start of the Black Sea Economic Cooperation (BSEC).

However, most of these agreements and treaties were of a declaratory nature. Ukraine's integration into the Black Sea region did not really take off until late 1997. In spring 1997 a panel of 42 Ukrainian foreign policy specialists (from the Ministry of Foreign Affairs, the Supreme Rada, the Armed Forces of Ukraine, as well as a group of journalists and academics) characterised the speed of Ukrainian integration into the Black Sea region as either medium (24 per cent), slow (55 per cent), or at zero (21 per cent).[4] The same panel concluded in spring 1998, however, that Ukraine's progress of integration into the Black Sea region was one of the most positive changes in Ukrainian foreign policy over the last year.[5] The main reason for this shift was the development of the GUAMU (Georgia, Ukraine, Azerbaijan, Moldova and Uzbekistan) sub-regional grouping, and the increased emphasis on the Black Sea region as a transportation focal point for trade (especially oil and gas) between Central Asia, the Caucasus and Western Europe.

The upsurge of integrational activities in the Black Sea region was given additional importance by the fact that the coinciding integration process with Western and Central Europe was relatively stagnant. Ukraine experienced great progress here from 1994/95, but by 1998 it seemed that Ukraine had achieved as much as it could expect to – certainly for the time being. At this point Ukraine had signed special agreements both with Nato and the EU, and achieved membership of the European council.

Ukraine does not regard the Black Sea region as isolated from neighbouring areas. Rather, Ukraine sees the Black Sea region as part of a larger Europe. At the BSEC meeting in Yalta (Crimea), held on 4-5 June 1998, Ukrainian foreign minister, Boris Tarasyuk, characterized the formation of a Euro-Black Sea economic community as the BSEC's main task.[6] Secondly, Vyacheslav Chronovil (the nationalist veteran, Soviet political prisoner, and long-time leader of the moderately nationalist Rukh – movement – party) had already launched the idea of a 'zone of peace and stability from the Baltic to the Black Sea' during Soviet times. After independence, this idea became a favourite theme in Ukrainian foreign policy, and was put forward on many occasions by both Presidents Kravchuk and Kuchma. Whether Russia should become a part of this 'zone', however, always remained unclear. It appears that in Russia this idea was interpreted as a Ukrainian attempt to isolate Russia from the rest of Europe, and, arguably, the most nationalist of Ukrainian politicians had such an isolation in mind. The idea was received with scant support in most European capitals, but was not abandoned by Ukrainian policy makers. One indication that Ukraine has not abandoned the idea was President Kuchma's proposal to hold a conference in Ukraine in September 1999 on the theme of 'Baltic-Black Sea cooperation: towards integration in Europe in the 21st Century without division lines'.

It is important to be aware that Ukrainian foreign policy in the Black Sea region does not create the same heated domestic debates as those generated by Ukrainian foreign policy towards Russia or the West. This is because Ukraine's position in the Black Sea region is not entangled with the question of identity to the same extent. The East or West debate in Ukraine is very much a question of identity. Consequently, debates on foreign policy become highly emotional, which leaves less room for pragmatic considerations. Ukrainian policy in the Black Sea region is affected by this problem only to the extent that Black Sea policy is seen as part of the East–West struggle. This is most characteristic in the strategic dimension and to some extent in the ethnic minority dimension. When it is not seen as part of the East–West struggle, Ukrainian foreign policy makers have a fairly free hand in formulating their Black Sea policies. This provides them with more room for compromise and manoeuvre.

The Strategic Dimension

By the strategic dimension I mean whether state-to-state relations in the region are generally peaceful or characterized by conflict and tensions. In relation to this I find the concepts of "balance of power" and of "security building" useful for structuring an analysis. "Balance of power" can be understood as the idea that no country or block of countries becomes so strong as to threaten the security of the others.[7] Security, and thereby stability, is achieved by the establishment of a balance of power between the states in a region. "Security building" can be understood as the idea that stability should be achieved through the pursuit of all-inclusive, confidence-building measures. The question to be addressed in this section can thus be phrased as follows: is Ukrainian foreign policy in the BS region more informed by the concept of "balance of power", or by that of "security building"?

Since Ukraine's independence three problem areas have been of particular significance to the Ukrainian-Russian relationship: the division of former Soviet military assets, Ukrainian territorial integrity, and Russian acceptance of Ukrainian independence – including an independent Ukrainian foreign policy. All three have a bearing on Ukrainian–Russian relations in the Black Sea region. Russia and Ukraine have continually fought over ownership of the Black Sea Fleet since the demise of the Soviet Union, and many Russian politicians have repeatedly questioned the Ukrainian status of Crimea – in particular the city of Sevastopol. In addition, they are involved in other territorial disputes such as the delineation of the Black Sea and Azov continental shelves and the ownership of the tiny Tuzla isthmus. In addition Russia fears that Ukraine may join forces with other countries in the region, Turkey in particular, in order to reduce Russia's political influence.

Catherine the Great established the Black Sea Fleet in 1771. After several successful clashes with the Ottomans, Russia obtained treaty rights to base a fleet in the Black Sea in 1774. Historically both the Black Sea Fleet and Crimea itself are of great symbolic significance to many Russian politicians.

Conflict over the future of the fleet was a recurring problem in Russian-Ukrainian relations after the Ukrainian declaration of 1991 that all military hardware on Ukrainian territory belonged to Ukraine. The conflict was finally settled in May 1997, when the two parties agreed on how the fleet should be divided. The agreement was ratified by both countries' parliaments during 1998 and early 1999.

The dispute was not simply over the question of sharing military hardware and of basing rights for the Russian fleet in Ukrainian Crimea. Russian military experts were, also, worried that a total Ukrainisation of the fleet would tilt the naval balance of power in the Black Sea region in favour of Turkey. They feared that this could have important economic and political consequences for Russia. The influential Russian daily, *Nezavisimaya Gazeta*, stated as follows: 'in reality, the question of the fleet is the question of who will have the ability to control the Black Sea as an important communication centre for the export of oil from Asia to Europe.'[8] The Commander of the Russian Black Sea Fleet, Admiral Victor Kravchenko, put the topic into a historical context: 'Let us turn to history. Our forefathers led a century long unyielding struggle for the possession of the Black Sea. And they achieved their aim. It is no coincidence that the Black Sea was called a Russian ocean. A great power cannot achieve economic progress without ocean waterways. And if we did not have a fleet, who would take notice of us?'[9]

The increased presence of NATO warships in the Black Sea has heightened Russian concerns. Some of these warships were invited by Ukraine to participate in naval exercises under the Partnership for Peace programme. Russia, however, regards the warships as tokens of NATO expanding its sphere of influence, at the expense of Russia's own sphere of influence. If such concerns persist and grow in Russia, there is a danger that the Black Sea region might lose some of its autonomy as an independent vector in Ukrainian foreign policy. Instead it might come to be seen as an additional arena for the domestic struggle between an eastward-oriented and a westward-oriented Ukrainian foreign policy. This could substantially limit the room for manoeuvre and for pragmatism in Ukrainian policy in the region.

The 1998 Major Treaty between Russia and Ukraine solved the question of Ukrainian territorial integrity, at least on paper. In this treaty Russia fully recognizes Ukrainian territorial integrity within the present borders (including Crimea and Sevastopol). The Treaty met heavy resistance both in the Duma and in the Federation Council, but the vote in favour was still decisive – 244 for in favour and 30 against in the Duma, and 106 for in favour and 25 against in the Federation Council. One of the most outspoken opponents of the treaty was Moscow Mayor Yuri Luzhkov. He denounced the Federation Council ratification of the Treaty, and said he would let Russian citizens know just who voted for the "surrender" of Crimea and Sevastopol.[10] Mr Luzhkov is considered to be a favourite candidate for the year 2000 Russian presidential elections. Fear of Russian intentions regarding Crimea will therefore remain strong in Kiev even after the Treaty.

What, then, are the main Ukrainian perceptions after almost eight years of co-existence with Russia in the Black Sea region? Grigory Perepelitsa, head of the department of military policy at the National Institute for Strategic Studies, was very plain-spoken when concluding a review of Russian foreign policy in the Black Sea region: 'The tendency is there for all to see, Russia is striving to achieve for itself a politico-military dominance in the Black Sea region. As long as this tendency dominates there can never be stability and peace.' Perepelitsa's advice to the Ukrainian leadership on how to respond to this Russian threat was equally blunt: 'It is in Ukraine's interest to work for a balance of power in the region excluding the possibility of any one state becoming dominant ... This interest is the main foundation for the new Ukrainian policy towards the Black Sea region.'[11] Mr. Perepelitsa's explicit balance-of-power thinking does not reflect a consensus in the Ukrainian political leadership on this issue, yet, as I will demonstrate, a diluted version of it is clearly one of the factors that determine Ukrainian foreign policy in the region. The National Institute for Strategic Studies is a government think tank that can be said to have more influence on policy than most other similar institutions in Ukraine. One politician who has especially close relations with this institute is Volodymyr Horbulin. He is the leader of the National Security and Defence Council, and one of the main architects of Ukrainian foreign and security policy during the Kuchma administration.

Former President Kravchuk's visit to Turkey in May 1992 was perceived as the 'thin end of the wedge' in terms of Ukraine's attempts to achieve a balance of power with Russia in the Black Sea region. Kravchuk hoped that Turkey would become an ally of Ukraine in the same way that he hoped Poland would become an ally of Ukraine in East-Central Europe. The pursuit of special relations with Turkey has remained a popular idea in the Ukrainian foreign policy establishment. A major analysis of the Ukrainian security situation conducted by the National Institute for Strategic Studies states:

'The creation of the geopolitical triangle Ankara–Kiev–Baku will provide Ukraine with the opportunity to most fully realize its economic and political potential in the Black Sea region. Promoting this policy is important for Ukraine also because the USA in this part of the world defines Turkey, Azerbaijan and Poland as prioritized partners. Ukraine is the necessary geopolitical link between the Baltic and the Black Seas in the US arch of interest, and this intensifies the American interest in the preservation and support of the territorial integrity and stability of Ukraine. (...) Of strategic interest for Russia in this regard, will be to stop the process of strengthening relations between Kiev and Ankara at any price.'[12]

As a caution against taking Ukrainian propositions of geopolitical triangles too seriously, however, it should be noted that such propositions seem to have become akin to a sport for Ukrainian political leaders. An observer of Ukrainian foreign policy, Rostyslav Khotin, counted seven different triangle proposals over the last few years.[13] Still, even if they are mostly words rather than deeds, they are nonetheless indicative of a Ukrainian desire for the formation of political blocs with which to counterweight Russia.

Turkey initially gave Ukraine ample cause to expect the will to partnership to be mutual. In July 1992 Turkey's minister of defence, Nevzat Ayaz, told his Ukrainian colleague, Konstantin Morozov, that Turkey would support Ukraine if it wanted to join NATO, and both ministers stressed that the new geopolitical realities had made military and technical cooperation between the two countries extremely important. Numerous other official Turkish statements in support of Ukrainian territorial integrity have contributed to a perception in Ukraine that Turkey is a political ally. For example this was especially the case when nationalist circles in Russia questioned Ukrainian territorial integrity.[14]

However, this mutual appreciation has not developed into anything that could be called an anti-Russian politico-military alliance. A researcher from the same National Institute for Strategic Studies, Boris Parakhonskiy, cautioned against such an alliance in October 1998. He asserted that relations with Turkey should be developed mainly within the frameworks of bi-lateral economic cooperation or within the framework of the BSEC. This is in order to avoid the development of cooperation into a politico-military alliance. He also advised that military-political cooperation between the two countries should only develop as a result of Ukraine's general cooperation with NATO.[15] On the Turkish side, the scholar Duygu Bazoglu Sezer has noted that 'the Turkish view attaches great importance to Ukraine's political independence and territorial integrity as a vital element of regional and European security.' She also admits that 'in fact, it is possible that the leadership in both countries have occasionally perceived the need to draw closer as their shared apprehensions about Moscow's regional intentions have increased.'[16] It appears that when it comes to openly joining forces against Russia there is considerable ambivalence in both countries. Both countries are aware that anything approaching a politico-military alliance would provoke Russia and the security situation in the region would deteriorate for all parties.

Romania was the only country besides Russia to make territorial claims on Ukraine after Ukraine became independent. In 1940, as a result of the Molotov-Ribbentrop Pact, the Red Army moved into Romania and annexed several territories to the Soviet Union. These territories were Northern Bukovyna, the northernmost part of Bessarabia and the Hertsa area (these areas now constitute the Chernivtsi oblast); Southern Bessarabia (now the southernmost part of Odessa oblast); and the little Serpent Island just off both countries' Black Sea Coast, reported to contain rich oil and gas deposits.[17] On 24 June 1991 the Romanian parliament condemned the annexation, and that November both the Romanian government and parliament protested the former Romanian territories' participation in the Ukrainian independence referendum. Romania demanded that any major treaty between the two countries should include a clause condemning the results of the Molotov-Ribbentrop treaty. This demand was interpreted in Ukraine as a badly-disguised territorial claim and for a long time it precluded the signing of a major friendship treaty between Romania and Ukraine.

However, in an attempt to be included in the first wave of NATO enlargement, Romania's foreign minister, Adrian Severin, announced a shift in Romanian foreign policy in January 1997. One aspect of this shift was expressed in a commitment to resolve remaining controversies that had arisen with Ukraine. As a result, on 2 June 1997 Ukraine and Romania signed a treaty of friendship and cooperation, a treaty that was later ratified by both countries' parliaments. In the treaty Romania backed down from its insistence that the Molotov-Ribbentrop treaty be condemned, and Ukraine agreed to Romanian demands regarding the status of the Romanian minority in Ukraine. Disagreements over the continental shelf remained unresolved.

At present relations between Ukraine and Romania are peaceful. Harmonious relations, combined with a common suspicion of Russia and a common desire for integration to the West, could have led to Romanian-Ukrainian balancing against Russian influence in the Black Sea region. Yet nothing of the sort has developed, probably for much the same reasons as in that of the Ukraine-Turkey relationship.

A major reorientation of Georgian foreign policy took place in autumn 1996. The Georgian parliament was disgruntled with Russian foreign policy in the Caucasus. It therefore asked the Georgian president to form a special committee to look into the possibilities of a reorientation of Georgian foreign policy, away from Russia and towards the West. This reorientation led to a search for new partners, and Ukraine was placed high on the list. The partnership that later developed is based on the following calculation of mutual benefit: Georgia will open up access to Caspian oil for Ukraine, while Ukraine will help Georgia to resist Russian pressure and try to 'open doors' for Georgia with the West. Most of Georgian Ukrainian cooperation takes place within the framework of GUAMU.

GUAMU is the only Ukrainian policy initiative in the Black Sea region that can truly be interpreted as an initiative to achieve a balance against Russia. GUAMU held its constitutive meeting on 25 November

1997 in Baku in Azerbaijan. The meeting produced a protocol defining four policy areas for cooperation: resistance to separatism and mutual support in the settlement of regional conflicts; a common approach to peace-keeping operations; development of transit routes; and preparation for eventual accession to West European and Atlantic institutions.[18]

All of the four policy areas singled out for cooperation have one thing in common: they represent policy areas where the member states have conflicting interests with Russia. Though all four participants have repeatedly stated that GUAMU was not established in opposition to anyone, it is hard not to notice the anti-Russian slant. In January 1999 a common approach to peace-keeping was taken one step further with the decision to establish a common GUAMU peace-keeping battalion. The GUAMU countries intend to use the battalion to protect the pipelines from Baku to the Turkish Mediterranean port of Ceyhan and the Georgian port of Supsa, and as a peace-keeping force in local trouble spots such as Nagorny Karabakh, Transdniestr and Abkhasia. This is an attempt to reduce Russian influence in the region by demonstrating the GUAMU's own ability to handle these problems. All of these countries consider the Russian peace-keepers in the aforementioned trouble spots to be tools for the support of Russian imperial control.

To a certain extent the other members of GUAMU consider Ukraine an example to be followed in resistance to Russian pressure. The chairman of the Georgian parliament Zurab Zhvanya said, during an official visit to Kiev in November 1997, that the success of Ukrainian independence provides 'a guarantee that also makes it possible for us to twist ourselves out of the brotherly [i.e. Russian] embrace.'[19] The other countries also seem to expect Ukraine to take the lead in cooperation. On the one hand this wish has been received with pleasure in Ukraine, as a token of the country's increasing prestige and international standing, but on the other hand it has led to domestic warnings that Ukraine should be careful not to take on obligations which it cannot fulfil.

In the Ukrainian document *Ukraine's National Security 1994-1996*, two competing configurations of states are identified in the Black Sea region: one is Russia, Bulgaria, Greece and Armenia against Turkey, the other is Ukraine, Azerbaijan and Georgia. The document further states that the strengthening of ties between the countries of the second configuration might 'weaken the dominating role of Russia in the Black Sea region, and prevent Russian countermeasures.'[20]

The establishment of GUAMU did not appear to cause any particular alarm in Russia. However in December 1997, the then Prime Minister Chernomyrdin complained about the 'dispersal to different corners' of

CIS member states,[21] and Federation Council chairman, Fedor Stroev, told journalists that the GUAMU 'cannot be seen as a friendly gesture toward Russia.'[22] It is unclear whether Russia's low-key reactions to GUAMU simply reflect the fact that Russia does not see GUAMU as important, or whether they reveal a foreign policy failure that the Russian leadership is hesitant to admit.

When it comes to security building, Ukraine has been one of the most active participants in the BSEC (Black Sea Economic Cooperation). The BSEC was established on the initiative of the then Turkish President, Turgut Özal, in 1992 to promote, in particular, economic cooperation in the Black Sea region. In this respect, Ukrainian authorities emphasize the possible spillover effect that economic cooperation might have on security politics. Ukrainian President Leonid Kuchma accentuated this aspect of cooperation during the June 1998 BSEC meeting in Yalta: 'The BSEC constitutes an important component of the new system of European security precisely by having an economic foundation.'[23]

At the second session of the BSEC Interparliamentary assembly in November 1993, the Ukrainian delegation proposed to introduce a security dimension to the organization. President Kravchuk repeated the proposal at a meeting of the BSEC in May 1994. Although the proposal was rejected at the time, in February 1998 the idea was taken up again but this time outside the framework of the BSEC. At a meeting at the Ukrainian embassy in Vienna representatives from Bulgaria, Georgia, Romania, Russia and Turkey agreed on a document entitled "Leading principles for the conduct of negotiations regarding efforts to strengthen mutual trust and security in naval affairs in the Black Sea". Though these negotiations are conducted outside any institutional framework, the participants decided to keep the Organization for Security and Cooperation in Europe regularly informed about the progress of negotiations. It is important to note that these negotiations will also deal with principles for the naval activity of non-Black Sea countries in the Black Sea. This is, perhaps, of special interest to Russia, which has voiced considerable concern over the American naval presence in the Black Sea. In September 1997 Russian Black Sea commander, Admiral Victor Kravchenko, told reporters that there was 'no need for the presence of third countries'.[24] In early 1999 these negotiations were followed up on the Turkish side by a proposal to create a joint naval force in the Black Sea for rescue, mine search-and-find and humanitarian aid operations.

As already indicated the countries most important to Ukraine in the Black Sea region are Russia, Turkey, Romania and Georgia. Russian-

Ukrainian relations in the region are characterized by an air of mutual suspicion. Ukrainian authorities fear Russian hegemony in the region, whereas Russian authorities fear that Ukraine might ally with other powers in the region against Russia. Ukraine, Turkey and Romania all share a common fear of Russia's preponderance in the region, but at present none of them consider explicit alliances against Russia to be the best solution. Also, none of them have the Black Sea region as their main priority on their foreign policy agenda. Georgia and the other GUAMU countries are more willing than Turkey or Romania to join forces with Ukraine in preventing Russian domination, but their capacities are considerably smaller.

The head of the department for military policy at the National Institute for Strategic Studies, Grigory Perepelitsa, indicates in his article on military developments in the Black Sea region, that Ukrainian balancing behaviour is a result of a disappointment with the reception of the Ukrainian security-building initiatives of 1993/94. The Ukrainian initiative for security-building measures in early 1998, however, indicates that Ukraine has not abandoned its belief in this strategy. The 1998 initiative reflects their continued belief in the usefulness of security-building measures, although it might also reflect their realization that major Black Sea powers such as Turkey and Romania, despite strained relations with Moscow at times, have shown only a limited interest in openly joining Ukraine in a balancing act against Russia.

Ukraine is simultaneously pursuing a balancing of power policy and a security-building policy in the region. This is reflected both in the Ukrainian debate on Black Sea issues, and in actual political behaviour. Initiatives reflecting both ways of thinking have occurred continuously since Ukraine became independent, and there are few indications that the Ukrainian leadership sees these two ways of thinking and acting as contradictory in any major sense. This double approach is most probably not the result of specific planning. No particular and consistent strategy for Ukrainian foreign policy in the Black Sea region appears to have been developed. Rather, this policy should be seen as the result of a continuously-changing mix between balance of power and security-building thinking, where particular events of the day in addition to the personnel configurations close to those making decisions often turn out to be highly decisive for the policy choices.

The Economic Dimension

In economic terms the Black Sea region is the third most important region for Ukraine. In the years 1996 and 1997 the Ukrainian trade turnover with the combined Black Sea countries was approximately the same as the Ukrainian trade turnover with Germany, but it was also on the increase. However it was still only about one-tenth of the trade turnover with Russia.[25] It is significant that Ukraine has a positive trade turnover with the combined BSEC countries and I will go on to discuss this.

The Black Sea region is considered by Ukrainian decision-makers to carry a significant potential for contributing to economic growth in Ukraine, and also for enhancing the geopolitical importance of Ukraine through economic factors. There are several areas in which the Ukrainian Black Sea coast is thought to have particular potential for contributing to the recovery of the Ukrainian economy; tourism, ship transport, ship-building, and the exploitation of Black Sea shelf oil and gas resources are all areas that have potential. However, it is as a transit area for the export of goods from the Caucasus and Central Asia – including Caspian oil – to the rest of Europe that the region is of most importance to Ukraine.

Tourism is of particular significance for Crimea, which during Soviet times was one of the most important resorts for the country's approximately 240 million inhabitants. After independence Crimea lost much of its tourist trade because of the unstable local political situation. A process of privatization of the major sanatoriums and hotels, the elements of which process were unclear, and the polarization of wealth in the former Soviet Union contributed to this problem. Further the majority of the population of the former Soviet Union became much poorer and therefore could not afford to travel anywhere during their vacations, and those who did earn enough to travel preferred Western destinations such as the Canary Islands and Greece to Crimea. However the potential for tourist trade in Crimea is still there and if the tourism branch were to be restructured and made more efficient, it should be able to attract tourists both from the former Soviet Union and Western countries. Already today tourism accounts for 8.2 per cent of the Ukrainian GNP, and 6.2 million tourists visited Ukraine in 1998.[26]

Ship transport is significant both because of the considerable capacity of the Ukrainian ports, and because of the fairly large merchant fleet that Ukraine inherited from the Soviet Union. Before 1991, the ports of Odessa and nearby Mykolayiv, together with Kherson and Sevastopol, were cornerstones of Soviet foreign trade. After 1991, however, trade through these ports declined rapidly, chiefly due to a sharp decrease in the Russian use of these ports. Russian merchants shifted much of their export to domestic ports in the sea of Azov and to Novorossiysk. By comparison since 1996 the Romanian port of Constantsa, alone, has had an annual turnover of approximately 40 million tons of goods, whereas in the same period all the Ukrainian ports combined have had an annual turnover of approximately 55 million tons of goods.[27] However, the capacity of these ports is far from exhausted. A certain return of Russian goods to Ukrainian ports could be discerned at the beginning of 1998 and this is an indication of a more positive trend. The main reasons behind such a return are that the Ukrainian ports are closer in distance for many Russian exporters than the Russian ports, combined with the fact that the Ukrainian ports lowered their tariffs for the handling of goods.

The Ukrainian merchant fleet – dominated by the state-owned company Blasco – is a perennial problem for independent Ukraine. Many of the ships are very old, and are continually being impounded in foreign harbours because of an inability to pay for the services used. Because of this, the management of Blasco has sold off a large number of vessels. These large-scale sales have led to numerous charges of corruption. According to the leader of the special Ukrainian parliamentary investigating commission for the merchant fleet, Yuri Karmazin, selling off sections of the fleet is more lucrative than the transport services the fleet provides.[28] The fleet is clearly in trouble, but most observers think that it has potential albeit in a modernized and scaled-down form. According to Blasco's president, Oleksandr Stognienko, in the future the fleet will consist of about 80 vessels with an average age of about 10 to 15 years.[29]

Ukraine had the largest civilian shipbuilding industry of all the former Soviet republics. Today most of Ukraine's shipbuilding capacity is still owned by the state (nine shipyards along the Black Sea coast in 1998), and 40 per cent of this capacity is concentrated in the city of Mykolayiv where three shipyards employ about 10,000 workers. The shipbuilding industry has gone through many of the same hardships as most other branches of the Ukrainian economy since independence.

There was quite a lot of optimism in the shipbuilding industry at the beginning of the 1990s. By the mid 1990s, however, much of this optimism had disappeared. The main reason for this was that the industry had fallen into great debt. According to journalist Vladimir Rybalka, the debt problem was the result of a flawed policy regarding contracts with western companies in the early 1990s – a result of Soviet managers' inexperience in dealing with Western capitalism. He writes: 'In those years business trips abroad to find foreign partners were especially encouraged. (...) These partners were astonishingly easy to find, and they proposed advantageous deals. That is, they seemed advantageous, and large long-term contracts were signed with fixed prices.'[30] Rybalka claims that Soviet managers, not anticipating the rise in raw material costs that would follow the introduction of capitalism to the former Soviet Union, accepted prices that were unrealistically low. He cites the example of a tanker built at a Kherson shipyard for a Greek company. In March 1998 the Greek company wanted to purchase the tanker, which was only 70 per cent finished, for 18 million US dollars, when the actual cost of producing the tanker had already risen to 25 million US dollars. There are probably a host of other reasons for this sorry state of affairs, such as low labour efficiency, but the bottom line is that the industry is seriously in debt.

In late 1997 Ukrainian authorities decided to make an effort to reverse this negative trend in the shipbuilding industry. The parliament adopted a special law for the shipbuilding industry in December 1997, and in October 1998 the three shipyards in Mykolahiv were awarded the status of free economic zones by presidential decree. In 1998 the industry gained several contracts with foreign partners, the Ukrainian weekly *Zerkalo Nedely* reported, in late 1998, the beginning of a 'psychological watershed' at least in some parts of the Ukrainian shipbuilding industry. The Black Sea coast is therefore likely to continue to be important for the Ukrainian economy because of its shipbuilding industry. For this to be a lasting trend, however, the industry has to scale down considerably, it also has to modernize, and become more efficient.

Ukraine's dreams of its Black Sea zone becoming an important transit area for goods from the Caucasus and Central Asia to Europe emerged early after independence. They mostly remained dreams, however, until the oil boom in the Caspian Sea, and until Ukraine's 1996 accession to the 1993 EU-initiated TRACECA project.

TRACECA is a programme for the development of transport links between Central Asia, the Caucasus, and Europe. It was originally signed to by the EU, the five former Soviet republics in Central Asia and the three former Soviet republics in the Caucasus. A major reason for the initiation of this project was the recognition that most of the developed transport routes in the Soviet Union ran in a north–south direction. To create transport routes going in an east-west direction would make trade between Europe and these new states easier. In addition the initiative was assigned a symbolic meaning by being presented as a kind of reopening of the old Silk Road.

Ukraine hopes that at least part of the Caspian oil exports to Europe will be transported over Ukrainian territory. In that event, the oil would be transported by tankers from Georgia (Supsa) to Odessa, and from Odessa by pipeline to Brody in Western Ukraine, where there is a connection to the major European pipelines. The Odessa-Brody pipeline is only finished halfway, but the other half is under construction.

Ukraine initially hoped that the Baku – Supsa – Odessa – Brody alternative would be chosen as the main route for the export of Caspian oil. The international companies that extract oil in the Caspian Sea, however, chose the Turkish Baku – Supsa – Cheyhan alternative as the main route. Still, this does not totally exclude the Ukrainian route. In February 1999 British Petroleum/Amoco was reported to be considering the Odessa–Brody pipeline as an alternative to the Baku–Cheyhan route,[31] and in the same month Polish Premier Jerzy Buzek proposed that a group of analysts should investigate the possibility of building a pipeline from Odessa to Gdansk.[32] Any arrangement for the use of the Odessa–Brody pipeline would increase the importance of the Black Sea region for the Ukrainian economy.

There are two main reasons for the Ukrainian emphasis on this project beyond the potential transport fees for oil that could bring much needed cash to the Ukrainian treasury. These are that in this way Ukraine can diversify its own sources of energy supply; and that being a transit focal point for oil to Europe would enhance the geopolitical importance of Ukraine.

At present Ukraine is totally dependent on Russia for energy supplies, a fact that is deplored by most Ukrainian politicians. In 1993, the chairman of the Ukrainian parliamentary commission for economic reform, Volodymyr Pylypchuk, complained that the 'Russian oil whip' negates the development of a sovereign Ukrainian state.[33] Russia supplies approximately 90 per cent of the Ukrainian oil demand, and more than 60 per cent of the gas demand.[34]

The connection between pipelines and geopolitics in Ukrainian political thinking was amply demonstrated by the leader of the Ukrainian parliament's sub-committee for energy, Ivan Diyaka, in an interview with the Ukrainian weekly *Segodnya* in December 1998: 'After the 'give away' of Ukraine's nuclear arsenal Ukraine is respected internationally only because its territory is crossed by a pipeline that combines the Russian gas and oil fields with European consumers. To remove this last lever would be enough to return our independent country into a province.'[35] The Russians have launched plans for building a new export pipeline to Western Europe through Belarus and Poland, circumventing Ukraine. These plans only heighten the geopolitical importance of the Odessa – Brody project in Ukrainian eyes. In an analysis of Ukraine's place in the geopolitics of pipelines, a scholar at the National Institute for Strategic Studies, Oleksandr Manachynskyi, wrote: 'Russian experts understand that the building of the transport line Baku – Supsa – Ukraine will decrease the importance of Russia on the Central-European oil market. Therefore Moscow, in our opinion, is likely to use a variety of means to try to prevent the project.'[36] The Ukrainian emphasis on GUAMU should also be seen in this light. The need to secure alternative sources of oil has been the main reason why Ukraine has tried to promote its position in the Caucasus.

However, although many in Moscow clearly see the Baku – Supsa – Ukraine route as a competitor to their own Baku – Novorossiysk route, the suspicions of Oleksandr Manachynskyi have not been totally validated. In fact, in June 1998, the Russian oil and gas companies Lukoil and Gasprom decided to join the development of the Ukrainian transport system rather than undermining it. Gazprom stated that it would like to increase the amounts of oil and gas transported across Ukraine, and Lukoil said the company would like to help to build the oil terminal in Odessa. Gazprom Chairman Rem Vyakhirev said his company would help finance a gas pipeline for Russia across southern Ukraine via Romania and Bulgaria to Turkey, and Gazprom also signed a deal with Crimean Chernomorneftegaz to collectively explore the Azov and Black Sea shelves. After this, Ukrainian President Leonid Kuchma even invited Vyakhirev and another Gazprom affiliate, Aleksandr Lebedev, to join his foreign investment advisory council.[37] Both companies enjoy close links with the Russian government. It could therefore be that Ukrainian security analysts read more geopolitics into the pipeline question than there are grounds for – and more than the Ukrainian political leadership does.

The TRACECA project has, according to the EU, not only an economic but also a political purpose: 'to enhance economic and political independence of the republics.'[38] TRACECA is for surface transport only, and has nothing to do with the transport of Caspian oil and gas. Ukraine, as well as Bulgaria and Romania, was included after the initial eight, because of a recognition that there was a missing link in the project between its western end (the Caucasus) and the European market. For Ukraine in particular, TRACECA meant that the port at Ilyichevsk south of Odessa received substantial rehabilitation funds from the EU. More importantly, however, for Ukrainian decision-makers the inclusion into TRACECA has meant that their insistence that Southern Ukraine has major potential as a geoeconomical transportation focal point has become more of a reality and less of an assertion. This point was also made in a 1998 EU evaluation report on its cooperation with Ukraine: 'Transport is a more than usually important sector in Ukraine on account of the country's geographic location, which makes it a potentially major transit point for trade between the NIS [Newly Independent States] and Western Europe, as well as to the wider world through the Black Sea ports.'[39]

From a geopolitical point of view it is important to note that TRACECA, if successful, will reduce the dependence of the participating countries on Russia, and possibly also Turkey and Iran for east-west trade. This point was explicitly recognized in a EU evaluation report on TRACECA: 'It has to be acknowledged that these countries [Russia, Turkey and Iran] have a major role in transport and trade and this is to some extent in conflict with the strategic objectives of the TRACECA programme.'[40] It is therefore possible that Ukraine in the future could experience a conflict between participating in TRACECA and participating in the BSEC, where both Russia and Turkey are influential members. Such conflicts could be prevented, however, if TRACECA and the BSEC find ways of co-ordinating their activities. The first steps towards such a cooperation were taken in Tbilisi in Georgia in April 1997, when members of TRACECA and the BSEC held a first joint meeting. This development was clearly in Ukraine's interest, and in May 1997 an International Black Sea Transport Conference was held in Kiev to further discuss, among other things, the topics arising from the Tbilisi meeting.

The BSEC is the main forum for Ukrainian initiatives on economic cooperation in the Black Sea region, but Ukraine has also signed bilateral economic agreements with most Black Sea littoral states. In addition, much of the dynamics of the Ukrainian initiatives in this regard are found at the sub-state level. A major initiator of Black Sea economic cooperation has been the city and oblast authorities of Odessa, and also, to a lesser extent the authorities of Mykolahiv and Crimea.[41]

Odessa was always a very internationally-oriented city. The city has continued this tradition as part of independent Ukraine. While the political elites of other major cities in Ukraine, such as Dnipropetrovsk and Donetsk, have their eyes focused on the struggle for political influence in Kiev, the political elite of Odessa has kept largely aloof from that struggle. Instead, the Odessa political elite has focused on promoting Odessa as a centre for trade, commerce, and economic cooperation in the Black Sea area. The Odessa oblast is probably the most affluent oblast in Ukraine.

The first initiative came during the Soviet era, in 1988. This was a proposal to create an economic free zone in Odessa. Although periodically repeated after 1991 by Odessa authorities, initially the proposal was not welcomed in the corridors of power in Kiev. The Odessa authorities later broadened the initiative with a proposal to include in the zone regions from neighbouring Moldova and Romania. This proposal recommends that the three countries first create their own zones in the region, and that some kind of a merger of these zones follows as a second step. Romania has already created such a zone in the county of Galats. Ukrainian authorities have so far been sceptical about joining territories from three different countries into one economic free-zone, and several Ukrainian ministries and expert groups have deemed the project almost impossible to implement for judicial reasons.[42] However, the Ukrainian leader of the Agency for free economic zones, Leonid Minin, indicated a change in attitudes to the question in March 1999. He said that a package of laws and technical-economic requirements for three economic free-zones in the Odessa oblast had been sent to the Ukrainian government for approval.[43] One of these zones is the Reni river port, which in the future could become part of a three-country zone.

The Odessa initiatives for increased economic cooperation in the bordering areas between Romania, Moldova and Ukraine have also been followed up at the state level. In June 1997 the leaders of the three countries agreed to establish the Lower Danube Euroregion.[44] The Odessa local authorities played no small role in the formulation of this initiative.

Another vehicle for cooperation in this region is the Commonwealth of Danube Countries. The leader of this organization from October 1996 to October 1997, was Governor of the Odessa oblast Ruslan Bodelan. Established in 1991 the organization consists of 34 regions and ten countries along the Danube. It cooperates with the Council of Europe, and one of its main functions is to facilitate such initiatives as the Lower Danube Euroregion.

In addition Ukraine has been fairly active in promoting environmental cooperation in the Black Sea area. For example, at the June 1998 Yalta BSEC summit, Ukrainian president, Leonid Kuchma, proposed that the organization should create a co-ordinating Council for Ecological Security, and establish a mechanism for monitoring pollution of the Black Sea ecosystem. The problem with this, and other similar statements and resolutions of the BSEC organs, is that they have a tendency to remain on paper. This is due more to a lack of funds than to an unwillingness to act. Therefore the government projects that have been initiated have largely been dependent on Western money.

The European Union has been particularly active in funding environmental projects in the Black Sea. In the years 1992-1997 the EU spent over 8 million ECU on environmental projects in the Black Sea region. Part of that money went to the establishment of the Regional Activity Centre for Pollution Monitoring and Assessment in Odessa, and the 1995 Danube Programme for Ukraine and Moldova. The Commission is also supporting the so-called Bucharest Convention for the Protection of the Black Sea. The signatories to this convention are, in addition to Ukraine, Bulgaria, Romania, Russia, Georgia, and Turkey.

Ukrainian authorities see the Black Sea region as a zone with a great potential for contributing towards the economic recovery of the country. There are distinct possibilities for a revival of tourism, shipbuilding and the commercial fleet, if these areas are modernized and made more efficient. The main importance of the region for Ukraine in economic terms, however, is as an alternative source of energy supplies and as a transport focal point between East and West.

Several of these economic projects contradict Russian interests. This does not prevent Ukraine from participating in the development of these projects, but the country is at the same time trying to increase its economic cooperation with Russia in the Black Sea region. This is taking place both bi-laterally (cooperation with Lukoil and Gazprom on the Black Sea shelf) and through the BSEC. It seems to be a common view in Kiev that increased cooperation in the economic sphere will be an important factor in promoting stability as well as trust in the political sphere.

The Ethnic Minority Dimension

The Ukrainian Black Sea region is the only region of Ukraine where Ukrainian authorities have experienced serious ethnically-based unrest – the separatist attempts of pro-Russian forces in Crimea in 1994 and 1995 (close to 70 per cent of the Crimean population is ethnically Russian), and the violent demonstrations by Crimean Tatars in June 1995.

Ethnic Russians account for about 22 per cent of the Ukrainian population, but Crimea is the only region where they are in the majority. Many other Ukrainians, however, use Russian as their daily language (some estimates say around 50 per cent). These Russian-speaking Ukrainians identify themselves alternately as Russians, Ukrainians, Soviets or just "locals". The Russians and the Russian-speaking Ukrainians are concentrated in Eastern Ukraine, and along the Ukrainian Black Sea coast. After Ukraine became independent there was widespread fear both in Ukraine and in the West that the country would break up along ethnic lines. In Eastern Ukraine some organizations were formed to promote such a development, and in the Ukrainian Black Sea areas there were some calls for the formation of a *Novarossiya* territorial unit as an independent state or as a part of Russia. However, there was hardly any serious ethnic mobilization against the Ukrainian state by the Russians. The only exception was Crimea.[45]

In January 1994 the separatist Yuri Meshkov won the Crimean presidential election. The Ukrainian authorities had never accepted the office of a Crimean presidency. In March the same year his parliamentary election bloc *Rossiya* won an absolute majority of the seats in the local parliament. Meshkov turned the clocks in Crimea to Moscow time, stated that Crimeans should do their military service only in Crimea, reactivated the strongly pro-independence 1992 Crimean constitution, and actively lobbied for Moscow support.

However, in spring 1995, the Ukrainian authorities peacefully subjugated the whole separatist effort by disbanding the Crimean presidency and placing the Crimean government directly under the Ukrainian government. One of the reasons why Ukrainian authorities could do this was that Meshkov had met with little sympathy for his policies in Moscow. Another reason was that the separatists had fallen out with one another over the division of property during the Crimean privatization process. Relations between Kiev and Simferopol remained problematic, but further serious attempts at separatism have not occurred. In March 1998 Leonid Grach, the charismatic and popular leader of the local Communist Party, was elected leader of the local parliament. This is the most influential political position in the autonomy. Some pro-Russian forces hoped for a revival of the separatist drive. Mr. Grach, however, who had, previously, harshly criticized most of the Ukrainian government's policies regarding Crimea, turned out to be a pacifier rather than a promoter of Crimean opposition to Kiev. It was thanks to Grach that a Crimean constitution satisfying both the all-Ukrainian and the local Crimean parliaments could be finally adopted in 1998.

Separating Crimea from Ukraine is, therefore, hardly on the political agenda any more, even in Crimea. Nevertheless, an opinion poll of the Ukrainian political elite in 1996 showed that four out of ten were still worried about Crimean separatism.[46] The fear of separatism is a fear that Ukrainian politicians share with politicians in other countries around the Black Sea, and one of the expressed aims of the GUAMU cooperation is to develop measures for jointly preventing ethnic separatism.

To understand the circumstances surrounding the Tatars in Crimea it is important to put these into an historical context. When the Golden Horde disintegrated in the middle of the fifteenth century, the Tatars in Crimea formed their own khanate in 1443. From 1478 this khanate survived as a semi-independent state under Ottoman suzerainty until Russia, under Catherine II, conquered it in 1783. In 1944 most Crimean Tatars were deported to Central Asia following allegations of cooperation with the Nazi forces. During the rest of the Soviet era the Tatars used every opportunity to campaign for their return, a right that was granted them in 1988. Since then there has been a stream of Tatars returning to Crimea, with a peak in 1992 and 1993, when 80,000 returned each year. Today there are more than 250,000 Tatars in Crimea.

The Tatars have been poorly integrated into Crimean society, and animosity between Tatars and Russians in Crimea has surfaced repeatedly since the beginning of the 1990s. The most serious incident happened in June 1995 after the local Mafia had beaten three Tatars to death because they refused to pay protection money; a large crowd of Tatars assembled to avenge the murders. Ukrainian anti-riot police stopped them outside the town of Sudak, and fired into the crowd. Two Tatars were killed and many more wounded. Further bloodshed was averted by moderate Tatar political leaders, who managed to calm the crowd down. (The political leaders of the Crimean Tatars are both moderate politicians and enjoy strong support from the Tatar population.)

Tensions again ran high, however, when about 85,000 Tatars were denied the right to participate in the March 1998 Ukrainian parliamentary elections. This was because Ukrainian bureaucracy had been extremely slow in arranging for them to obtain Ukrainian citizenship.[47] This denial of the right to participation in the elections led to clashes between police and several thousand Tatars in Simferopol on 24 March 1998. In December 1998 the Ukrainian parliament approved a special constitution for Crimea. The peninsula was recognized as an autonomy within Ukraine in 1991, but the division of authorities between Kiev and the autonomy had so far not been worked out in detail. The constitution seriously provoked the Tatar community. Earlier the Tatars had had a fixed quota of the seats in the Crimean parliament, but this provision was removed from the new constitution. For this and other reasons there were again rallies of thousands of Tatars in Simferopol 8 April 1999. Crimean and central Ukrainian authorities have only accommodated Tatar demands to a very limited degree, and future ethnic unrest in Crimea cannot be ruled out.

The Tatars have also received some moral and financial support from Turkey. Turkey considers that it has a special responsibility for the Turkic-speaking Crimean Tatars, and a powerful lobby of Tatar descendants in Turkey maintains this feeling of responsibility. However in both Crimean and Russian circles this support has been interpreted as a form of hidden Turkish imperialism. The Russian scholars Sergey Kazennov and Vladimir Kumachev wrote in an article in 1998: 'Turkey's intentions regarding the northern Black Sea are more than transparent. A good example here is the mass resettlement of Crimean Tatars [i.e. in Crimea] that to a large extent, according to certain sources, is directed and financed by Turkey. Because of this, Ukraine's policy of solidarity with Turkey will only lead to an expansion from the south that is closing in on Ukraine's own borders.'[48] It was therefore a very positive development when Turkey sent an official trade delegation to Crimea in February 1999, not specifically to meet with the Crimean Tatars, but to meet with the general Crimean business community. Facilitating this development was the 1998 Ukrainian – Turkish trade agreement, and the adoption of the Crimean constitution, which specified Crimea's degree of autonomy in economic affairs. In 1998 Turkey became the most important trade partner for Crimea. Total exports from Crimea to Turkey totalled 15 million US dollars, and total imports to Crimea from Turkey totalled four million US dollars.[49]

After Ukrainian independence, the Ukrainian Black Sea region was considered to have a substantial potential for ethnic unrest, and repeated statements from leading politicians in Moscow questioning the Ukrainian status of Crimea added to the fear in Kiev. The GUAMU focus on the danger of ethnic separatism should be seen in this light. Ukraine fears that local ethnic unrest could be used by Moscow as a pretext for interfering in Ukrainian internal affairs, and lead to an increased Russian military presence as it has done in Georgia. Russia could also prevent the possible intervention of the UN in such a conflict, because of its veto right in the UN Security Council. It would be more difficult for Russia to do this if the GUAMU countries could point to a peace-keeping capacity of their own.

However ethnic separatism now seems very unlikely among the Russians of Eastern and Southern Ukraine, or, increasingly, among the Russians of Crimea. However, tension between the ethnic Russians and the Tatars of Crimea is still a problem.

The Civil Society Dimension

There is an emerging civil society in Ukraine, but its influence on political decision-making so far remains scant. The Ukrainian Non-Governmental Organizations (NGOs) are critically short of funds, they are insufficiently protected by Ukrainian law and – probably most important of all – Ukraine did not inherit from the Soviet era any tradition for organizational life independent of the state, or the state bureaucracy to listen to NGOs.

In a 1999 article Oleksandr Lavrynovych, a central politician in Ukraine since independence and a member of the moderately nationalist Rukh parliamentary faction, summarized the insignificance of Ukrainian NGOs for political decision-making in the following way: 'In Ukraine during the last years there has not appeared one influential non-governmental organization (excluding political parties) that has been able to substantially influence government policy within its sphere of interest.'[50]

In line with Lavrynovych's conclusions is the experience of several central Kiev environmental NGOs in preparation for the 1998 Arhus international conference on the Convention for Public Access to Ecological Information. They tried to arrange several round table conferences between NGOs and government officials on the topic, but few representatives from the bureaucracy cared to participate. However, at a later forum called "The Promotion of the Populations Information Level on Environmental Issues", organized by the EU TACIS programme, both Ukrainian parliamentarians and governmental officials took part.

By the beginning of 1998 there were a total of 1258 officially registered NGOs in Ukraine, 53 of these were political parties. However, according to Oleksandr Lavrynovych, some experts estimate that if you count all types of non-registered organizations in Ukraine, there are about 10,000. The Ukrainian population numbers slightly less than 52 million people. For a comparison, Germany, with a population of 82 million, has approximately one million different public organizations.[51]

Ukrainian civil society activity in the Black Sea region has largely been concentrated in two areas: cooperation among Black Sea littoral cities, and ecological activism.

The cooperation among Black Sea littoral cities was formalized by the establishment of the International Black Sea Club (IBSC) in December 1992. One of its initiators was Odessa. The IBSC is a forum for consultation and cooperation on economic, cultural and ecological matters among 19 cities in the Black Sea region. The Club has the status of an observer in the BSEC, and of a consultative organ with the UN Economic and Social Council. It is also a member of the International Union of Local Government and the European Council for Small Business, and Odessa had chairmanship of the Club from 1995 to 1998.

Within the framework of the IBSC, particularly close cooperation has developed between Odessa and Istanbul. The universities of the two cities have established comprehensive cooperation programmes, several commercial projects are being developed, and in early 1999 a direct passenger and goods ferry-line was put into operation. The mayor of Odessa, Edvard Gurvits, joked in December 1997: 'Today in Odessa it is more difficult to find a person who has not been in Istanbul than to find a person who has not been in Moscow or St. Petersburg.'[52] The two cities signed a special agreement regarding cooperation and friendship in late 1997.

The environmental NGOs have, arguably, been more important than most other kinds of NGOs in independent Ukraine because of the 1986 Chernobyl accident. The Green World Association (*Zeleny Svit*) was established in 1987 as a direct result of the catastrophe, and, according to the British scholars Taras Kuzio and Andrew Wilson, the Green World Association became: 'a flag of convenience for many other radicals, while environmental discourse permeated throughout political life, and became a useful shorthand for criticism of Ukraine's lack of control over its own destiny.'[53] The reasonably good results for the Green Party in the Ukrainian parliamentary elections in March 1998 (5.5 per cent and fourth largest) testifies to continuing support for green ideas in the Ukrainian population.

There are about 15 different major environmental NGOs in Ukraine today. Of these, four are of particular importance to the Black Sea: the Ecological Information Centre in Crimea, the Odessa Socio-Ecological Union, the National EcoCentre of Ukraine, and the Green World Association. The Ecological Information Centre in Crimea promotes public education about environmental issues, it provides information to the local media, and it maintains a library on ecological issues. The National EcoCentre has as one of its most important activities the study of the state of the Azov water basin, and the Centre has established local branches along the Black Sea and Azov coasts, in Berdyansk, Mariupol, Mykolayiv and Kherson.

Most active, however, seems to be the veteran Green World Association. According to its own November 1997 report, the association has, on a number of occasions, been able to influence government policy regarding ecological issues. Just to mention some of the Green World initiatives in the Black Sea region: the Bolgrad Green World (Odessa region) managed to convince the local authorities to formulate a district environmental programme; due to joint activity between the National EcoCentre in Mykolayiv and the local Green World Association, the local authorities have increased the total area of natural reserves four times between 1992 and 1997; in March 1996 the association held a conference for 23 Ukrainian and two Moldavian NGOs on how to increase NGO participation in the various programmes for the protection of the Danube; the association organized together with other environmental NGOs the Black Sea day of Ukraine 31 October 1996; it also organized together with other environmental NGOs a meeting of the Azov-Black Sea Forum of Ukrainian NGOs in Kerch in Crimea in November 1996; and the association participates, together with governmental structures in the development of a National Action Plan for the Azov and Black Sea environment protection.[54]

Civil society in Ukraine is nascent and, despite numerous impediments, it is growing. The influence seems to be mainly on the local level, but at least the activities of the Green World Association to some extent modify Lavrynovych's description of the unimportance of the NGOs. So far most of the NGO activity has taken place within Ukraine's borders, but the first steps have been taken towards cooperation with foreign NGOs. One example is a joint seminar between NGOs from Romania, Moldova and Ukraine to discuss the lower Danube region, in Cahul in Moldova in October 1998.

Cross-border civil society activity might become a factor promoting cooperation in the Black Sea region in the future, but for the time being it is too weak to have this ability. NGO activity has not, so far, had any substantial influence on whether Ukrainian authorities should opt for a balance of power or a security-building approach in its policy towards the Black Sea region.

Conclusion

The Black Sea region continues to be less important for Ukrainian foreign policy than for the Eurasian and Euroatlantic regions, but its relative importance has increased over the last couple of years. The two main reasons for this are that its importance for the transport of oil, gas and other goods from Central Asia and the Caucasus to Western Europe is now internationally recognized, and that Ukraine has found partners in the region (Azerbaijan, Georgia and Moldova) with whom it can join in efforts to balance against Russian influence.

I have analysed Ukrainian perceptions of the Black Seas region along four dimensions. One question remains to be answered, however, and that is how these dimensions interplay to produce the overall Ukrainian perception of cooperation and conflict in the region. This question basically concerns how the three other dimensions influence the strategic dimension. The strategic dimension concerns the problem of war or peace, and therefore refers to the most important concern for any state, the question of its own survival. The three other dimensions are also clearly important in their own right, but little of their potential for cooperation is likely to be developed unless there is peace (understood as absence of war or the threat of war) in the region.

There are in the Black Sea region at least three non-strategic factors that can qualitatively influence the strategic dimension in favour of reducing the role of balance of power, not just with the Ukrainian government but with all Black Sea governments. These are: the importance of the Black Sea region as a transportation focal point between east and west: the need to co-ordinate the exploitation of joint natural resources, especially oil and gas; and the need for concerted efforts to save the Black Sea environment.

All Black Sea states will, in different degrees, profit from the region becoming a transport focal point. Clearly, this could also be a source of conflict, since most of the states want as big a slice of the pie as possible. However, if the situation deteriorates in the direction of violent conflict, there will be no pie at all. Western Europe will then find other, more secure, ways of transportation. Ukraine at the moment seems to consider the transport issue as a zero-sum game, and therefore developments in this sector support balance of power in the strategic dimension.

On the question of natural resources, Ukraine has quarrelled with both Russia and Romania about continental shelf borders and with Turkey about fishing rights. However, there are signs that Ukrainian authorities, at least in some cases, have come to the conclusion that this is not necessarily a zero-sum game. Joint exploitation might be preferable both to a continued fight for resources and to separate exploitation. The joint Russian-Ukrainian explorations of the Black Sea and Azov Sea continental shelves indicate such reasoning is in operation. If this cooperation is broadened that could, in time, work to reduce balance of power in the strategic dimension.

With regard to the Black Sea environment, all affected governments acknowledge the need for concerted efforts. The main problem here is not the will to co-operate, but the funds necessary to move beyond statements and declarations. Here, the active role of the EU has been of particular importance. Continued Western support for these efforts can promote effective cooperation among Black Sea governments on environmental issues. This could in turn reduce the level of political tension, and thereby reduce the tendency to think in terms of balance of power for most governments in the region.

However, even if developments in all the three non-strategic dimensions would motivate security building rather than balancing behaviour, this would still not be enough to tilt the balance in favour of Ukraine pursuing a predominantly security-building approach. Ukrainian Black Sea policy is to a large extent hostage to the overall Russian–Ukrainian relationship.

The most important question for Ukraine in the Black Sea region is therefore the following: should better and more stable relations with Russia be seen as a precondition to be fulfilled before opting for the security-building approach, or should opting for this approach be seen as a way of improving relations with Russia? This is a dilemma that the Ukrainian leadership is still trying to resolve.

* I am grateful to Anders Kjolberg and Sven Gunnar Simonsen for commenting upon earlier drafts of this chapter. Whenever I cite Russian or Ukrainian language sources in this chapter, the translations are my own.

Notes

1 Quoted in Yuri Shcherbak, 1998, The Strategic Role of Ukraine – Diplomatic Addresses and Lectures (1994-1997), Harvard Papers in Ukrainian Studies, Harvard University Press, Cambridge, Massachusetts, p. 13.

2 See especially: Sherman W. Garnett, 1997, Keystone in the Arch, Carnegie Endowment for International Peace, Brookings Institution Press, Washington, and Taras Kuzio, 1995, Ukrainian Security Policy, The Washington Papers, Center for Strategic and International Studies, Washington D.C. For an analysis of Ukraine and Central Europe see: Oleksandr Pavliuk, 1997, "Ukraine and Regional Cooperation in Central and Eastern Europe", Security Dialogue, vol. 28, no.3, September, pp.347-362, and for an analysis of Ukraine and NATO see: Tor Bukkvoll, 1997, "Ukraine and NATO: The Politics of Soft Cooperation", in Security Dialogue, vol. 28, no.3, September, pp.363-374.

3 One exception is: Grigory Perepelitsa, 1996, "Osnovnye voennye tendentsii v Chernomorskom regione: ukrainskaya perspektiva" (Main military tendencies in the Black Sea region (the Ukrainian perspective), in Irina Kobrinskaya and Sherman Garnett, Ukraina: problemy bezopasnosti (Ukraine: problems of security), Carnegie Endowment for International Peace, Moscow, pp.25-47.

4 "Foreign and Security Policy of Ukraine Expert Poll: January – March 1997", in Foreign & Security Policy of Ukraine April to June, provided by the Ukrainian Center for Peace, Conversion and Conflict Resolution Studies, p. 82.

5 "Foreign and Security Policy of Ukraine Expert Poll: April-June 1998", in Foreign & Security Policy of Ukraine April to June, provided by the Ukrainian Center for Peace, Conversion and Conflict Resolution Studies, p. 87.

6 "Ykrayina – CHES: Vyznannya pravilnosti kursu" (Ukraine and the BSEC: acknowledging the right course), Polityka i Chas, no. 7, July, 1998, p.83.

7 For this and other definitions, see: Michael Sheehan, 1996, The Balance of Power – History & Theory, London, Routledge, pp. 2-4.

8 From *Nezavisimaya Gazeta* quoted in Volodymyr Pankeev, "Velykiy naftovyi peredil" (The great oil partition), Den, no. 38, 1998.

9 Interview with Admiral Victor Kravchenko in *Interfax-AIF*, no. 11, 16-22 March 1998.

10 RFE/RL Newsline, 18 February, 1999.

11 Ibid. p. 31.

12 Belov, Binko and Pirozhkov (ed.), 1997, Natsionalna bezpeka Ukrayiny 1994 – 1996 rr. (The National Security of Ukraine 1994-1996), National Institute of Strategic Studies, on the Internet at http://www.niss.gov.ua/book/otch/roz05.htm, chapter 11. Zovnishnopolitychni aspekty (Foreign policy aspects).

13   These proposed geopolitical triangles were: Ukraine – Turkmenistan – Iran, Kyiv – Ankara –Teheran, Kyiv – Kishinev – Bukharest, Kyiv – Bukharest – Warsaw, Warsaw – Kyiv – Ankara, Ukraine – Turkey – Israel, and Kyiv – Ankara – Washington. Rostyslav Khotin, "Heopolitychna heometriya Kyeva" (The geopolitical geometry of Kiev), Den, no.31, 1998.

14   The Turkish foreign ministry made an official announcement to the press in support of Ukrainian territorial integrity in April 1995, the Turkish President, Suleiman Demirel made a similar statement in November 1996, and such a statement was also made by the Turkish delegation to the meeting of the BSEC parliamentary assembly in Tbilisi in December 1996. See: Nataliya Mkhytaryan, "Ukrayina i Turechchyna v ramkakh CHES" (Ukraine and Turkey in the framework of the BSEC", Polityka i Chas, no.4, April 1997, pp.42-46.

15   Boris Parakhonskiy, 1998, "Pivdenni dyvidendy – suchasna politychna sytuatsiya na Blyzkomu Skhodi ta stratehichni interesy Ukrayiny"(Southern dividends – the present political situation in the Middle East and the strategic interests of Ukraine), Polityka i Chas, no.10, October 1998, pp. 48-49.

16   Duygu Bazoglu Sezer, 1995, "Balance of Power in the Black Sea in the Post-Cold War Era: Russia, Turkey, and Ukraine", in Maria Drohobycky, Crimea – Dynamics, Challenges, and Prospects, American Association for the Advancement of Science, Rowman & Littlefield Publishers, Inc., London England, p.182.

17   By the southernmost part of Odessa oblast is meant the counties of Reni, Bolhrad, Izmayil, Kiliya, Tarutine, Artsiz, Tatarbunari, Sarata, and Bilhorod-Dnistrovsky. See, Boechko, B, "Severnaya Bukovyna i Pridunavye—iskonnaya territoriya Ukrainy", Polityka i Vremya, no. 5, 1992, pp. 47-51 and no. 6, pp. 66-71.

18   See *Jamestown Monitor*, vol. 3, issue 222, 26 November 1997.

19   Alena Pritula, "Politicheski-izbiratelnoe gruzinskoe gostepriimstvo" (Political-electoral Georgian hospitality), *Zerkalo Nedely*, no.44, 1 November 1997.

20   This analysis of most aspects of Ukrainian security is made by the close to government think tank National Institute of Strategic Studies, and it is written under the auspices of the secretary of the Ukrainian Security Council and close Kuchma aidè Volodymyr Horbulin. The document is available in Ukrainian on the Internet at http://www.niss.gov.ua/book/otch/roz12.htm. The quotation is taken from the chapter The Crimean problem in the context of Ukrainian-Russian relations under part 11, Foreign policy aspects.

21   See: RFE/RL NewsLine, 8 December, 1998.

22   RFE/RL NewsLine, 3 December 1997.

23   Nikolay Semena, "Budet li OCHES cchastlivee SNG ?" (Will the BSEC be happier than the CIS ?), *Zerkalo Nedely*, no. 23, 6-12 June, 1998.

24   RFE/RL Newsline, 29 September 1997.

25   Calculated from figures presented in Anatoly Humenyuk, "Stratehiya poshuku priorytetnykh zovnishnikh pynkiv zbutu" (The strategy for the

detection of priority foreign markets), Ekonomychny Chasopis, no. 11-12, 1998, on the Internet at http://www.harvard .kiev.ua/ist

26   Interview with the chairman of the Ukrainian State Committee for Tourism, Valery Tsybukh, Zerkalo Nedely, No. 19, 15-21 May, 1999.

27   Nina Perstneva, "Stanet li bolshaya Odessa morskimi vorotami Evropy ?" (Will Odessa become the naval port of Europe ?), Zerkalo Nedely, no. 44, 31 October – 5 November, 1998.

28   Mykhailo Aksanyuk, "Yuriyi Karmazin: torhovelnyi flot Ukrayiny – na mezhi obvalu" (Yuri Karmazin: the merchant fleet of Ukraine – on the border of collapse), Den, no.176, 1997.

29   Stefan Korshak, "Debts threatening to sink Blasco", Kiev Post, 17 April 1997.

30   Vladimir Rybalka, "Ne v meru razvity, ottogo i bedny", (Not sufficiently developed, and therefore also poor), Zerkalo Nedely, no. 13, 3-9 April, 1999.

31   RFE/RL Newsline, 2 February, 1999.

32   RFE/RL Newsline, 25 February, 1999.

33   David R. Marples, "Ukraine, Belarus, and the Energy Dilemma", RFE/RL Research Report, no. 27, vol. 2, 2 July, 1993, p.40.

34   Oles M. Smolansky, 1999, "Fuel, Credit, and Trade – Ukraine's Economic Dependence on Russia", Problems of Post-Communism, vol. 46, no.2, p.49.

35   Interview with Ivan Diyaka in Segodnya, 29 December, 1998.

36   Oleksandr Manachynskyi, "Yevraziya: velykyi naftovyi pasyans" (Eurasia: the great oil patience), Polityka i Chas, no.4, April 1998, p. 35.

37   For details see: Tom Warner, "Russian energy barons throw Kyiv gas life-line", Kyiv Post, 26 June 1998, available at the Internet at http://www.thepost.kiev.ua.

38   See TRACECA evaluation report at the official EU web-site, http://europa.eu.int/comm/dg/evaluation/tacis_tranceca/31.htm

39   See Ukraine evaluation report at http://europa.eu.int/comm/dg1a/evaluation/ukraine

40   See evaluation report at the official EU web-site, http://europa.eu.int/

41   Oblast is a territorial unit of Ukraine.

42   For details on this project, see Nina Perstneva, "Prizrak brodit po Dunayu(prizrak volnoy zony" (A ghost is roaming over the Danube (the ghost of an economic free-zone), Zerkalo Nedely, no. 47, 21-27 November, 1998.

43   Interview with Leonid Minin in Kompanion, no. 13, March 1999, available on the Internet at http://www.maximum.com.ua

44   "Euroregions" are economic and ecological cooperation agreements that can apply for financial support from the EU Phare Cross-Border Cooperation Program. The Lower Danube Euroregion is proposed to consist of the Odessa oblast, the Moldovan provinces of Kagul, Kantemir, and Vulkaneshti, and the Romanian provinces of Brelia, Galats and Tulcha. See: Nina Perstneva, "Evroregion Nizhniy Dunay: Pervaya rabochaya vstrecha proshla bez uchastiya Moldovy" (Euroregion Lower Danube: The first

working meeting proceeded without the participation of Moldova), *Zerkalo Nedely*, no. 41, 10-16 September, 1998.

45 For an analysis of why there was little or no ethnic mobilization of the Russian population of Eastern and Southern Ukraine, see: Tor Bukkvoll, 1997, Ukraine and European Security, Chatham House Papers, Royal Institute of International Affairs, London, pp. 45-54.

46 Paul Goble, "Analysis: Kiev's New Security Map", RFE/RL Analyses, 26 July 1996.

47 15,000 of these were stateless, and 70,000 were citizens of other former republics because Ukraine and these republics had not agreed on a process for transferring these people's citizenship.

48 Sergey Kazennov and Vladimir Kumachev, "V kakoe buduschee dreyfuet Ukraina?" (Into what future is Ukraine drifting ?), Natsinalnaya elektronnaya biblioteka, on the Internet at http://www.nns.ru/analytdoc/ukraina/html

49 See: Vyacheslav Lebedev, "Turetskie smotriny v Krimu" (Turkish ... in Crimea), (the word smotriny refers to an old tradition whereby the groom's relatives visit the home of the bride to get to know her and her family better), *Nezavisimaya Gazeta*, 16 February, 1999.

50 Oleksandr Lavrynovych, "Chy mozhlyve v Ukrayini hromadyanske suspilstvo?" (Is a civil society possible in Ukraine?), *Hromadski Initsiatyvy*, no. 12, February 1999, a journal for Ukrainian NGOs available on the Internet at http://www.ZURC.Org/GI/GI

51 Oleksandr Lavrynovych, "Chy mozhlyve v Ukrayini hromadyanske suspilstvo?"

52 *Odessa*, no.11-12, 1997, available at the Internet at http://www. paco.net/odessa/media/odessa/1097/42.html

53 Taras Kuzio and Andrew Wilson, 1994, Ukraine: Perestroika to Independence, MacMillan, London, p. 77.

54 This information can be found on the Internet site of the Center for Civil Society International, http://solar.rtd.utk.edu/~ccis/nisorgs/ukraine/kyiv/zsvtinfo.htr

CHAPTER SIX

Security Cooperation in the Black Sea Basin

Plamen Pantev

The issues of security cooperation in the Black Sea basin, the need and the feasibility for it as well as the maturity of its design, stem from the many conflicts that broke out in the post-Cold War era in the Black Sea area and the adjacent Balkan, Caucasian and Caspian regions. The other major source of the interest in these questions is the existence of various economic, social and political factors that stimulate the rise of real opportunities for cooperation in the Black Sea basin, for shaping prerequisites of local countries to join the Eastern enlargement of the European and the Euroatlantic civic and security zone, and the globalizing economy too. The reception of such opportunities has not been that of unanimous acceptance, whence follow new interstate contradictions and tensions.

The patterns of security and foreign-policy behaviour of regional actors in the last decade vary greatly, reflecting the different domestic environments, the conceptual orientations of the respective societies, their international affiliations and the still immature level of regional cooperation.

The security situation in the Black Sea basin and the utilization of the region-building opportunities is the focus of research for many observers from different parts of the world. In 1996 Ronald D. Asmus, F. Stephen Larrabee and Ian O. Lesser – prominent experts from the RAND Corporation – described the formation of two arcs of crises on the European continent, which cross each other dangerously in the triangle "Middle East – Balkans – Transcaucasia". The first arc divides Russia and Germany and from Northern Europe reaches to the Balkans. The second splits the Mediterranean Sea: starting from North Africa it cuts through the Middle East and extends to South-Western Asia. The Black Sea basin and the littoral territories acquire a key strategic meaning and role within these arcs of crises.[1]

Unlike the RAND experts this paper does not equate the strategic meaning and contents of the two arcs of tensions and crises. The situation in Europe, in the EuroAtlantic space and the OSCE zone is incomparable to the conflict potential of the "Southern" crisis arc. The persistent and purposeful policy of NATO, EU/WEU to build, together with Russia and the OSCE, a new and more effective interlocking institutional security system has dramatically diminished the conflict potential of the first crisis arc. The formula for achieving this is characterized by a difficult compromise between enlarging NATO and EU interests, Russian security interests and a definite unwillingness in the Central/Eastern/Southeastern European countries to serve as a "strategic buffer" between the West and the East alongside a clear will to participate actively in the eastward expansion of the civil space and the zone of stability and security in the Euro-Atlantic-Asiatic components of the OSCE area. A historical responsibility of the Central/Eastern/Southeastern European countries is to support the complex process of reaching strategic compromises between the security interests of their own countries, of the EU/WEU, NATO and of Russia. If such compromises are achieved the evolving Northern arc, inherited from the Cold War, bears the potential to dilute and neutralize the harmful effects of the Southern one.

This is the analytical framework necessary for the consideration of Black Sea basin security issues together with their interaction with conflicts in the Balkans and in the Transcaucasian-Caspian subregions. Apart from other factors these conflicts are influenced by leading world power centres which are trying to redefine geopolitical spheres on the basis of evolving geoeconomic conditions and interests. The zone that stretches from the Adriatic Sea through the Black Sea and to the Caspian Sea has already assumed the character of a world region, a meeting point for the interests of the USA, the EU and Russia. Moreover, this broader region is part of the enlarging EU as well as part of the Union's neighbourhood. Thus these perspectives also enable us to assess the role of the Black Sea region in the process of shaping a manageable system of Atlanto-Euro-Asiatic security and that of a key ingredient of this system: the capacity for crisis management (or conflict settlement) across this particular area and its adjacent regions.

The Need for Security Cooperation in the Black Sea Basin

Any 'security cooperation' is linked to the need to overcome certain risks, concerns or threats to the security of particular countries as well as to the protection of other interests. The Black Sea basin, which comprises the territories of the eleven member-states of the Organisation for Black Sea

Economic Cooperation (BSEC), calls for security cooperation for three basic reasons: the existence of specific sources of conflict that need to be treated and dealt with; present and potential conflicts as well as post-conflict developments that require a cooperative approach to their settlement; the evolution of real opportunities to develop the region and the individual countries economically and to gradually mould an area of more extensive cooperation.

Coping with Sources of Conflict in the Black Sea Basin

The sources of real and potential conflicts in the region are as discussed in this section. Firstly there is the birth of new state actors after the collapse of the Soviet Union, inadequate state-building stability and the reflection of this in the configuration of interstate relations in the adjacent regions of the Caucasus, Caspian Sea basin and the Balkans. Involvement and integration are the tools needed to cope with these issues.

Also to be taken into account is the changing military balance, mainly among the three largest armed forces in Europe – those of Russia, Turkey and Ukraine. Acquisitions of armaments in the Black Sea and in the neighbouring regions are both huge in quantity and of high quality. This is also true for the industrial capacity of the region for armaments. Major issues have emerged in relation to the naval balance of the Black Sea – between Russia and Ukraine as well as between Russia and Turkey. The implementation of the 1936 Montreux Convention about passage through the Straits is a major point of contention. The activity of PfP countries' navies in maritime exercises may also lead to disputes. There is almost no system of confidence-building measures (CBMs) in the maritime environment of the Black Sea. Questions surrounding the higher ceilings for force deployments of Russia and Turkey than those permitted by the initial agreements of the Vienna Conventional Forces in Europe (CFE) negotiations are controversial and still unsettled. Issues related to the level of civilian and democratic control over the armed forces in the littoral states may also lead to the escalation of regional tensions. All these questions need an in depth and sound approach and resolution.

The Black Sea basin is an area in which economic systems are not homogeneous as well as an area experiencing grave ecological problems. Pollution is the worst of these. It is linked to the activities of coastal and other European states through the Danube, Dniestr and Dniepr rivers and this circumstance may lead to internal political instabilities and disputes over the origins of pollution. The economic prosperity and environmental health of the region are obviously not solely the responsibility of countries from the Black Sea basin.

After 16 November 1994 the Convention of the Law of the Sea (1982) came into force and new geopolitical problems arose from this, problems concerning the delimitation of the Exclusive Economic Zones (EEZ), including the continental shelf, and of the sea spaces (territorial waters, geographic centre of the Black Sea, agreements between the neighbouring littoral states, etc.). Legal clarity is indispensable to ensuring a solid legal basis for both economic and the military activity in the Black Sea.

The imperfect political stability of the transitional countries of the region, the emergence of highly-organized crime linked to the global structures in this sphere combined with the absence of a regional security system provide potential for local conflicts. Turkey – the major naval power of the Black Sea and a key strategic country – permanently faces three grave problems which could produce explosive effects in the region: these issues are those of Islamic fundamentalism, the Mafia and the Kurdish question. Turkish-Greek tensions add to the depression of the political climate in the area. While Turkey and Greece belong to NATO, all former Soviet Union states of the region are part of the military umbrella of the CIS. Bulgaria and Romania are NATO applicants and EU-associated countries. Common denominators concerning security matters are indispensable in this situation – more than is suggested by OSCE and PfP/EAPC.

The Black Sea and its littoral states are potentially becoming either battlefields or fields of cooperation for the oil and natural gas pipelines from Russia and the Caspian Sea basin. The diversification of energy supplies may result in a significant shift in European and North American dependencies away from the Middle East and the Persian Gulf oil reservoirs. The solution to this problem may itself lead to conflicts of various proportions – although it may also lead to opportunities for the mutual benefit of the actors involved.

The risks of terrorist activities in Chechnya and in those regions with Kurdish resistance organization form obstacles of a different kind from the normal transportation of oil and gas through and around the Black Sea. All countries with an interest in the oil and gas supplies should profit from a lasting and stable resolution to the Chechen conflict and to the complex Kurdish question.

Conflict and Post-Conflict Settlement in the Black Sea Area

A broad array of conflict and post-conflict issues exist in the Black Sea basin area; these need to be tackled in a cooperative way within security structures. First is the question of Chechnya: this raises a mixture of ethnic, religious and territorial problems which calls for major Russian attention to the resolution of internal conflict, conflict that has the potential to detonate broader areas and issues.

Next are the conflicts in Ingushetia, North Ossetia, Daghestan, Abkhazia, Southern Ossetia, Ajaria and Karabakh. These bear what are understood as both conflict and post-conflict features and both a cooperative and responsible approach to these conflicts is required if their destructive potential, in an area that has a lot of opportunities, is to be diminished.

It is probable that this should also be the perspective adopted when approaching an issue as highly complex and serious as the Kurdish one. Along with the anti-terrorist rhetoric there lies a major conflict which destabilizes an important country like Turkey and threatens a broader area, one with huge and positive geoeconomic potential – the Balkan-Black Sea-Caspian Sea zone. A more persistent, benign and cooperative way of dealing with this issue is in the interests of all the actors involved in this region.

Greek-Turkish contradictions over the Aegean Sea, Cyprus and Western Thrace contribute to the conflict potential of the broader region. Greek-Turkish relations consume a great deal of the attention as well as the political energy of NATO which by now, effectively, keeps these bilateral conflicts under control.

The Transdniestria conflict in Moldova, Russian-Ukrainian tensions over the Crimea, the Black Sea navy and those concerning economic issues further shape the conflict and post-conflict picture of the region.

Constructive opportunities in the BSEC area

While all the issues listed and analysed in the previous paragraph, as well as the need to deal with them, are a major incentive for efficient security cooperation, there are existing factors which directly stimulate this, and these factors will now be outlined. The effective utilization of the potential of the energy sector is one factor of the utmost importance for future cooperative efforts in and about the region. Similarly the involvement of the private sector, as well as the private industries in general, will aid in pioneering the technological modernization of a broader region, which covers the belt stretching from Central Asia and the Caspian Sea basin through the Caucasus and the Black Sea area to Southeastern Europe. The modernization of the telecommunications and transport infrastructures is just one aspect of this. It should also be noted that developing trade relations will contribute to the expansion of the potential for cooperation of this broad zone.

The institutionalization of the BSEC and the transformation of the forum into a regional economic organization for 11 countries of the broader area formally places these national actors on track for promoting peace and prosperity, in a form which is based on pluralist democracy, the respect of human rights, the rule of law and a free market economy. Multilateral economic cooperation based on free-market principles is a significant stepping stone towards the integration of the region, as a prospective free trade area, into the activities of the WTO on a global scale. Additionally it may improve the options of the EU to extend its market eastwards to more than 190 million people (in the case of Russia only the littoral regions are counted).

The institutionalized economic relationships of the 11 BSEC members introduced three important political areas of cooperation in the area: the parliamentary, the governmental and that of the local authorities. There is no doubt that this will raise the general cooperative potential of the region. Moreover the BSEC has the minimum capacity for an adequate framework for the evolution of CBMs. The regional cooperation may profit from the environment of a working system of CBMs.

The stable, peaceful and friendly bilateral relations between various pairs of countries, of the 11-strong group, is another major incentive for the multilateralization of the cooperation on a regional scale and an important factor in the improvement of relations among countries that have not yet foregrounded their bilateral links as cooperating partners.

The strengthening of links between the BSEC, European and Euroatlantic institutions is a significant catalyst to regional cooperation and development. For most of the 11 BSEC countries the EU is their ultimate institutional objective.

Developing cultural and educational links is another stimulus to cooperation in the region. One example of this is a Bulgarian idea to draft common history books for secondary-school students in the Black Sea region, as a step towards diminishing ethnic and ideological tensions and as a means of promoting the spirit of cooperation among younger generations.

The building-up of regional cooperation is hindered by the multiplicity of countries and the diversity of their interests, as well as the fact that some of them prefer other foreign-policy instruments than the BSEC for reaching their objectives. The absence of a tradition of cooperation; BSEC's inadequate potential to develop, combined with the primacy of the EU orientation of most of the countries; the lack of capital resources for the funding of Black Sea economic cooperation projects (with some exceptions concerning Turkey, Greece and Russia) – all these are factors which decrease the potential for cooperation in the region. Nevertheless, the foundations for an economic, social and cultural cooperation in the Black Sea area have been laid.

All of the above factors combined with the potential of the Black Sea basin and its adjacent territories to assume the features of a prospective geoeconomic world region, as well as a field of both EU enlargement and a prosperous EU neighbourhood, logically require an adequate and effective regional cooperation over security that would guarantee the stability of economic, social and political relations.

Forms of Security Cooperation in the Black Sea Basin

It is no news at all to post-Cold War security-studies experts that precautions in the economic field – privatization, the banking system, the budget, a modernized infrastructure of transport, energy and telecommunications – constitute significant elements in the conceptual framework for regulating the international community's conflict prevention actions.[2] In conceptual terms arising from security studies the BSEC, though a "purely" economic organization, fulfils major security and conflict-prevention functions in what is an ethnically and politically volatile region.

The terminology surrounding important issues in that area is somewhat confused: a distinction is made between "conflict prevention", "crisis management", "peaceful settlement of disputes" (or "conflict settlement") in Chapter III of the Helsinki Document of 1992. Victor-Yves Ghebali is right to underline the fact that such a distinction tends to assume the existence of three different situations requiring three different approaches: conflicts capable of being prevented; crises in need of management; and disputes subject to settlement.[3] V. Y. Ghebali goes on to point out that the distinction between "prevention", "management" and "settlement" has no solid justification. Any successful preventive management amounts to settlement. So "prevention" and "settlement" are comparable forms of "management" which just take place at different times.[4]

Drawing on this broader conceptual perspective the answer to one traditional question about the BSEC: "Is there a political and security dimension?" is definitely "yes". The organization was created by a political decision and the institutional regulation of economic relations has a political normative nature. The ratification of the Charter of BSEC by the member-states will result in the strengthening of the political character of the institution through the assumption of legal features of the relationships. In addition BSEC has a definite security dimension. Black Sea cooperation is not exempt from the spectrum of security roles open to other subregional groups in Central/Eastern Europe[5]:

The existential level of security provides the most obvious form of cooperation in this field in the Black Sea area – whether or not the founders of the forum for BSEC, and later the organization, planned it. Originating in the national strategic interest of Turkey to extend its influence to the east and to the south while avoiding open confrontation with Russia, BSEC provided a forum which was especially significant for the newly-born states in the area, whose national representatives both experienced and learnt to experience their identity in non-confrontational terms. People from BSEC countries meet regularly at personal, municipal, governmental and parliamentary levels to consider private, business, political, cultural, educational or legal issues. Mutual knowledge and understanding of one another is developing. Nascent feelings of local community and solidarity are developing in a region rich in historical rivalries and hatreds. Inherent in economic cooperation within the region – albeit small scale – is the conscious acceptance of the principle of not using force against members of the forum/organization. This is not just for the reason that the founding documents require respect of the UN Charter and the OSCE Acts but because it has become customary practice in the region. This improves the chances to establish communication channels between persons who previously knew one another in potential crisis situations. Hence, the chances of discouraging an outbreak of violence during a crisis in interstate relations are increased.

So-called 'soft security' is another form of possible security cooperation in the Black Sea basin. Without implementing any defence programmes the prevention or removal of internal and international sources of conflict is achieved through averting non-military threats to security. This is carried out by improving the economic conditions of individual participating countries and by an improved transport, energy and communications infrastructure. Increasing the economic interdependence of the neighbouring regions of BSEC countries, raising public awareness of a commonality of interests (through academic, educational and cultural exchanges), easing the visa regime and joint handling of migrant workers in border regions (Bulgaria and Greece), cooperative management of water resources (Bulgaria and Turkey, Bulgaria and Greece) – these are all ways to improve the security situation in the broader region.

The BSEC devotes particular attention to the protection of the Black Sea environment, both to the joint response to, and handling of, emergency situations and to cooperation in combating organized crime, international terrorism, illegal migration and illicit drug-trafficking. The achievement of these ends is facilitated by the existence and implementation of a Strategic Action Plan for the Rehabilitation and Protection of the Black Sea and regular meetings and agreements among Law-Enforcement Ministers, the Ministers of the Interior and by the Working Group on Emergency Situations coordinating implementation of the Agreement on Collaboration in Emergency Responses. In addition BSEC's Parliamentary Assembly is monitoring and encouraging the work done in this 'soft security' zone forming an important link with national parliaments in order to elaborate on appropriate legislation.

Another notable form of possible security cooperation concerns explicit security issues. These are relations for coping with new, 'non-traditional' threats to security such as terrorism, drugs, crime, illegal migration, ecological threats and natural disasters. However engagement with this security aspect in the Black Sea basin of countries contending for EU/WEU/NATO membership such as Bulgaria and Romania, does not distract them from their main integration efforts.

Less successful are initiatives to outline and adopt a system of CBMs in the Black Sea. Ukraine proposed this in November 1993, and in June 1994, confirming its wish to strengthen confidence in military and naval relations in the Black Sea. Bulgaria, Georgia, Romania, Russia and Turkey supported the idea but preferred to deal with it using other organizational frameworks. However the Russian-Ukrainian agreement concerning their Black Sea Fleets may bring fresh impetus to this proposal.

In 1996 Ukraine again moved to propose a more substantial BSEC security role in order to respond to issues of a pan-European nature. This may be of particular importance in shaping a coordinated approach to peacekeeping and crisis-management scenarios. Another explicit security role may be that of the collective mediation of disputes.

The BSEC countries are parties to the CFE and participate in efforts to improve it. Nevertheless there is room to develop unilateral, bilateral and multilateral initiatives for arms control and disarmament measures in this over-militarized region.

Another possibility to be considered is to seek a 'BSEC' division of labour in the UN, OSCE and PfP for the purposes of the verification and monitoring of conflicts.

In addition there is a potential form of security cooperation which relates to 'hard security' issues. This is considered not only unusual for the Black Sea basin but also unrealistic and by some even impossible – which does not mean that there have not been attempts to deal with these issues. In 1992 at the Istanbul summit that launched the BSEC initiative the President of Georgia, E. Shevardnadze, suggested a Council of Defence and Foreign

Ministers be established to tackle subregional crises. The idea was not taken up because the BSEC was destined to avoid security or political issues.

In the last two years Turkey has launched the idea of creating a multinational Black Sea Navy of the six littoral states. A navy unit is expected to develop the Black Sea economic cooperation and add to the formation of a multinational rapid reaction force of Southeastern Europe. The idea is that security on land must be developed through security at sea. Command is to rotate between members each year. Twice a year the navy unit will carry out one or two-week exercises for rescue operations and the prevention of ecological catastrophes.

Hard security roles involving the de-militarization or de-nuclearization of the region can hardly be expected. But joint navy crisis-management forces for rescue operations may well evolve in a sea that has six coastal countries that need to help one another. With the creation of an interface between BSEC and the OSCE/EAPC/PfP this prospect seems an even more realistic one. While the OSCE/EAPC/PfP interlocking can produce practical results in the area, the involvement of a subregional organization not focused on security, such as the BSEC, may assist the formulation of clearer objectives as well as economic ways of crisis management. The need to start talking "subregionally" on security issues is also linked to economic efficiency.

Another form of security cooperation designed to improve the capacity to settle conflicts is the practical establishment of an interface between the BSEC and European institutions with political and security effectiveness – the OSCE, EU, WEU, NATO/EAPC/PfP.

The OSCE is the premier organization for the promotion of human rights and democracy in Europe. OSCE is the specialized Euro-Atlanto-Asiatic institution for early warning, conflict-prevention, crisis and post-crisis management and rehabilitation. OSCE has already experienced missions in countries of the region – Russia (in Chechnya), Georgia (in South Ossetia), Azerbaijan (in Nagorno-Karabakh), Moldova (in Transdniestr), Ukraine and Albania.

EU is another major actor that has an interface with the BSEC. Already the Union has clearly determined its future Southeastern boundaries by integrating Bulgaria and Romania in 10-15 years. The BSEC is calling upon the EU for the establishment of a BSEC Fund, entrusted to the EBRD and replenished through voluntary contributions of EU Member States – BSEC Observers and the EC as well, similar to that set up for the CEI. This would require the adoption by the EU of a comprehensive cooperative approach to the BSEC as a region.[6]The EU is already financing rehabilitation projects in both Abkhazia and South Ossetia. The Union also has the unique opportunity through the EU-BSEC interface to enact the contents of the European Energy Charter, signed in December 1991 it covers the whole of Europe, the former Soviet Union and all other Western industrialized nations. Its purpose has been the establishment of a common code of conduct for the exploitation of energy resources and their transport, thus providing a legal guarantee for investors in particular, but also to set environmental standards.[7]

The interface of BSEC and the EU is important for security in the region in another way: the Union provides instruments for conflict prevention – economic, diplomatic and military. The economic group includes a conditional common trade policy, development aid (association agreements and financial aid), commercial sanctions (embargo and interdiction of financial transactions), non-proliferation of weapons (nuclear weapons and conventional weapons) and humanitarian aid as influential instruments in conflicts. The diplomatic instruments are as follows: mediation, fact finding and special envoys; "informal" diplomacy; diplomatic sanctions; coordination of member-state policies within other organizations; surveillance of democratic and social standards; support of democracy and human rights programmes and regional cooperation. The military instruments are: strictly military as provided by the Maastricht and the Amsterdam Treaty for EU; operations conducted by paramilitary forces (police missions, drug enforcement missions and special missions).

As already discussed the PfP and the EAPC along with two NATO states have a solid presence in the area. BSEC may profit by reaching a mutual reinforcement with the Alliance if it opens communications on issues of common interest. It has already begun on environmental issues and has the potential to evolve on such questions as cooperation in disaster relief and rescue efforts. Logically the latter are linked with the growth of the Black Sea region's economic potential.

While the WEU prefers to develop the bilateral dialogue with BSEC countries, its experience of cooperation in the Adriatic and the Danube during the sanctions regime against FRY should not be neglected. An evolving Common European Defence may find it useful to utilize the crisis management potential of WEU in the Black Sea area too.

An important form of security cooperation that would inevitably evolve in the Black Sea basin is that concerning the democratic control of the armed forces. As discussed earlier in this paper the OSCE/PfP framework can be more effectively utilized in the Black Sea region. The democratic organization of civil-military relations is a fundamental prerequisite for the social and economic modernization of the area in general and an indispensable stepping stone to other forms of security cooperation.

In conclusion, the region of the Black Sea basin is not only profiting in security terms from a changed, post-Cold War environment but is also contributing to the stability and development of the area. A broader definition of security and a more intensive interface with the EU/WEU, OSCE, NATO/EAPC/PfP may increase the role of the BSEC in settling particular conflicts, in cooperation on hard security issues and for eastward extension of the EuroAtlantic civil and security zone.

The Relations between Russia and Turkey and the Security Cooperation in the Black Sea Basin

Relations between Russia and Turkey — the most powerful actors in the Black Sea basin – are particularly important for the improvement of security cooperation in the Black Sea basin and of its conflict settlement potential. There exists a historical relationship of mistrust linked to the record of the thirteen wars they have fought against each other in the last five centuries, and so some misperceptions of each other's intentions and capabilities are only to be expected. It is instructive, however, to be reminded that this record has been halted during the greater part of this century due to a pragmatic and cautious policy of restraint since the 1920s when fundamental bilateral agreements were reached which have been respected.

After the first three years of the BSEC – years characterized by Russian suspicion and reluctance to cooperate – Russia changed its attitude to the forum. The temporary Russian economic recovery, coupled with chances to improve the great power's role and influence in the Black Sea area and to re-establish its leadership role, led to changes in Russia's attitude towards the forum. Participation in the Parliamentary Assembly (PA) of BSEC is no longer viewed as no more than an opportunity for Turkey to promote its political objectives in Central Asia, the littoral states and the Balkans, but is now also regarded as an open window for Russia's foreign policy. The balance of Russian and Turkish interests in and around the BSEC is fundamental in the drive towards the wider cooperation of the 11 members of the BSEC.

The biggest challenge is that of how to regulate this balance. In this respect both the USA and the EU have important roles to play. US strategic priorities have strongly shifted to the Caspian basin because so many American private investors are engaged in that region. Also the INOGATE projects of the EU have made the Union a major geostrategic and geoeconomic actor in this region. The New Silk Road or TRACECA – a major plan for infrastructure improvements of the region – is intended to promote the westward transit of goods and energy resources from

Kazakhstan and Turkmenistan, from the Caspian Sea (under and across it) to Azerbaijan, Georgia and Turkey, and to Europe and the USA.

Understanding that Russia has a critical role to play – both in the transit of oil and gas supplies and in the transport corridor construction – is vital for the success of these projects. The involvement of the USA and the EU in negotiations with both Russia and Turkey is indispensable to improving the security situation in the region. The USA and the EU are in a position to neutralize the 'fuelling-up' of Russian-Turkish competition for leadership in a situation which requires cooperation and coordination. The EU has a much better chance of implementing the TRACECA project if it succeeds in balancing its support for US economic interests in this project with other economic and financial incentives in favour of Russia. With regard to this project the Russian perception is that Russia is being cut off from transporting through routes to the north of the same energy supplies. Turkey is unable, both culturally and linguistically, to cover the countries from the Southern tier of the former Soviet Union and Russian influence remains strong. Hospitable acceptance of the European project in this area is contingent on the balancing of Russian interests.

US support for the Baku-Ceyhan oil pipe-line that is of major Turkish interest should be balanced by America's insistence on keeping the Bosphorus and the Dardanelles open for oil-tankers with Caspian oil according to the rules of the law of the seas. Generally speaking, the West's Black Sea basin strategy should give preference to the 'engagement' option in its attitude to Russia and leave aside the 'containment' and 'disengagement' ones. This option would mainly correspond to the NATO-Russia relationship – a significant instrument in influencing the global strategic balances.

EU-Turkish and EU-Russian relationships and their careful mutual balance may become the key lever for driving the zones of stability and prosperity eastwards. The job is not easy but it cannot be postponed for long.

From Security Cooperation to a Black Sea Basin Security Community of Nations

Alongside the 'trial and error' approach to shaping closer security cooperation in the Black Sea basin the broader conceptual incentive of the "security community" may accelerate this positive process.

At the beginning of the 60s Karl Deutsch defined the security community as "a group which has become integrated, where integration is defined as a sense of community, accompanied by formal or informal institutions or practices, sufficiently strong and widespread to assure peaceful change among members of a group with reasonable certainty over a long period of time."[8] There is not that much literature on this issue[9], though there is an agreement among the experts that the Atlantic Alliance, the European Union and the group of Scandinavian countries in the Nordic Council should form security communities.

Most characteristic of the approach of member countries of the security community is the belief that the use of military force is unthinkable and inapplicable in case of a dispute among them.[10] The security community is a realistic political concept, affording a brighter perspective, though requiring the realisation of many pre-conditions if it is to be successful.[11] The very process of adaptation and the realization of requirements reassures the individual actors, who have interests in the Black Sea region, that they share a common practical political programme for action. Each of the pre-conditions is necessary, but the goal of creating the security community can be achieved only if they interact with all the others. The pre-conditions seem to be as follows:

Compatibility of the values of the societies and states in the group. Compatibility of values has a special meaning when shared by the politicians, who take the most responsible political decisions. There can hardly be any doubt that the progress of democracy and freedom, including the evolution and activity of the free associations and non-governmental organizations is an important indicator of the development of the process.

Acquiring mutual predictability in the behaviour of the decision-makers of individual countries. One factor that may positively influence confidence and predictability in the political field is the promotion of the role and implementation of the principles of international negotiations. The mere fact of an approach towards hard regional issues through dialogue, negotiations, involving existing governmental and non-governmental expertise to improve stability and the security situation in general would in practice stimulate the process of building-up a Black Sea basin civil society.

The democratization of the societies of member states of the community is important. Strong civil societies are an essential pre-condition of the community's efficiency. The national criteria for attaining democracy and developing civil societies do not differ from R. Dahl's "procedural minimal conditions": inclusive citizenship; rule of law; separation of powers; elected power-holders; free and fair elections; freedom of expression and alternative sources of information; associational autonomy, and civilian control over the security forces.[12]

Good communication is essential to foster mutual understanding between the countries. The free movement of people, goods, capital and services and the limitation of illegal migration are significant requirements for countries of the community. A specific aspect of the issue is that of upgrading the degree of responsiveness among the governments, which should react to all acts of cooperation with a readiness to communicate.

Another important factor for improving communication is the development of a qualitatively different information environment, including on security issues. Good-neighbourly relations, stability, security and cooperation need to be supported by a permanently-functioning system of information exchange on defence and national security issues and the conscientious enlargement of areas of mutual transparency.

Confidence-building measures may be strengthened if new and active regional players, such as the non-governmental organzsations (NGOs) dealing with international and security studies, contribute to diminishing the level of unpredictability in the regional interrelationships through their expertise.

Then there is the issue of economic growth. Economic guarantees of security in the framework of the community are the solid foundation for all other aspects. The area, especially the Balkan countries, strongly needs the comprehensive economic support of the international community for the heavy losses suffered from the UN embargo regime during the conflict in Bosnia and Herzegovina and later during the ethnic cleansing in Kosovo and the NATO campaign against FRY.

Another factor that must be taken into account is the existence of core areas for the community. This is a matter of well-developed politico-administrative systems, consisting of a country or group of countries, playing a key role in developing integration processes. Developed civil societies in the countries of the core area of the community may give a strong impetus to the process of building-up security community.

Further there is the expectation of mutual benefits for countries in the community in the economic, military and environmental areas. This is quite a natural expectation, that can only be satisfied by proving the higher degree of cost-effectiveness within the security regime as opposed to outside it.

A higher level of political efficacy is needed: this would provide necessary public support for building up the security community. Political systems in each country and their efficiency are extremely dependent on the implementation of the Dahl's criteria for democracy.

Another pre-condition is the constructive management of ethnic and national conflicts. One can hardly underestimate the obstacles in this field, but they are not insurmountable in the context of improved social and economic conditions.

Successful arms control and disarmament is essential. The realization of this requirement is facilitated by the improved European strategic environment. The CFE Treaty, the Dayton agreements and the new round of negotiations for the conventional forces in Europe with participation of the countries on an individual basis "frame" the process in a positive way.

There needs to be a shared perception of the risks, challenges, threats and dangers of the broader international environment. A settled institutional relation of the Black Sea basin countries to NATO, EU, OSCE and the WEU and regulated details of their interlocking mechanisms for security may rationalize the threat perception system in the area.

The shaping of common regional interests and their realization by the political elites of the countries of the security community is another pre-condition. NGOs may be quite helpful in supporting and influencing governmental attitudes on these issues.

Finally there is the realization of the necessity of compatible and consistent national security strategies of member countries of the community. The military defence aspect of the issue is of a particular importance.

Despite the various problems, the time to formulate the policy of building-up a security community in the Black Sea basin is approaching. The success of this policy would depend on the effective interaction of three eventual levels of its formation, targeted at building a regional security community:

On the national level parallel to official governmental policies in the region is the growth of the role of the so called "third sector" – the non-governmental organizations. These are assuming the capability, together with leading intellectuals in the area and forward-minded representatives of the media, to shape public opinion in the direction of advising or supporting governments in building up a security community.

On the regional level the evolution of Black Sea economic cooperation may significantly improve the chances of moulding a Black Sea basin regional community. NGOs within the region may also contribute to the evolution of a positive regional social and political atmosphere, the sense of belonging to a common region and its philosophic link with the Euro-Atlantic security community.

On the international level the involvement of the EU, NATO, the UN, the OSCE, the WEU, the CE, and of the USA in a cooperative way is indispensable for the evolution of the security community in the Black Sea basin. These organizations and the only superpower – the United States – must display both example and moral leadership if they are to have a positive influence on efforts to build a security community in the Black Sea basin countries and be able to engage a power as great as Russia in the region-building activity.

Conclusion

It is our understanding that security cooperation in the Black Sea basin is not impossible. Certainly, the process has not yet evolved to the point of effectiveness and is still far from a security-community type of relationship. However, the need for a commitment to cooperate on security issues is real for all countries from the region, stemming from the various sources of conflict, from the actuality of active and post-conflict situations that require settlement and from obvious opportunities to boost the area economically.

A stable Black Sea basin becomes crucial as part of a longer chain with strategic subregions such as the Balkans, the Caucasus and the Caspian Sea basin. The benign involvement of leading powerful external and local actors in creating this stability is the major prerequisite. This call is far from founded in idealism and wishful thinking. Rather it is the only real basis for utilizing the geoeconomic potential of the region and preventing a dangerous geopolitical and geostrategic clash of interests.

Notes

1 Ronald D. Asmus, F. Stephen Larrabee, Ian O. Lesser, 'Mediterranean Security: New Challenges, New Tasks', in: NATO *review*, May 1996, p.25.

2 See Sophia Clément, 'Conflict Prevention: A Conceptual Approach', in: Conflict Prevention in the Balkans: Case Studies of Kosovo and the FYR of Macedonia, Chaillot Papers 30, December 1997, pp.7–13.

3 V. Y. Ghebali, 'Preventive Diplomacy As Visited From the OSCE', in: V. Y. Ghebali, D. Warner (eds), The OSCE and Preventive Diplomacy, GIIS, G., July 15/98, pp.55–56.

4 Ibid., p. 56.

5 Alyson JK Bailes, 'The Role of Subregional Cooperation in Post-Cold War Europe: Integration, Security, Democracy', in: Andrew Cottey (ed.), Op. cit., pp.153–183. I extend my special thanks to Alyson Bailes – a devoted student and conceptualizer of Central/Eastern European regional arrangements and their security aspects.

6 BS/INFO.98.719, 14.12.1998, Draft-Platform for Cooperation between BSEC and EU, pp. 2–3.

7 Frankfurter Allgemeine Zeitung, 21 August 1997.

8 Karl W. Deutsch, 'Security Communities', in: Rosenau (ed.), International Politics and Foreign Policy, 1961, p. 98.

9   See: Joseph S.Nye, 'Peace In Parts': Integration and Conflict in Regional Organi-
    zation, Boston, Little Brown, 1971; Luc Reychler, 'A Pan-European Security
    Community: Utopia or Realistic Perspective?', in: Armand Clesse and Lothar
    Rühl(eds.), Beyond East-West Confrontation: Searching for a New Security Struc-
    ture in Europe, Nomos Verlagsgesellschaft, Baden-Baden, 1990, p. 202–210; John
    Roper, '"Security Community" Between Concept and Reality', in: Revue
    Roumaine d'Etudes Internationales, XXV, 5–6(115–116) 1991, p. 315–316; 'The
    Vulnerable Content: Western European Security in the 21st Century', in: Eurob-
    alkans, No 22–23, Spring-Summer 1996, p. 27–28; Plamen Pantev, ' "Security
    Community" in the Balkans: Prerequisites, Factors, Contents, The Role of
    Bulgaria', IIR Research Paper, Sofia, 1993; Coping With Conflicts in the Central
    and Southern Balkans, St. Kliment Ohridsky University Press, 1995, pp.40, etc.
10 See: Karl W. Deutsch et al., Political Community and the North Atlantic
    Area, Princeton University Press, Princeton, New Jersey, 1957.
11 See: Luc Reychler, Op. cit., p. 203; Plamen Pantev, 'Bulgaria and the Euro-
    pean Union: The Security Aspect', in: The Southeast European Yearbook
    1993, ELIAMEP, Athens, 1994, pp.55–63.
12 R. Dahl, Dilemmas of Pluralist Democracy, Yale University Press, New
    Haven, 1982, p.11.

CHAPTER SEVEN

Can the Marine and Coastal Environment of the Black Sea be Protected?

Laurence David Mee[1]

One of the most difficult problems facing the countries surrounding the Black Sea, is the environmental degradation of its marine and coastal environment. How can the countries surrounding the Black Sea restore and protect this joint heritage in times of profound political and economic change? The present chapter examines the nature of the environmental crisis, the measures adopted to overcome it and the continuing obstacles to implementing them.

Examining the Symptoms of Environmental Degradation

It does not require a profound knowledge of oceanography to appreciate the unique nature of the Black Sea. Any physical map of Europe is sufficient to reveal its huge drainage basin; two million square kilometres covering over one third of Europe and including major portions of 17 countries. It will also show the basic characteristics of the sea itself, its comparable surface area to the Baltic or North Seas; its great depth, over two kilometres in places; and its isolation. The Black Sea is connected to the Mediterranean through the narrow, twisting Bosphorus, 700 metres wide and less than 60 metres deep in places, and through the Sea of Marmara and the Dardanelles. The Bosphorus annually carries 600 cubic kilometres of surface water flowing from the Black Sea and 300 cubic kilometres of deep water replacing it from the Mediterranean. In addition it carries some fifty thousand cargo ships (including 1500 tankers) annually, and flows through the middle of megalopolis Istanbul.[2]

The Black Sea is one of Europe's newest seas. It was formed a mere seven or eight thousand years ago when sea level rise caused Mediterranean water to break through the Bosphorus valley refilling a vast freshwater lake tens of metres below the prevailing sea level. The salty water sank to the bottom of the lake, filling it from below and forming a strong density gradient (known as a pycnocline) between the Mediterranean water on the bottom and the freshwater mixed with some seawater near the surface. The depth of this natural density barrier depended (and still depends) upon the supply of fresh water from rivers and rain, and the energy available from the wind and the sun for mixing it with the underlying seawater. The oxygen in the incoming water was quickly exhausted by the demands of bacteria associated with decaying biota and terrestrial organic material falling through the density gradient into the bottom water. Within a few hundred years, the Sea, below some 100 – 200 metres depth, became depleted of oxygen. The bacterial population switched to organisms capable of obtaining their oxygen by reducing dissolved sulphate to toxic hydrogen sulphide and the resulting water body became the largest volume of anoxic water on our planet.

So for several thousand years only the surface waters, down to the "liquid bottom" pycnocline, have been capable of supporting higher life forms. Though not very biologically diverse compared with open seas at similar latitudes, the Black Sea developed remarkable and unique ecosystems, particularly in its expansive North-Western shelf where the sea is relatively shallow. The seabed in this part of the Black Sea was well oxygenated since it is well above the pycnocline. This area, and the adjacent shallow Sea of Azov, also receives the inflow of Europe's second, third and fourth rivers, the Danube, Dnieper and Don. A particularly unique ecosystem developed based on the 'keystone' benthic (bottom living) red algae, Phyllophora sp., which formed a vast bed with a total area equivalent to that of Belgium and The Netherlands. The term 'keystone' is not used lightly: like the keystone in the middle of a stone bridge, its removal causes the entire structure to collapse in a precipitous manner. This particular keystone was a place of great beauty, vast underwater fields of red algae, home to a myriad of dependent animals, linked together in a complex web of life.

Despite its uniquely fragile natural physical and chemical characteristics, the Black Sea ecosystem appears to have been relatively stable. During the first half of the twentieth century, perhaps until three decades ago, there was little evidence of human impact on the Sea or on its flora and fauna. Some changes had occurred however, and these were precursors of much worse events to come. Sensitive monk seal populations, for example, began to decline from the late nineteenth century, driven from their breeding grounds by human activities. Nowadays the rarely-sighted miniscule population of these seals seems likely to be doomed. Indeed, there is no certainty that any of these animals remain in the Black Sea. Another early change came about through the introduction of a number of exotic animal species, introduced by accident from the hulls, bilges or ballast tanks of ships, and which flourished to the detriment of the Black Sea's characteristic fauna. The predatory sea snail Rapana thomasiana, for example, arrived from waters around Japan in the mid-1940s and devastated beds of the Black Sea genotype of the common oyster, Ostrea edulis. It is one of a list of some twenty-six species introduced through human activity (accidentally or intentionally) since the beginning of the century and which have profoundly altered the Black Sea ecosystem.[3]

Another gradual change was taking place on the coastlands of the Black Sea. Urban construction occurred in an unplanned and haphazard manner. The Black Sea was an increasingly popular tourist venue, particularly for the peoples of the former Soviet Union and the other Eastern and Central European COMECON countries. This, together with competing demands for space from shipping, industry and coastal settlements (mostly with inadequate waste disposal), placed increasing demands on coastal landscapes. The damming of many rivers brought hydrological changes, particularly through the decrease in sediment flux to the coast, a phenomenon that led to major problems of erosion.[4] This, in turn, was often ineffectively combated by the construction of a very large number of structures to protect beaches (groynes). These further degraded the landscape and exacerbated pollution problems. In the competition for coastal space, the natural environment was the, seemingly, inevitable loser. This is not only a problem of former communist countries but also in Turkey, where high levels of economic growth have sometimes been at the expense of environmental protection. Throughout the entire coastal area of the Black Sea, the human population has continuously encroached on the ecosystem that it is part of and upon which it depends.

From the late 1960s to the early 1990s, events occurred in the Black Sea that can objectively be considered as an environmental catastrophe.[5] The strongest single symptom of the catastrophe was the virtual elimination of the Phyllophora ecosystem of the Black Sea's north-western shelf in a matter of some ten years. The chain of events leading to the decline of this ecosystem started with an increase in nutrient flux down the major rivers, particularly in the late 1960s when fertilizer use increased markedly as a result of the 'green revolution'. This brought about a decrease in light penetration in the sea due to the increased intensity of phytoplankton blooms (eutrophication). Deprived of light, the red algae and other photosynthetic bottom dwelling (benthic) species quickly died. Their function was lost as a source of oxygen to the bottom waters of the shelf seas and as a habitat for a wide variety of organisms. The bottom waters of the northwestern shelf became seasonally hypoxic (very low oxygen) and even anoxic (no measurable oxygen). Thousands of tons of benthic plants and animals were washed up on the shores of Romania and Ukraine and the seabed became a barren area with a very low biological diversity.

The loss of the northwestern shelf ecosystem had an impact on the entire Black Sea. It coincided with a period of expansion in the fisheries industry and the application of high technology fish-finding hydroacoustics and more efficient, though unregulated and destructive, purse seining and bottom trawling gear. The consequence was a decrease in the diversity of commercially exploitable fish species from some 26 to six, in less than two decades. As eutrophication advanced in the Black Sea, the smaller fish species such as anchovies and sprat were favoured since they depend upon the phytoplankton-driven pelagic ecosystem, rather than the benthic one. Furthermore, their predators had often been removed by overfishing or habitat loss. As a consequence, fishing effort switched to these lower value species. Annual catches of anchovy for example, rose from 225,000 tons in 1975 to some 450,000 tons a decade later.[6]

In the mid-1980s, another exotic species arrived in ships' ballast waters, the ctenophore Mnemiopsis leidyi, sometimes known as the comb jelly.[7] This species was brought from the eastern seaboard of America and, without predators, flourished in the eutrophic Black Sea environment where it consumes zooplankton including fish larvae. Perhaps the word "flourished" is an understatement. At its peak in 1989-90, it is claimed to have reached a total biomass of about one billion tons (1,000,000,000 tons wet weight) in the Black Sea, more than the world annual fish harvest! This massive population explosion had an enormous impact on the Black Sea's ecosystems and commercial fish stocks. The loss of zooplankton allowed huge populations of phytoplankton to develop in a series of blooms that reduced the mean Secchi depth (the maximum depth to which a white disk lowered into the sea from a ship remains visible) from the normal average of twenty metres, to only five metres. Anchovy catches plummeted in 1990 to only 60,000 tons.

The situation in the Black Sea was mirrored by another environmental stress on its coasts. The economic decline of the Black Sea coastal countries and the political upheaval of transition to a market economy led to a lack of maintenance of waste treatment facilities for domestic sewage and industrial waste. Of course, many cities had never had effective sewage treatment but the general decline was evidenced by an increased frequency of outbreaks of waterborne diseases such as cholera and frequent beach closures due to unsanitary conditions. In Ukraine, for example, 44 per cent of bathing water samples taken in 1995 did not meet the national microbiological standards.[8] This environmental problem, coupled with the decline in standards of tourism infrastructure and limited spending power of people in the region, also led to a sharp decline in tourist numbers and in the local economies.[9]

The state of the environment in the Black Sea in the early 1990s gave little reason for optimism. However the economic crisis did give some respite for pollution. Farmers were often unable to apply the quantity of fertilizers used in the former centrally-planned economies. Many large energy-inefficient and polluting industries were forced to close. By 1996 there was already some evidence of recovery of the benthic ecosystem on the northwestern shelf of the Black Sea, albeit small. Furthermore, Mnemiopsis populations started to decline and the anchovy fisheries recovered, almost to their mid-1980s level. Most local economists and ecologists agree, however, the pressure on the environment will return as the economies recover, unless urgent measures are taken to limit the environmental impact of renewed growth.

As the new century dawns, additional environmental pressures are emerging as a result of the rapid increase in the use of the Black Sea as a maritime transport route, particularly for the shipment of oil en-route from the newly-opened Caspian oil fields. This issue has given rise to major political differences between the coastal countries of the Black Sea as the countries compete for revenue-generating pipeline routes across their territories or defend their rights to use the Black Sea as an international shipping route. Unfortunately, the eagerness to join this perceived bonanza is often leading to the failure to follow proper environmental impact assessment procedures or to invest in measures to protect the natural environment and assure sustainable development.

International Action for Protecting the Black Sea

Protection of the Black Sea environment requires a concerted approach between the six coastal countries. This must be accompanied with measures implemented at the national level. The present section examines the international dimension: how the countries around the Black Sea are responding to the deterioration in its ecosystem and to the environmental crisis around its shores.

The Varna Fisheries Agreement and the MARPOL Convention – early attempts to take international action.

A fisheries convention (the Varna Convention) was signed by the Black Sea members of ComEcon: Bulgaria, Romania and the USSR in 1960. This convention did not contemplate regulation of fisheries but focused on data gathering and exchange. Turkey remained outside this agreement. It thus had no significant impact on restraining the fisheries effort or managing stocks.[10] Bulgaria, Romania and Turkey cooperated within the framework of the General Fisheries Council for the Mediterranean, but the USSR was not a member and the Council had little or no impact on management of fishing in the Black Sea.

Black Sea Fisheries remain internationally unregulated to this day. There are frequent accounts of conflicts and at least one death due to the violation of territorial waters, particularly but not exclusively by Turkish fishermen. With the collapse of centrally planned economies in the North (and of their fishing industries in the Black Sea), Turkish fishing now accounts for some 90 per cent of the economic value of all landings in the Black Sea.[11] The stakes are high for an international management policy (including quotas) to be completed but the individual country perspectives on an equitable division of resources may be divergent. Serious negotiations for a new Black Sea Fisheries Convention have been underway since the early 1990s; 'final' draft conventions are circulated from time to time but progress is painfully slow.

Another early international convention is MARPOL 73/78, a global convention that was signed in its original version in 1973 and is designed to protect the sea from ship-based pollution. Though ratified by all Black Sea countries (and legally fully in force in the region), its provisions have not been fully nor consistently applied. MARPOL 73/78 offers a possi- bility of extra protection for the Black Sea region, having designated the Black Sea as a 'especially protected area' within several of its Annexes.[12] Under this regime, if in force, discharge of oil or garbage within the region would be prohibited. In order to enforce this regime, however, Black Sea countries will need to provide for sufficient reception facilities in their Black Sea ports. Effective enforcement, however, will also require clarity concerning the delimitation of exclusive economic zones, a process likely to be rather lengthy. It will be in the economic interest of the coastal countries to implement the special area provisions, as they will be able to increase tariffs for ships entering Black Sea ports. The use of the Black Sea as an oil tanker super-highway makes the implementation of this legisla- tion an urgent priority for environmental protection.

With respect to MARPOL, there is an interesting recent development in the region. Three of the Black Sea countries are now in pre-accession to the European Community. The new EC port waste Directive will impose even stricter controls than MARPOL. Harbour masters are concerned that the new provisions will increase some port charges and influence the trade to their ports. They have recently formed a Black Sea Ports Association, involving all six countries, and are calling for the new regulations to be applied in a uniform manner and for grants and credits to be given in order to equip their ports to appropriate standards.

The Bucharest Convention

Development

In late summer 1986, at the initiative of the then USSR, representatives of the then four countries of the Black Sea (Bulgaria, Romania, Turkey and the USSR) met to discuss the possibility of drafting a Convention for the Protection of the Black Sea Against Pollution. This was to be largely modelled on the Regional Seas Conventions of UNEP, notably the Barcelona Convention, though the negotiating process was conducted between the four countries with no external participation. The opening of this chapter in co-operation was a direct consequence of 'Perestroika' in the Soviet Union and marked a new era in relations with its neighbours which was to see dramatic developments in a short space of time. The negotiating process continued for a period of six years during which time the Soviet Union itself was to break up. The four countries became six – Bulgaria, Georgia, Romania, Russian Federation, Turkey and Ukraine but all parties demonstrated their commitment to complete the process.

The Convention and its three Protocols[13] were adopted by the Diplomatic Conference on the Protection of the Black Sea against Pollution held in Bucharest on 21 April 1992, and deposited with the Government of Romania. The Convention, as well as the Land-Based Sources Protocol and the Emergency Response Protocol, entered into force on 15 January 1994, in accordance with Art. XXVIII of the Convention, i.e. sixty days after their fourth ratification.

Structure and Contents

The name "Bucharest Convention" actually refers not only to the framework convention itself, the Convention for the Protection of the Black Sea, but also to its five Resolutions, and three Protocols: the Land-Based Sources Protocol, the Emergency Response Protocol, and the Dumping Protocol. The Land-Based Source Protocol and Dumping Protocol are accompanied by annexes containing so-called black and grey lists. In accordance with general practice, pollution by the substances and matter on the black lists (Annexes I), categorized as hazardous, needs to be prevented and eliminated by the Contracting Parties. Pollution by substances on the grey lists (Annexes II), categorized as noxious, need to be reduced and where possible eliminated. In the case of land-based sources, there is an additional Annex III, which prescribes restrictions to which discharges of substances and matters listed in Annex II should be subject. Furthermore, dumping of wastes and materials containing the noxious substances contained in Annex II requires a prior special permit from 'the competent national authorities', while, according to Annex III, dumping of all other wastes and materials requires a prior general permit.

The Convention addresses five of the six generally recognized sources of marine pollution[14]: land-based (in Art. VII and Protocol), vessel-source (Art. VIII), ocean dumping (Art. X and Protocol), exploitation of the seabed of the continental shelf or margin (Art. XI), from or through the atmosphere (Art. XII). The only source not covered is exploitation of the seabed of the international Area, simply because the Black Sea does not contain territory which falls under this definition. It also deals extensively with emergency response (Art. IX and Protocol), a term which refers to the use of techniques to prevent pollution arising from accidents, since the Black Sea, but especially its entrance, the Bosphorus Straits, has been confronted with a considerable number of accidents.

Implementation

The provisions of the Bucharest Convention require implementation by the six Contracting Parties: the Black Sea coastal states. They are bound to implement the provisions since the Convention is part of the legislation of all six countries. In practice however, some countries were not immediately capable of implementing it, mostly because of economical constraints, and in some cases they may be unwilling to take action to implement all of its provisions. The Convention does not provide for special enforcement techniques, such as a dispute settlement mechanism (the traditional enforcement technique, which is however not necessarily useful in case of environmental matters, where prevention rather than resolving or restoration is required) or a compliance reporting procedure, but, "in order to achieve the purposes of the Convention", it does provide for the establishment of a Commission for the Protection of the Black Sea, which shall consist of at least one representative of each Contracting Party (Art. XVII). The Commission shall, i.e., "promote the implementation of the Convention, inform the Contracting

Parties of its work, and assist them by making recommendations on measures necessary for achieving the aims of the convention, and on recommendations of possible amendments to the convention and protocols" (Art. XVIII). The Convention further determines that the "Commission shall be assisted in its activities by a permanent Secretariat" (Art. XVII).

Unfortunately, despite the determination of the Parties to complete the ratification process, the full implementation of the Convention has not followed suit. The Commission has been established, and had its first meeting in May 1995. The Commission decided to adopt the name of 'The Istanbul Commission' as its Secretariat, still to be established, will have its premises in Istanbul, Turkey. The Commission however, has not yet proven to be the active, supervisory body as intended by the Convention. Full and active functioning of both bodies is essential if the Convention is to succeed. It will also be necessary for the process of further elaborating a 'Protocol Concerning Cooperation in Controlling Transboundary Movement of Hazardous Wastes and Combating Illegal Traffic Thereof', and possibly in elaborating a Biodiversity Protocol.[15] Experience in earlier Regional Seas programmes has shown that the existence of an organizational structure, providing for a coordinating body, increases chances of success of a convention. The delay in integration of the coordinating body has been mostly due to the failure of the Parties to secure the necessary funds for its integration. The economic circumstances of many of the Parties have led to severe restrictions on overseas spending. This is coupled with a series of diplomatic problems regarding the agreement for establishing the Secretariat. The current log-jam for example, appears to be a conflict between Russia and Turkey regarding the provision of immunities and privileges for the staff of the Secretariat. Sadly, a very low priority has been afforded to the implementation of the Convention by the Parties (perhaps with the exception of Turkey). It is currently hoped that the Secretariat will be in place in 2001, seven years after ratification of the Convention.

As mentioned earlier, the Bucharest Convention is closely modelled on the format and substance of the UNEP Regional Seas Conventions[16], most notably the Barcelona Convention for the Protection of the Mediterranean. However, in the 20-year lag time between the approval of these earlier Conventions and the Bucharest Convention, there have been many improvements in the available legal tools. The Barcelona Convention in particular has been completely revised, together with its respective Protocols.[17] One of the earliest tasks of the Istanbul Commission will be to re-examine the provisions of the Protocols and whether or not these need to be readjusted to current international circumstances.

The Odessa Ministerial Declaration: A Statement of Common Policy

Development

The Bucharest Convention itself is a legal and diplomatic tool for joint action and does not set out to establish environmental policy goals (e.g. targets for reducing the loads of specific pollutants etc.). It also does not establish any regulatory mechanism for exploitation or development of the natural environment (e.g. straddled marine resources or specially protected areas). In order to develop a common policy framework, a clear "Declaration of Environmental Quality Objectives" was considered necessary. Following the initiative of the Government of Ukraine and employing the stewardship of UNEP, a Ministerial Declaration was formulated during nine months of negotiations and signed by all six countries in Odessa in April 1993 (the "Odessa Declaration"[18]). This Declaration is a pragmatic and innovative policy statement that sets environmental goals and a time frame to guide management regimes and associated investments. It was the first policy agreement on regional seas to reflect the philosophy of UNCED, Agenda 21, and features a heavy emphasis on accountability, periodic review and public awareness. These features represented a major conceptual shift in a public statement from countries of the region, particularly those emerging from totalitarianism.

The "Odessa Declaration" is remarkable in two ways. The first is the spirit of consensus. While negotiations were going on, Ukraine and Russia were engaged in a dangerous conflict about ownership of the Black Sea naval fleet and Georgia was suffering civil war. "The environment has no political boundaries," explained Professor Sherbak, the then Minister for the Environment of Ukraine. The second remarkable feature was the commitment to a new approach to environmental policy making in the region, including much greater public participation and accountability. The Declaration also represented the first public policy statement in the region to endorse the Precautionary Principle[19], an important departure from the earlier *de-facto* acceptance of rivers and seas as waste receptacles.

Structure and Contents

The "Odessa Declaration" consists of a preamble, a general policy statement and nineteen specific actions. These actions were designed to facilitate the rapid development of practical measures for controlling pollution from land-based and marine sources (including the harmonization of environmental standards); to restore, conserve and manage natural resources; to respond to environmental emergencies; to improve the assessment of contaminants and their sources; to introduce integrated coastal zone management policies and compulsory environmental impact assessments; and to create a transparent and balanced mechanism for reviewing and updating the Declaration on a triennial basis. The Declaration was designed to provide a basis for a flexible but continuous process for taking decisions on coordinated national action towards common goals at present and in the future. Its clear objectives and specific time-frames were to guide and stimulate implementation of the Bucharest Convention.

Implementation

On the 7 April 1996 the first triennium came to its end. A report commissioned by UNEP[20] evaluated to what extent the "Odessa Declaration" has succeeded to serve as 'agenda' for implementation of regional measures, in accordance with the Bucharest Convention. The results of this analysis were encouraging even despite the lack of formal implementation of the Bucharest Convention. The "Odessa Declaration" had given a strong signal to donors, particularly the newly-created Global Environment Facility, that the Black Sea countries were willing and able to cooperate on restoring and protecting this severely damaged and unique shared environment. This paved the way for financial assistance to be granted for implementation of the "Odessa Declaration".

In June 1993, as a result of the Declaration, a three-year Black Sea Environmental Programme[21] (BSEP) was established with US$9.3 million funding from the Global Environment Facility (GEF) and over US$5 million collateral funding from the EU, Austria, Canada, Japan, the Netherlands and Norway. The BSEP was designed to improve the capacity of the Black Sea countries to assess and manage the environment, to support the development and implementation of new environmental policy and laws for protecting the Black Sea, and to facilitate the preparation of sound environmental investments. A Programme Coordinating Unit (PCU) was established to coordinate the activities of BSEP. In order to share the task of programme implementation between countries, each Black Sea country agreed to host a BSEP "Activity Centre", a specialist institution which addresses one aspect of the Black Sea environment, such as: Emergency Response to oil spills (Varna, Bulgaria); Fisheries (Constanta, Romania); Pollution Assessment (Odessa, Ukraine); Coastal Zone Management (Krasnodar, Russia); Biodiversity (Batumi, Georgia); and Pollution Control (Istanbul, Turkey). The BSEP also created a Black Sea Data System and a Black Sea Geographic Information System. The networks of institutions enabled specialists to "reconnect" with one another and external funding provided additional training and modern equipment. Non-governmental organizations began to play a key role in the BSEP, holding national and regional fora. The programme also included organizations such as the Black Sea Economic Cooperation, specialized UN agencies and international NGOs. Amongst many other things it generated an urgent investment portfolio, implemented by the World Bank and instrumental in levering almost $100 millions of new investments with environmental benefits.

The "Odessa Declaration" was seen from the outset as an interim policy arrangement. Its signatories called upon the GEF partners to assist them with the development of a medium/long-term action plan for the protection of the Black Sea. It thus set the wheels in motion for a much more comprehensive strategy of which the Declaration itself was to be one of the building blocks.

The Black Sea Strategic Action Plan

Foundations – the Transboundary Diagnostic Analysis

The Development of the Black Sea Action Plan followed a carefully implemented technical process spanning over two years. The first step was the integration of an effective institutional network, a matter described in the previous section. The network was then asked to conduct an analysis of Black Sea problems within the field of specialization of each "Working Party" (Biodiversity, Emergency Response, Fisheries, Pollution Levels and Effects, Pollution Sources, Legislation, Integrated Coastal Zone Management, etc.) The thematic analyses were conducted at a national level and then integrated regionally. In the case of sources and levels of pollution, new reliable information had to be gathered and much of the data used in the present book was obtained during this preparatory period, a remarkable accomplishment in such a short time and one which required the cooperation of many national and international actors. A similar situation occurred in the case of fisheries. The thematic analyses were then gathered together and studied intensively by a group of regional and international specialists in order to construct a "Transboundary Diagnostic Analysis"(TDA) of the Black Sea.

The Black Sea TDA is a technical document[22] which, in a highly analytical manner, examines the root causes of Black Sea degradation and options for actions which may be taken to address them. It examines each major environmental problem, the "stakeholders" involved in the problem (who is responsible? who has to act?) and the uncertainties in the information describing the problem (do we need more information and if so what kind?) It then proposes solutions, often giving various options and attempts to set a time frame and cost for the solutions. Some of the solutions require policy changes, some require capital investments. They are all part of a holistic management approach that does not limit itself to end-of-pipe solutions but encourages the development of more environmentally-sustainable economic activities.

The relationship between perceived problems and their social and economic underlying causes is the starting point for the TDA. Many of the environmental problems share common root causes and these cannot be addressed by a single sector which constitutes a conundrum facing environmental agencies. "Environment" has been defined as a sector of government rather than an issue that permeates all sectors. Environmental ministries are often too weak to resolve problems at the level of their underlying causes because the causes are within the authority of other, more powerful sectors. Environmental agencies in the Black Sea region are often blamed for inaction but are rarely empowered to intercede in the work of other ministries. Environment sector budgets are generally minuscule in comparison with those of other ministries and this has a cascade effect on the entire regulatory framework. The institutions which depend upon the Ministry of Environment for support often get too little too late and cannot fulfil their functions. Staff are paid salaries well below the cost of living and have to seek employment somewhere else in order to feed their families. Usually, the State Institution itself becomes the part-time job. This situation often applies to those professionals who are supposed to be providing essential data for environmental protection or the inspectors who are supposed to implement state and local legislation.

The Action Plan – Development, Structure and Contents

The BS-SAP[23] was developed from June to October 1996 as a direct consequence of the TDA. It is a negotiated document, prepared during a series of meetings between senior environmental officials of all six Black Sea coastal countries and adopted (following in-country cabinet consultations) at a Ministerial Conference, celebrated in Istanbul on 31 October 1996. The Plan, only 29 pages in length, contains 59 specific commitments on policy regarding measures to reduce pollution, improve living resources management, encourage human development in a manner which does not prejudice the environment, and to take steps towards improving financing for environmental projects. In adopting this plan, the Black Sea governments have committed themselves to a process of profound reform in the manner in which environmental issues are addressed in the Black Sea and its basin.

The structure of the Plan itself is simple. It starts with a set of "opening statements" which link the BS-SAP to the on-going process in the region, the Bucharest Convention and the Odessa Declaration. It recognizes that a considerable number of efforts have already been made to save and protect the Black Sea but that there is a "pressing need to take further actions both locally and regionally".

The first formal chapter of the BS-SAP is entitled "The challenge: the state of the Black Sea environment". It describes the priority issues facing the Black Sea countries and identified in the Transboundary Diagnostic Analysis (TDA): eutrophication; insufficiently treated sewage; harmful substances, especially oil; the introduction of exotic species; poor resources management and the loss of habitat and landscape. The challenge is summarized by a single statement: *The challenge which the region now faces is to secure a healthy Black Sea environment at a time when economic recovery and further development are also being pursued.*

The overall aim of the Plan is presented in a rather evocative manner: It is to *enable the population of the Black Sea region to enjoy a healthy living environment in both urban and rural areas, and to attain a biologically diverse Black Sea ecosystem with viable natural populations of higher organisms, including marine mammals and sturgeons, and which will support livelihoods based on sustainable activities such as fishing, aquaculture and tourism in all Black Sea countries.* Why marine mammals and sturgeons? Apart from humans, marine mammals and sturgeons are the largest life form sustained by the Black Sea. Their presence is more than symbolic. Both depend upon a healthy unpolluted and diverse Black Sea ecosystem. Dolphins depend on the healthy connection of the Black Sea with the world's oceans and sturgeon depend upon clean rivers for breeding as well as a clean Black Sea. The message is a clear one: the Black Sea offers opportunities for human development in co-existence with the most sensitive ecosystems.

The second chapter of the BS-SAP sets down policies that form the basis for international cooperation. These consist of a set of principles regarding *the concept of sustainable development, the precautionary principle, anticipatory actions, the use of clean technologies, the use of economic instruments, considerations on environment and health, close cooperation among Black Sea coastal states, cooperation among all 17 Black Sea basin states, better recognition of stakeholders, and last, but certainly not least, transparency and public participation.* The chapter continues with a detailed analysis of the institutional arrangements for implementing the Bucharest Convention and the BS-SAP. Here, the BSEP Working Parties were transformed into *Advisory Groups* to the Commission, many with new mandates. The concept of Activity Centres is retained and further strengthened. Finally measures are proposed to promote *wider cooperation* throughout the Black Sea basin and beyond.

The third, and longest, chapter of the BS-SAP looks at specific policy actions. These Actions are bold and innovative but were carefully tempered by the political realities perceived by each of the parties at the time of adoption. The agreed actions are summarized in below but the text of the Plan is well worth studying in detail.[24] Each action is accompanied by a timeframe for implementation.

Below is a summary of the twenty major points of the Black Sea Strategic Action Plan:

adoption of a new institutional framework for the Black Sea, building on the achievements of BSEP and including the creation of a project implementation unit within the Secretariat of the Istanbul Commission;

encouragement of a basin-wide approach to certain policy areas;

implementation of profound fiscal reform – the implementation of the polluter pays principle for pollution source control by 1999 – through the adoption of permitting and licensing procedures addressing common Water Quality Criteria for specific types of water use;

abatement of priority hot spots by the year 2006 – public progress reports in 2000 and 2005;

development of specific plans for waste water treatment plants for sewage in all coastal cities by 2000;

adoption of measures to control pollution from vessels using the 'port State Control' approach with meaningful incentives and penalties;

implementation of packages of measures for dumping, transboundary movement of hazardous waste, emergency response, etc.;

publication of five-yearly 'state of the Black Sea' reports based upon a joint monitoring system and regular surveys of land-based sources of pollution;

introduction of a regime for the joint control of fisheries based upon a quota system for capture and the rehabilitation of key ecosystems which act as nursery grounds;

development of a new Protocol on Black Sea Biological and Landscape Diversity;

the design of a comprehensive package of investments in conservation areas (wetlands and marine ecosystems);

the introduction of compulsory Environmental Impact Assessments, Environmental Audits and Strategic Environmental Impact Assessments with harmonized criteria;

development of a regional strategy for Integrated Coastal Zone Management with associated legal instruments by 1999;

economic development in the areas of sustainable aquaculture and environmentally-friendly tourism;

increased attention to public participation, based upon a comprehensive package including local authorities, NGOs, private sector, Regional Environmental Centres, schools, etc.;

enhanced transparency through rights of access to information and improved public awareness;

continuation of the BS-SAP process at the national level through the development of National Black Sea Strategic Action Plans;

organization of five-yearly donor meetings including the development of blended packages of investment based upon revisions of the NBS-SAPs;

completion of a feasibility study of the Black Sea Environmental Fund which could be supported by regionally-applied economic instruments and would address incremental costs;

regular and transparent revision of progress on implementation and the updating of the SAP objectives.

Notable features of the BS-SAP include its emphasis on integration of pollution control efforts with those of the Danube River, the adoption of a system of economic instruments to regulate existing sources of pollution (and to avoid new ones), enhanced protection status for sensitive coastal and marine habitats, intersectoral planning and management of coastal regions and greatly improved transparency and public participation.

The actions agreed to control pollution are a good example of the Plan's pragmatism: In adopting the BS-SAP, countries agreed to a system of harmonized water quality objectives which are reviewed every five years. Simply expressed, these objectives describe the desired quality of water for each use of the sea and rivers, including the use as a natural system. Each country, on the basis of its own legislation then introduces a discharge permitting system (and associated economic instruments) for polluters which enables it to meet the objectives and to obtain necessary revenues from permits, fees and penalties, levied on the polluters. Permit holders are clearly informed that the terms of the permits will be reviewed, and probably tightened, after five years. This provides the double benefit of achieving successive improvements in environmental health and in providing an incentive to install improved pollution control technology. The water quality objectives themselves will be set on the basis of common research and monitoring programmes coordinated through the institutional network of the Istanbul Commission.

The BS-SAP is completed by three small chapters entitled: *IV. National Black Sea Strategic Action Plans; V. Financing the Strategic Action Plan and, VI. Arrangements for Future Cooperation.* These demonstrate the point that the BS-SAP is a dynamic and flexible document which is process-oriented. The National Black Sea Strategic Action Plans, in particular, will provide a nationally-driven mechanism for ensuring that the BS-SAP is properly implemented at a local level. This is further supported through the Plan's strong commitment to public participation, including greater public awareness and transparency.

Implementation

Implementation of the BS-SAP is currently well behind schedule. This does not imply that there is no implementation at all but recent reports[25] clearly indicate that the governments are not meeting the deadlines they set for themselves. There are many reasons for this, including the delays in completing the institutional arrangements described earlier and the continuing economic difficulties confronted by many of the countries. The fact remains however that even basic requirements for pollution management, such as a reliable monitoring system, are not being implemented, despite continued support from the international community. This is reason for considerable concern.

Activities which are moving ahead are those related to the development of National Black Sea Strategic Action Plans and some programmes for public participation and public awareness. The National BS-SAPs are another important feature of the overall process. It is relatively easy for governments to agree on regional plans because they include many generalities that define principles rather than detailed implementation plans. The political reality however is that actions are taken on a country or even municipal level. All Black Sea countries therefore committed themselves to defining and implementing National Plans that include details of how and when the regional plan is to be implemented at a domestic level and, most importantly, announce the implementation of new measures including legal and economic instruments. At the time of preparing this report, all six National Action Plans are nearing completion.

The Next Step: Investing in the Black Sea

Many of the problems of the Black Sea can be ascribed by economists to a lack of "internalization" of environmental externalities.[26] The most significant "free" use of the Black Sea and its tributaries is for the disposal of waste from human activities. Some of the pollution problems of the Black Sea result from a lack of investment in adequate treatment of effluents, others such as the diffuse discharge of nitrogen and phosphorus compounds, are the result of more complex issues related to agricultural practices and poor pricing of fertilizers in a heavily subsidized and distorted national and international market.

The Black Sea Environmental Programme placed an initial emphasis on tackling point sources of pollution by trying to stimulate the necessary investments. At the early stages of the programme, shortly after approval of GEF funding in 1993, the World Bank took charge of developing a Priority Investment Portfolio which consisted of one project of undisputed urgency from an environmental perspective per country. Of these projects, only those in Georgia, Romania and Bulgaria were fully implemented and the remaining projects are still at various stages of approval, though pre-investment studies have been finalized. The reasons are many as will be discussed further, but one of the main lessons learned is that investments with an environmental benefit take a very long time to negotiate and the acceptance by governments of a portfolio is only one of the earliest steps.

Practical Problems with the Development of an Investment Portfolio

Several specific investment projects have been identified in the Black Sea region (many more than those featured in the Urgent Investment Portfolio), expensive feasibility studies made and hopes raised. But some of the studies remain on shelves, gathering dust. There is insufficient space in this article for analysing the reason for this in depth but a few common causes are worth reviewing.

The first is inadequate prioritization. Projects need to be prioritized initially according to whether or not they address real environmental concerns. Then, two other issues need to be settled, whether countries are willing to borrow money for the projects and whether they are able to pay back the loans, since a loan is not a free gift and must be returned with interest. The project itself must also be evaluated in terms of the suitability of the technology applied and whether indeed a technological solution is appropriate in the first place.

The practical reality is more complex. To begin with, the "shopping list" of proposed investments usually contains a range of projects from large and expensive industrial waste-water treatment plants costing tens of millions of dollars to very small loans for upgrading existing municipal utilities. International financial institutions (IFIs) are often shy of the mega industrial projects because of uncertainties in the viability of industries that may still be state owned. The industries themselves are sometimes unwilling to take loans, fearing that the cost of waste treatment may make them unprofitable, if indeed they are in the first place. The author has heard of teams of IFI experts that have been shut out of an industrial plant by an aggressive director, fearful of closure. The directors have little fear of existing state environmental legislation, it is usually cheaper to pay or ignore fines than invest in new treatment technology. Public pressure to change this situation in centrally planned economies is usually minimal, the apathy being driven by the feeling of powerlessness of the individual in the system, lack or knowledge of real alternatives or from fear that actions may result in job losses.

At the other end of the spectrum, the author recalls many wastewater treatment plants that have not functioned for some years owing to the need for a major overhaul or missing pumps. The IFIs are often uninter- ested in making US$0.5-1 million loans needed to restore and upgrade them and the countries in the region have no experience in dealing with "green" banks or small-scale donors. As a result, nothing gets done unless a costlier replacement plant is proposed.

Loan portfolios therefore, usually start at the middle of the spectrum, often with municipal utilities but sometimes with industrial plants. They still have to cross the barriers of "willingness to borrow" and "ability to pay". Again, inspectorates of pollution may not be adequately empowered to enforce revenue-gathering charges and fines from industry despite the importance given to the "Polluter Pays Principle" in the Black Sea Stra- tegic Action Plan. Economic instruments for paying for municipal serv- ices, drinking water and waste disposal, are often ineffective. In some cases, local economies are so depressed that the users cannot afford to pay the full costs of utilities. It is necessary to reform all parts of the economy together in order to distribute the benefits as well as the costs. Social interests cannot be ignored. In BSEP, collaborating with the IFIs, the development of investment packages has been encouraged where, together with a loan, grants are included for strengthening economic instruments, monitoring and enforcement and public awareness of the benefits of paying for services. The economic instruments are also needed to pay for maintenance, which is often ignored but is often equal to the capital cost of a plant over its operational lifetime.

The final barrier however, is often the selection of the technology itself. The case comes to mind of a municipal garbage incinerator in a Black Sea coastal resort built by a foreign company using "best available technology from Western Europe". It stands idle, two years after completion. Prior to construction, the manufacturers failed to study the different composition of local garbage from that of their own country. The incinerator was unable to reach the high temperatures needed to operate safely in an environmentally acceptable manner. Garbage with such a high organic content could have been separated and partly composted, but such techniques require new consumer practices, new attitudes by the authorities and do not result in such lucrative deals with foreign companies.

Developing a New Investment Portfolio and New Financing Mechanisms

The initial experiences with the development of an urgent investment portfolio taught some important lessons. The GEF Black Sea Project was extended in 1996 for a second "bridging" phase in which National Action Plans, a Priority Investment Programme and a Black Sea Environmental Fund were to be developed.

The current development of a portfolio is a complex process that balances a series of interests of the banks and their potential clients. The GEF, for its part, is only able to finance the "incremental costs" of a project.[27] The incremental costs are the difference between the investment a government or organization would make to satisfy its domestic interests and those that would address transboundary problems of global concern. GEF finance could potentially soften the overall conditions of a loan but cannot cover the entire cost of a project unless this is entirely transboundary in nature (very unlikely). Negotiations are therefore presently focused on 'packages' which include loans by banks or private investors for domestic pollution control projects, supplemented by grants from the GEF and bilateral grant agencies to cover incremental costs of upgrading technology or policies to tackle transboundary issues.

Money for "end of pipe technology" is only a small part of the problem of putting together an effective programme for environmental protection. The Black Sea Transboundary Diagnostic Analysis clearly shows the need for three other fields of action requiring initial investment and policy actions: investment in protected areas; new environmentally-friendly business ventures; and, basin wide initiatives for controlling trans-boundary contamination from non-coastal countries.

If the actions to protect the Black Sea indicated in the BS-SAP are to be sustainable, a reliable source of funding must be found for its management. The funding for management regimes for most of the Regional Seas is based upon voluntary contributions of the countries involved, based on a scale of assessment, originally developed by the United Nations. In practice, this approach leads to large funding uncertainties as experience has taught that funds flow on a very irregular basis and full quotas are rarely met. In the case of the Black Sea, the countries have recently investigated the possibility of establishing a Black Sea Environmental Fund, based upon contributions raised through the region-wide application of certain economic instruments.[28] As an example, the countries may wish to charge a small additional levy to ships using Black Sea ports as a used fee for the Black Sea. There are very large institutional barriers to be overcome if such a fund is to be created. It seems likely that difficulties in funding the Istanbul Commission, and the actions described in the BSEP, may be a major constraint to their success.

Towards a More Holistic Approach to Management

The policies and measures described in the previous sections of this article are all part of a more holistic approach to pollution control and prevention. There are still some missing ingredients however and these will be summarized in the present section.

A Basin-wide Approach

The key problem of eutrophication cannot be resolved without integrating the nutrient reduction strategies of all seventeen Black Sea basin countries, even though some of them are landlocked and may feel no responsibility towards the Black Sea nor enjoy the benefits of its restored health. To the best of our knowledge[29], some 14 per cent of total nitrogen reaching the Black Sea is from Bulgaria, 27 per cent from Romania, 12 per cent from Ukraine, ten per cent from the Russia Federation, less than one per cent from Georgia, six per cent from Turkey and about 30 per cent from the non-coastal countries (Austria, Belarus, Bosnia and Hertzegovina, Croatia,

Czech Republic, Former Yugoslavia, Germany, Hungary, Moldova, Slovakia, Slovenia). In the case of phosphorus, the figures are Bulgaria, five per cent; Romania, 23 per cent; Ukraine, 20 per cent; Russia, 13 per cent; Georgia one per cent; Turkey 12 per cent and 26 per cent, for the remaining countries; a similar story to that of nitrogen. The importance of showing these numbers is to illustrate that nobody is "innocent", not even the Georgians whose low percentage input reflects the current collapse in the coastal economy, probably a temporary feature.

As illustrated above, at the time of the 1995 study, the largest single contributor of nutrients was Romania. Romania's entire territory drains into the Black Sea, mostly through the Danube. The industrial and agricultural practices adopted during the former political regime paid little regard to environmental protection, especially in the "green revolution". Now that the economy of Romania is market-based, many subsidies on fertilizers have been removed and large animal production complexes are closing. The decrease in fertilizer use is beneficial to the environment but unless alternative and cost-effective agricultural practices are adopted, there will be enormous social problems of unemployed farm workers unable to compete with cheap food exports from places where cheaper production techniques are applied. A similar situation prevails in neighbouring Moldova where large animal complexes have also closed but where smallholders now have excessive numbers of animals literally in their back gardens, in very unsanitary conditions. Human health is already declining in these places and shallow wells, the main local water supplies, are polluted. There are no simplistic solutions to these problems unless consumption patterns themselves are changed – and how can countries with rampant over-consumption in the west demand changes of their poorer neighbours in the east?

Over 50 per cent of the dissolved nutrients reaching the Black Sea arrive via the Danube river. The Danube river basin has its own management regime which includes a Convention and an Action Plan.[30] The Danube Pollution Reduction Programme (a GEF funded project) has helped to define new strategies for reducing pollution, including nutrients, in the entire Danube Basin. Similarly, in the Dnieper River (shared by Ukraine, Belarus and Russia), a GEF-supported programme is developing a new Action Plan. If there are to be effective reductions in the flux of nutrients entering the Black Sea, it is important that a Basin Wide Approach is developed in which the objectives of the different river basin projects with respect to protection of the Black Sea are matched with the needs of the coastal countries for implementing the Black Sea Action Plan. This does not imply the creation of a new 17-country programme, rather the provision of a forum for the various programmes to agree on some common policies.

A first move in this direction was the creation of an ad-hoc working party in December 1997, between the Danube and Black Sea Commissions. The group freely exchanged scientific and policy information between experts from all parts of the Danube basin and the Black Sea coast. It agreed[31] to recommend to the Parties of the two Conventions to take measures to maintain the discharge of nutrients to the Black Sea at or below the levels recorded in 1996. Furthermore, this group foresaw the need to monitor the recovery of the Black Sea very carefully to determine the effectiveness of this measure.

Unlike the Istanbul Commission, the International Commission for the Protection of the Danube River is currently very active, perhaps partly due to reliable funding from the upper riparian countries (Germany and Austria) and from the European Commission. The wider international community has already warmed to the proposal of the ad-hoc group and a new phase of closely co-ordinated well-financed Danube and Black Sea GEF projects for nutrient reduction has been proposed. These would be intersectoral, integrating agricultural policy reforms, wetland protection and restoration, legal measures, economic instruments, incentives and public participation. The major obstacle for this to happen is the continued political stalemate surrounding the integration of the Secretariat of the Istanbul Commission and the implementation of the Black Sea Strategic Action Plan.

Ensuring Public Support for Protecting the Black Sea

Greater public awareness is a key to promoting action for protecting the environment, but it is naive to regard awareness campaigns as being sufficient. They have to lead to an understanding that there are viable options for sustaining the natural environment and human welfare. Also it has to be understood that the situation requires a personal and collective commitment by all individuals in society. This is easier said than done in societies in which people are barely able to cover the material needs of their families, spend inordinate amounts of time confronting dehumanizing bureaucratic obstacles, and often feel that individual action will be ignored or repressed.

Until recently, in countries with a communist regime, individual or collective action on environmental issues was insignificant unless conducted within the limits defined by the government or through the channels of the communist party itself. The situation was different in

Turkey of course, but it should be remembered that Turkey had significant periods of military rule in the last two decades and these periods were not conducive to the development of a strong civil society. In the entire region therefore, the "environmental movement" is a new one. In a rather short period of time, non-governmental organizations have emerged, grown and gathered strength, though in many cases, they fragmented and faded. One of their problems is that many NGOs were, and remain, small groups of specialists or enthusiasts, trying to raise funds for their projects and seeing the world through their own technical perspective. This function sometimes fills a vacuum left by weak government agencies. There are very few genuine community-based NGOs however. Perhaps many people are still not fully aware of their democratic rights or are so preoccupied with the demands of survival in a transition economy that they have little spare time to seek other avenues to assert their rights.

The Black Sea has national NGO fora and a regional forum. These did not develop spontaneously but were the product of initiatives supported through outside donors. The NGO forum spends much time questioning its own purpose since there is little coherence between these groups if they were mostly established as technical clubs rather than in response to deeply felt concerns amongst the general public. This is not to decry their usefulness and genuine intentions. The problem is that many donors have not understood this situation and have seen these NGOs as the only key to enhancing democratic processes, which is not necessarily true.

There are some recent examples of NGO action which are, however, remarkable and suggest that there is a limit to the apparent apathy shown by some local communities. In the city of Zonguldak in Turkey, a local community-based NGO, predominantly organized by local women, successfully took the Government to court over the direct discharge of fly-ash to the Black Sea from the local thermoelectric power station. The station has now been equipped with the necessary treatment facilities. Near the Black Sea port of Novorrossiysk, the construction of an oil terminal is planned. The Black Sea is rapidly becoming an oil super-highway, driven by the unabated demands for energy from western markets – a new cause for concern for an ecosystem that is already sick. Partly as a result of efforts by the local NGO Aquatoria, the local public were mobilized and, in a public hearing, rejected the results of an official environmental impact assessment which supported the construction on a site considered to be of great natural beauty. The stakes are very high, as the terminal is a key element of Russia's oil export plans.

Central governments and other centralized organizations are not adept at transferring the benefits of technical assistance from capital cities to the regions and fully involving them in the decision making process. Until recently many local authorities have remained unaware of over $20 millions of international efforts to protect the Black Sea and may still feel in a role as observers rather than full participants in guiding the overall effort. The current development of National Black Sea Action Plans involving key sectors at the local level may improve this situation. Different sectors in local settlements need to be brought together if a community spirit is to exist at all. In this respect, the institution of 'International Black Sea Day', annually celebrated throughout the Black Sea on 31st October, has been important in catalyzing the involvement of local authorities, donors, NGOs, business groups, schools and the media. The initiative focuses the often disperse efforts of these groups on a single common objective. The fact that practical activities are being undertaken in many towns in six countries on the same day excites the imagination and gives a sense of international solidarity which the media is quick to grasp. Unfortunately, incentives for individual or collective environmental action at the local level are virtually absent. These would help to stimulate citizen initiatives and give a higher status to environmental protection in society.

The message of *awareness-choice-commitment-action* is one that finds most fertile ground in younger generations. The importance of environmental education should not be understated – not just formal education in the classroom but bringing children in direct contact with nature in a manner which inspires them and promotes deep feelings as well as knowledge. Children need to become aware that the litter in their parks, streets and beaches is just as important a source of environmental degradation as the factories belching fumes and toxic wastes which they may only read about in books or see on the television. Raising funds for environmental education in the Black Sea region however, is very difficult. In the West, we are reticent to recognize that much of our foreign aid is focused on improving trade and little is available for fostering the transfer of knowledge and wisdom to a new generation of citizens who will have to tackle the legacy of our current very unsustainable lifestyles.

Conclusion: Are We Closer to Saving the Black Sea?

Apart from its incalculable intrinsic value, the Black Sea is used to produce considerable economic revenues for its coastal states and the region as a whole. Most of these revenues depend on maintaining a healthy sea. However, part of the current economy is supported by destroying the health of the marine and coastal environment through free waste disposal or by urbanizing natural areas. If this unsustainable trend continues, the Black Sea environment will decline even further, leaving a tragic legacy for future generations.

The more environmental destruction is allowed to occur, the less the scope for economic growth. If, for example, legislation for integrated coastal zone management is not agreed and imposed in many parts of the Black Sea, the coastline will become cluttered with a maze of ugly holiday homes, ports, factories and highways. The use of the sea as a repository for garbage or untreated sewage is evidence of a low societal value given to its protection. The beauty of the coast is already deteriorating in many parts and biological diversity is being lost through natural habitat destruction. Roads or monotonous rows of summer residences are now dominating large stretches of the coast of Turkey. Everybody strives to own a key piece of the landscape but in so doing destroys it. Many tourists are already going elsewhere in search of a more attractive coastline. Both aesthetic and economic values are being lost. By careful planning and legislation, economic and aesthetic values can be assured and destructive impact minimized.

The current annual value of fisheries, tourism and maritime transport can each be measured in billions of dollars. Russia and Turkey, for example, have recently agreed on a multi-billion dollar "Blue Stream" sea-bottom gas pipeline. In contrast, it is almost unbelievable that many Black Sea governments are not prepared to finance the Istanbul Commission, currently the only statutory mechanism for collaboration to protect the Black Sea. In 1997, an attempt was made[32] to integrate an interim mechanism for implementing the provisions of Bucharest Convention. Some US$180,000 was raised from international sources for 1998 and individual governments each agreed to contribute about $19,000 co-funding, with the Government of Turkey providing the infrastructure. Apart from Turkey, no government honoured this commitment, mostly declaring themselves unable to afford this sum or unwilling to do so in the absence of the others. This sad story reflects the failure of Black Sea governments to embrace environmental issues or to properly understand the relationship between environment and development in the case of the Black Sea. The small momentum for joint environmental action initiated at the time of "perestroika" seems to have ground to a halt.

Some hope remains for the Black Sea however. As mentioned earlier, the economic misfortune of many of Eastern and Central European countries has given rise to a partial respite from eutrophication. Most of the countries in the Danube Basin, and recently Turkey, have entered into the process of accession to the European Union. One of the prerequisites for accession will be approximation to EU environmental legislation. This will provide an important incentive for protecting the Black Sea and for improving the management of its fisheries. On the other hand, there is a significant risk of creating a new east-west division across the Black Sea, further complicating the implementation of plans to protect it for its own good and that of future generations.

Acknowledgements

The author wishes to express his thanks to his many colleagues in the Black Sea region, particularly the staff of the Black Sea Project Co-ordination Unit in Istanbul for sustaining their efforts during the past seven years of rapid change, punctuated by feelings of déja-vu. This chapter was prepared thanks to the support of a Pew Fellowship in Marine Conservation, an initiative of the Pew Charitable Trusts in Partnership with the New England Aquarium. Interpretations of current events in the Black Sea do not necessarily reflect the official position of the Pew Charitable Trusts or Pew Fellows Program in Marine Conservation.

Notes

1 Laurence Mee is Professor of Marine and Coastal Policy at the University of Plymouth, UK. From 1993-98 he was Co-ordinator of the Black Sea Environmental Programme based in Istanbul, Turkey.

2 BSEP (1997) Black Sea Transboundary Diagnostic Analysis, (Ed. L.D. Mee) United Nations Publications, New York. ISBN 92-1-126075-2, August 1997, 142pp.

3 Zaitsev, Yu., 1992. Recent changes in the trophic structure of the Black Sea. Fish. Oceanogr., 1(2): 180–189.

4 Kosíyan, R.D., & O.T. Magoon (eds) (1993). Coastlines of the Black Sea. Proceedings of the 8th Symposium on Coastal and Ocean Management, Coastal Zone í93. Coastlines of the World, American Society of Civil Engineers, 573pp.

5 Mee, L.D. (1992) The Black Sea in crisis: The need for concerted international action. Ambio 21(4): 278–286.

6 MacLennan, D.N., T. Yasuda and L.D.Mee, 1997. Analysis of the Black Sea Fishery Fleet and landings. Black Sea Environmental Programme, Istanbul, 25pp.

7 GESAMP (IMO/FAO/UNESCO-IOC/WMO/WHO/IAEA/UN/UNEP Joint Group of Experts on the Scientific Aspects of Marine Environmental Protection), 1997. Opportunistic settlers and the problem of the ctenophore Mnemiopsis leiydi invasion in the Black Sea. Rep.Stud.GESAMP, (58):84p.

8   op cit 2.

9   BSEP (1996) Black Sea Sustainable Tourism Initiative (Background report), Istanbul, Turkey, 322pp.

10 Reynolds, A.E. 1987. The Varna Convention: A regional response to fisheries conservation and management. Int. J. Est. Coast. Pol. Law., 154–170.

11 McLennan et al. op cit.

12 MARPOL 73/78 has five Annexes, concerned with: oil (Annex I), noxious liquid substances in bulk (Annex II), harmful substances carried by sea in packaged forms (Annex III), sewage (Annex IV), and garbage (Annex V). Acceptance of Annexes I and II is obligatory for all contracting parties.

13 Protocol on Protection of the Black Sea Marine Environment Against Pollution From Land-Based Sources (Land-Based Sources Protocol), the Protocol on Cooperation in Combating Pollution of the Black Sea Marine Environment by Oil and Other Harmful Substances in Emergency Situations (Emergency Response Protocol), and the Protocol on the Protection of the Black Sea Marine Environment Against Pollution by Dumping (Dumping Protocol).

14 See Douglas Brubaker, Marine Pollution and International Law: Principles and Practice, Belhaven Press, London and Florida, 1993, p. 33. The classification is reflected in UNCLOS III, Part XII. Prior to UNCLOS III, it was common to "combine" the pollution source "from and through the atmosphere" with "land-based pollution".

15 Elaboration and adoption of such Protocol was agreed by the Commission at their September 1996 session. It is referred to in the Black Sea Strategic Action Plan.

16 For a recent review of the Regional Seas Conventions see Mee, L.D. (1998), International cooperation in the Regional Seas, International Centre for Water Studies, Amersfoort, 35pp.

17 Barcelona Convention for the Protection of the Mediterranean Sea against Pollution (1976, ratified 1978, amended 1995). Protocols on dumping (1976,1995), emergency response (1976), LBS (1980, 1996), specially protected areas and biodiversity (1995), seabed exploration and exploitation (1994), transboundary movement hazardous waste (1996).

18 Hey, E. and L.D. Mee, (1993) The Ministerial Declaration: An Important Step, 23 Environmental Policy and Law 2, 215–220.

19 Several different definitions have been given of this principle, which is also embodied in the Odessa Declaration. One definition is contained in Principle 15 of the Rio Declaration: "In order to protect the environment, the precautionary approach shall be widely accepted by States according to their capabilities. Where there are threats of serious or irreversible damage, lack of full scientific certainty shall not be used as a reason for postponing cost-effective measures to prevent environmental degradation." See for further information: Ellen Hey and David Freestone (eds), The Precautionary Principle and International Law, Kluwer Law International, The Hague, London, Boston, 1995.

20 UNEP (1996) Triennial Report on the Implementation of the Odessa Declaration. UNEP, Geneva, September, 1996.

21 Detailed information on the development of the GEF Black Sea Environmental Programme may be found in its Annual Reports (for 1994 – 1997) and its regular newsletters. These may be obtained from the BSEP Project Implementation Unit, Harekat Köskü II, Dolmabahce Sarayi, 80680 Besiktas, Istanbul, Turkey.

22 BSEP (1997) Op cit.

23 BSEP (1996) Strategic Action Plan for the Rehabilitation and Protection of the Black Sea, Istanbul, Turkey, 31 October 1996, 29pp.

24 A guide to the BS-SAP, entitled 'How to save the Black Sea' has recently been published in English, Russian, Ukrainian, Georgian and Romanian. It is available from the Black Sea PIU at the address given in supra (21).

25 For example: BSEP (1998) GEF Black Sea Environmental Programme, 1997 Annual Report. UNDP, Istanbul 40 pp.

26 An externality occurs when an activity by one agent causes a loss of welfare to the other agent that is not compensated.

27 Full information on the concept of incremental costs may be obtained from a series of studies published by the GEF Secretariat, see http://www.gefweb.org

28 Cosslett, C.E. and L.D. Mee (1995) Regional Financing for Protection of the Marine Environment. Advisory Committee on the Protection of the Sea, London, May 1995, 10 pp.

29 Topping, G., H. Sarikaya and L.D. Mee (1998) Sources of pollution to the Black Sea. In: Mee, L.D. and G. Topping (Eds) Black Sea Pollution Assessment. Vol. 10, Black Sea Environmental Series. UN Publications, New York, ISBN 92-1-129506-8. 380pp.

30 EPDRB (1995) Strategic Action Plan for the Danube River Basin, 1995–2005, Environmental Programme for the Danube River Basin, Vienna, 109pp.

31 ICPBS/ICPDR, 1999. Eutrophication in the Black Sea: causes and effects. Summary report by the Joint ad-hoc Technical Working Group established in January 1988 between the International Commission for the Protection of the Black Sea and the International Commission for the Protection of the Danube River, based on the studies by Black Sea scientists and the discussion of the 'Group', UNDP Danube Programme Coordination Unit,. Vienna, 1999, 70pp.

32 BSEP (1998) op cit.

CHAPTER EIGHT

Russia and the Black Sea Realities

Nikolai Kovalsky

The Black Sea Region may be said to have left the deepest traces in the Russian people's memory. Christianity came to Russia through the Black Sea zone and the eighteenth century was one of struggle for Russian access to the warm Black Sea, especially in the time of Peter the Great and of Empress Catherine II. Many thousands of Russians fell in battle or were killed by disease or other hardships associated with such campaigns as Russia, gaining strength, addressed access to the Black Sea as one of the problems facing its development. Historically, therefore, Russia has been concerned with developments in the Black Sea. A long-standing preoccupation with the Black Sea is demonstrated by the frequent appearance of images of the Black Sea in the works of prominent Russian novelists, poets and painters, such as Pushkin, Lermontov, Dostoevsky, Gorky, Aivasovsky. In more recent times, since the disintegration of the Soviet Union, new considerations have arisen which impact on a Russian approach to the Black Sea area's problems.

The New Geopolitical Context of Russian Regional Interests

Today's Russia has to admit that its influence on the Black Sea region diminished after the Soviet era. Although Russia regards this region as a geopolitical priority, its reduced presence in the Black Sea impedes implementation efforts. The Black Sea coastline inherited by the Russian Federation from the USSR is a modest 30 plus per cent of the former length. Russia acquired only three of the 20 major coastal cities and only one technologically-advanced seaport – Novorossiisk. Gone are the days when the Russian empire and the Soviet Union controlled the entire northern and north-eastern coast of the Black Sea.

Yet even today the Russian political class feels the need to preserve its firm presence here, reasons for this as well as the manner of such a presence are discussed here. Many Russia regions have maintained strong economic links with the Black Sea area. Thus, the central part of Russia, the Volga region, Siberia and the Ural region cooperate closely with the areas adjacent to the basins of the Black Sea and the Azov Sea, even those that have become part of Ukraine, Georgia or Moldova. For example, cooperation with Moldova has taken the form of exchange, that of Russian natural gas and electricity for Moldovan instruments and wine. In addition, the Black Sea has always been a gateway to the world ocean for Russia. Black Sea routes accommodate about 25 per cent of Russian foreign trade. Such routes will gain in importance in the future as the Russian economy gets stronger, its foreign trade diversifies and it branches out into new markets. The Black Sea also constitutes a natural security zone for Russia. Even though there is virtually no direct military threat emanating from this region at present, the Black Sea and bordering areas are marked by a string of potentially destabilizing factors (a festering crisis in the Balkans, an alarming situation in Transcaucasia and the Northern Caucasus, the Kurdish problem, the charged situation around Iraq and Iran, etc.) Thus one of the priorities of Russian defence policy is to provide a Russian presence in the Black Sea area. Obviously this task can be realized only in conditions of peace and stability in the region.

But many dangerous challenges exist for Russia in the area. These include economic destability crises and attendant difficulties. These difficulties are both macroeconomic and structural, for example living standards have dropped sharply. The southern regions of Russia – Rostov Region, Krasnodar and Stavropol Territories – are in a grave economic predicament. The economic potential of the Northern Caucasus is being whittled down by ethnic conflicts, among other things, which, for this sizeable region, is also the shortest route to economic isolation from other territories of Russia. Crises include ethnic aggravation, increasing nationalism and secessionism. They became particularly evident in the course of armed clashes and conflicts in the Caucasus (including Chechnya) and Trans-Dniester.

Ethnic animosities in the Black Sea region may be related to the extraordinary ethnic diversity of the region, with more than 20 different large ethnic groups and nationalities. Moreover these nationalities are dispersed across the territories of different countries, where the national minority often plays a substantial role. For instance, ethnic Russians constitute 22 per cent of Ukraine's population, 13 per cent of that of Moldova's and 8 per cent of the Georgian population. Many ethnic Ukrainians reside in territories adjacent to their country, Ukraine: 300,000 of them live in the adjacent Rostov region, and another 600,000 in Moldova.

The Crimea is known for its ethnic entanglements, as its population of 2.5 million is composed of 1.7 million ethnic Russians, 600,000 Ukrainians and 250,000 Tatars.[1] The situation here is aggravated by the fact that local authorities cannot provide enough jobs and housing for Tatar settlers.[2] In addition the issue of national borders and territorial claims has assumed an acute dimension in the region. This is further complicated by the fact that several newly-independent states have failed to demarcate their borders. In Armenia, international demarcation treaties dating back to the early 1920s were perceived as unfairly discriminating by the late 1980s and early 90s.[3]

In the Caucasus, administrative and national borders frequently lie in sharp contrast to the ideas of the local populace about the entitlement of certain ethnic groups to specific territories (Ingushetia-North Ossetia). This situation is particularly fraught for Russia, as some segments of its southern borders have not been legally formalized. The striving of smaller ethnic communities for the attributes of a nation comes into conflict with previously established, but now obsolete, borders. This obsolescence occurred largely because of forced and spontaneous migrations. This part of the Black Sea region is marked by a fierce bloody tussle over territories, combined with struggles for independence. In some countries public opinion seems to suggest an emphasis on the desire for the restitution of territories deemed to have been somehow lost at different historical points.

This region is also marked by a high level of social tension largely caused by the pains arising from recent transition in several countries. The results of social conflicts may seriously destabilize the whole region. Additionally the populace is experiencing problems linked to evident failures in the promotion of social progress, as well as the enhancement of social security, health care, education, professional training, etc.

The situation of refugees and forced migrants is clearly outstanding in this context. Droves of refugees, amounting to 600,000,[4] have fled the Northern Caucasus to settle in the Krasnodar and Stavropol territories. Ethnically, the refugees are mostly Russians and Armenians or members of various Caucasian communities who have escaped bloody skirmishes in their native land. As many as 250,000 to 300,000 refugees from Abkhazia have come to settle in Georgia.[5] Crowds of refugees, estimated (as of 1993)[6] at 900,000 by the UN High Commissioner on Refugees, fled Nagorno-Karabakh for Azerbaijan. But official Azerbaijan figures are higher, 12,000,000.[7] High migration flows were also triggered off by the war in Chechnya.

It has been suggested that the fact that a large proportion of refugees are socially marginal may make them susceptible to extremist ideas and that younger people may attempt to satisfy pecuniary needs through anti-social or downright criminal endeavours. The inability of authorities in Russia and other post-Soviet republics to provide requisite social assistance for refugees leads to truly deleterious consequences. The inevitable tumult and disorder in a conflict can provide a fertile breeding-ground for organized crime and drug-dealing rings. There is a very real and confirmed danger of turning the region – lying at the cross-roads of merchant routes from Asia to Europe – into a haven for international drug traffickers. Taken in conjunction, these factors may induce the growth of organized crime, especially in the eastern part of the region.[8]

Environmental problems are increasingly detrimental to Russian interests in the Black Sea region. The sea, with coasts providing homes for about 160 million people[9], is becoming one of the most polluted in the world. The intensification of oil shipments, construction of oil terminals and oil and fuel spills from vessels result in still greater contamination of the water, which has an adverse impact on the fishing industry and tourism. The same fate befell the Azov Sea, which was turned into a dumping ground for the industry of Donbas and neighbouring areas.

The destabilizing factors cited above are rarely manifested individually. More often the evolution of a confrontational incident into a conflict will be brought about by a whole set of intertwined causes, with no apparent prevalent and secondary factors. This situation may be common to all major conflict entanglements in the Black Sea region. The conflict in the Caucasus is probably the most intractable, as bloody clashes spark off now and then in various parts of its territory. The situation in North Ossetia, Ingushetia, Abkhazia and Nagorno-Karabakh has not been settled so far, even though Russian peacemaking and intermediary efforts, undertaken jointly with the UN and OSCE, produced some results. Currently the situation in Chechnya appears to be particularly dangerous, because of its potential consequences.

Russo-Ukrainian relations are a significant geopolitical factor for the situation in the Black Sea area. The bilateral Treaty on Friendship and Cooperation was signed on May 28, 1997, after several years of talks, and ratified by the Duma in December 1998. The problem of the division of the Black Sea fleet and the status of its major base – Sevastopol – has also been officially resolved. In March 1999 the Ukrainian parliament ratified three agreements concerning this problem, which was among the conditions specified by the Russian side.[10]

But there are a whole cluster of difficult problems in bilateral relations associated with the Crimean issue. The Crimea was part of Russia from the late eighteenth century until 1954 and its population is 70 per cent ethnic Russian. Kiev observes the pro-Moscow stance of the Crimean Russians with an anxious disposition that is mixed with rivalry. However a closer analysis may reveal many common interests for Russia and Ukraine, spanning the Black Sea region among other fields. Consequently, the other side of their relationship is one of cooperation. For example, after many years of procrastinating, the delimitation of their common border has begun.

The role of the Black Sea is gaining in importance for Georgia which possesses all the required preconditions to be included into the world community as a sea power having naval bases and trading ports. The favourable geographical position of Georgia has always supported its efforts for the development of navigation. As early as sixth century BC when south of the Caucasus Mountains was the state of Colchis, it was famous for its shipbuilders and trade connections. Nor should it be forgotten that the shores of the Black Sea constitute nearly a quarter of its frontier.

Goods in transit from Armenia and Azerbaijan, as well from Central Asia, may be transported via Georgia, in particular via Batumi. In order to appreciate Georgia's potential it is useful to remember that in the past the cargo turnover of its trading ports accounted for approximately 2.5 per cent of the total cargo turnover of the USSR. The war in Abkhasia undermined the political, military and economic potential of Georgia. Nevertheless this country, in the long term, will maintain its influence in the Black Sea-Mediterranean region. Moldova also needs to have access to the Black Sea. For Moldova this is not simply a matter of prestige but a condition for its effective economic development. In addition Russia has to acknowledge the new roles of Turkey, Bulgaria, Romania and other Black Sea nations.

Factors that may complicate the situation in the Black Sea region in the future include a full set of differences over the shipment of the Caspian oil extracted from the shelf and land fields throughout this area. The choice of a route for the oil main line affects the interests of Russia, Turkey, Georgia, Azerbaijan, Kazakhstan, Iran, Armenia, Greece, Bulgaria and several other countries and major oil multinationals. Russia seeks to make the most intensive use of the existing oil pipeline, linking Baku and Novorossiisk, as its modernization will be far less costly (to an estimated factor of five) than the construction of a new pipeline via Georgia, putting aside the technically complicated and even more capital intensive project of a pipeline stretching across Turkey.[11]

So Russia has extensive and comprehensive interests in the region, which overlap with the interests of other countries. The range of international involvement in the region has visibly increased. Only two major political alignments were active there until the 1990s: on one hand the socialist countries as signatories of the Warsaw Treaty, on the other Turkey, a country backed by the NATO mechanism. Today, however, the Black Sea process involves over a dozen countries and international organizations. Consequently, Russia has come to face a situation where the Black Sea region is attracting ever greater attention from the international community. Judging from the most recent developments, this trend may accelerate. On the one hand, this may indicate that the Black Sea region is being rapidly integrated into the global system of international relations, while on the other, the large number of non-coastal states that wish to be involved may complicate the process of resolving existing issues. One new phenomenon is the increasing political, economic and military activity of the Western powers in the Black Sea area.

The Russian and Western presence in the Black Sea region

Obviously the interest of such Western powers may be related to the intermediate position of the Black Sea, being between Europe and Asia, and by its proximity to the Mediterranean and the Middle East. The presence of Western powers in the region helps them to solve their political, military, and economic problems in the Caucasus, the Caspian Sea region, and Central Asia as well as providing access to Russia's southern boundaries. The Black Sea region thus acquires an international significance.

All of these interests find expression in the Western powers' concrete and intensive activities. Specific aspects of their reactions deserve to be noted. First of all, the West cannot ignore the central role which Russia has long been playing in the region. While opinions on this vary, one general impression may be that, at present, the West has no interest in an excessive weakening of Russian influence in the Black Sea region. Further it is evident that the Western powers, including the United States, are disinclined to be too much involved in the physical settlement of Black Sea conflicts. However the West is against any increase of Russia's influence as it appears that a number of Western politicians would regard this as a revival of Russia's traditional 'imperial' aspirations.

Among other regional factors that should be taken into account is the role of the area as a transport corridor from Europe to Asia (TRACECA, 'Great Silk Way'). An additional consideration is the Caspian oil and the problem of pipe-lines which became an important incentive for the outside powers' activity on territory which is, historically, an area of Russian interest. With regard to US regional politics it is useful to mention the analysis made by the Institute for Security Studies (Western European Union):

'The United States considers the Black Sea region as particularly important, not only because of its energy resources but also because of its geography: proximity to Russia, Central Asia, the Mediterranean, south-eastern Europe and the Middle East. In addition, the region is important in determining whether, and if so to what extent, Russia is re-extending its influence over the Eurasian continent... US policy in the region is becoming less and less constrained by concerns about Moscow's reaction.'[12]

Western powers may be said to devote special attention to Ukraine as a Black Sea state, which is perfectly logical in view both of the size of the country and its place in international relations. However it is revealing that the support for Ukraine expressed by certain Western politicians tends to demonstrate an anti-Russian stand. Some of these politicians seem to regard Ukraine as a trump card which could be used to exert pressure on Russia, see Zbigniew Brzezinski for an example of such a stance.[13]

Georgia is the Transcaucasian country that has particularly extensive contacts with the West. This is understandable given that, since the days when the Soviet union was still there, the West has known Eduard Shevardnadze better than any other Transcaucasian leader. But an assessment of public opinion in Russia suggests a sensitivity to the new Georgian foreign policy orientation.[14] Turkey as a member of Western alliances has also come to play a conspicuous role in the region. Until recently, an assessment of public opinion in Russia, regarding Turkey, suggested that the Turkish initiatives aimed at promoting various ties with its northern neighbours (above all Russia) had made a favourable impression. For some time past, however, there has been evidence of an increasing concern about Pan-Turkist propaganda and a tightening of the control of the Black Sea Straits. Active cooperation with Turkey and elimination of complexities in the Russo-Turkish relations are required.

NATO is actively establishing itself in the Black Sea. NATO's instrument for this policy is the programme known as the Partnership for Peace (PfP), which all Black Sea countries have joined. In the new situation developing in the region, as a result of the conclusion of relevant accords, NATO's southern flank is shifting northward, which means that the Black Sea has become one of its components. Never have NATO-member warships sailed the waters of the Black Sea so often as today. It has become a regular NATO practice to hold joint exercises in the area, which the Russian military regards with some concern. In late 1998 such exercises took place in Ukraine (Fall, 1998 and Shield of Peace '98) and in Romania. Russia, by the way, refused to take part in the many exercises held under the PfP program in the Black Sea area. In 1990 the region was visited by five foreign ships, in 1996 29 ships from NATO spent about 400, in aggregate, days there. NATO's attention is not only focused on applicant countries such as Romania and Bulgaria, but also on Moldova and the Ukraine, and even on the republics of Transcaucasus, as was demonstrated by the General Secretary J. Solana.[15]

The increasing activity of NATO along Russia's southern borders has provoked discontent in Moscow. In 1996 the then President Boris Yeltsin declared that Russia would react strongly to any efforts 'to transform the Black Sea into a jumping-off place for the fleets of NATO and non-Black Sea countries.'[16] Thus there is reason for concern in Russia over NATO activities, previously indications are that reactions to NATO were influenced by the characteristics of the Cold War period. Of course the situation can be improved if NATO establishes a true partnership with Russia which takes into account not only its own interests but also the security concerns of Russia.

The appearance of the ghost of NATO in the Caspian area is, in Russia, considered somewhat threatening. The officials of Azerbaijan believe that 'NATO has to pay more attention to the security in the Transcaucasian space' and try to use the relations with the US and NATO for pressing Armenia in the Nagorny Karabach conflict.[17]

To understand the geopolitical situation in the Black Sea area it's necessary to take into account the fact that the eastern Balkans are an integral part of this area. The Balkans have always been an area of significance to Russia. Geographically the Balkans are close to Russian territory. If military bases with nuclear armament and missiles of enemy states or alliances were to be deployed here, this would constitute a threat to Russia's security. In economic terms the Balkan states are appreciated by Russia as good business and commercial partners. The further development of these relations has characterized recent decades. Other economic factors to take into account here are the problems associated with sea trade routes from the Black Sea, Europe, Asia, Africa, and the Western hemisphere. In addition there is an emotional and spiritual dimension which should be noted; this is based on an association, in Russian national consciousness, with the Balkans to important events in Russian history. It was from here the Slavonic alphabet and Byzantine culture came into Russian lands.

For the reasons outlined what happens in the Balkans has substantial implications for Russian domestic policy and for political life inside the country. Now, of course, Russia is paying special attention to the crisis on the territory of former Yugoslavia which, for decades, was its strategic partner in the region.

Two periods can be distinguished in recent Russian diplomatic activity in the Balkans. For the early 1990s it typically followed the Western powers' leadership. It might be said that in the name of solidarity with the West, Russian politicians were forgetting the real interests of their own country. This was a period identified by Stanislav Kondrashev, eminent columnist of *Isvestia*, as the time of 'romanticism in Russian foreign policy' and by Vladimir Lukin, former Russian ambassador in Washington and presently Chairman of the Duma's foreign policy committee, as an 'infantile pro-Americanism'.[18] During this period Russian diplomacy tried not to allow contradictions between the Russian and American lines to appear. Following the Western line Russia gave diplomatic recognition to the new sovereign states which sprang up after the disintegration of Yugoslavia. The Russian delegate in the UN's Security Council voted for the sanctions.

Evolution of Russian diplomacy towards the second stage of its Balkan activities was provoked by the Western policy of gradually isolating Russia from the decision-making process in Yugoslav affairs. A turning point in Russia's attitude was reached during the first months of 1994. At that point Russia achieved an evident success in preventing NATO bombardments when the Serbs adopted the proposals of the then Russian President Boris Yeltsin. Nevertheless, some weeks later, NATO carried out their operation against the Serbs without preliminary consultations with the Russian government. It became evident that the model of military intervention by NATO or by the US to end the war in Bosnia was unacceptable for Russia, as was NATO's further extensive involvement in the regional situation. Since that time Russian diplomacy began, rather firmly, to stand up for its line. It appeared that public opinion in Russia public displayed greater and greater suspicions about NATO's role in the Balkans.

Obviously the problem of the future situation in the Balkans must be discussed at both bilateral and multilateral levels and priority be given to the UN and its Security Council. At the same time it is not only the Balkans but the Black Sea region itself which needs more attention from the UN. The UN could do a great deal towards establishing stability and prosperity here, therefore providing for the elaboration of the regional programme for peace and cooperation.

Many Russian experts believe that the Organization for Security and Cooperation in Europe (OSCE) – the only truly all-European organization with 52 member states – is a most important tool for shaping a model of common and comprehensive security in Europe for the twenty-first century and for bringing peace and stability in the continent. In this respect the OSCE, given that it is an international organization, should involve itself more with the problems of the Black Sea region if it is really determined to elevate its role in European life. At any rate, its agenda and final documents should reflect the problems of the Black Sea region. It is important that the OSCE perceives activities in this region as an integral part of the building of Europe, while the systems of the Black Sea Economic Cooperation (BSEC) should be linked to the economic endeavours of the OSCE.

The Black Sea region needs the OSCE to hammer out an effective mechanism for conflict prevention and resolution and to implement its decisions in this field expeditiously and efficaciously. The expertise accumulated by OSCE missions in the region, in particular in Nagorno-Karabakh and Chechnya, indicates that this organization is capable of acting as a medium for conflict resolution. The Black Sea region with its intricate ethnic relations could make use of a charter for national minorities' rights drafted within the OSCE. Such a charter is long overdue, while the structure and nature of the OSCE make it the most appropriate agency for this kind of endeavour.

In a nutshell, the OSCE programme for Europe might well include a section describing the complexity of, as well as ways to untangle, the problems of the Black Sea region. It should also be noted that the OSCE could play an important part in resolving the environmental problems of the Black Sea region. Obviously, OSCE activities in the Black Sea region correspond to Russia's principal and objective interests.

As for the activity of the European Union in the Black Sea region, it could become an important factor in the political and economic life of the Black Sea countries, especially after the conclusion of European Agreements with Bulgaria and Romania, and the partnership and cooperation treaties with the Ukraine and Russia. Now is the time to realize the content of these documents. The EU deploy some technical assistance projects in the region, in specific fields: transport, energy, privatization, support for enterprises, etc. Probably the EU could establish a special Black Sea Programme. In short, the EU can act as catalyst to promote the Black Sea regional development.

The same proposal can be addressed to the Council of Europe, which could make its own effective contribution to the process of democratization in the new independent states as well as to the construction of civil society. Surely the Council of Europe has contacts with all Black Sea countries, yet it lacks a strategy for its regional activity in this field. Obviously good will and friendly cooperation are necessary prerequisites for a fair solution to all the difficult problems of the Black Sea Region.

Russia and the BSEC, Organization of Regional Fully-Fledged Cooperation

The regional organization Black Sea Economic Cooperation (BSEC), which consists of 11 member-states (Albania, Armenia, Azerbaijan, Bulgaria, Georgia, Greece, Moldova, Romania, Russian federation, Turkey, Ukraine), is central to Russian foreign policy. The signing of the Istanbul Declaration, in June 1992,[19] regarding the BSEC's establishment was among the first major foreign policy efforts undertaken by the new leaders of the Russian federation after the Soviet union fell apart.

The President of the Russian Federation declared that by signing the Declaration Russia pursued several specific objectives. In particular was Russia's aim to bolster good-neighbourly relations with the Black Sea nations and, primarily, with the CIS countries. This aim was pursued as a means to ensure peace and tranquillity at Russia's southern borders and to turn the Black Sea region into a zone of peace and prosperity. In doing so, Russia had displayed some interest in expanding and enhancing cooperation in the economic field, including commerce and industry, research, technology, and environmental protection. On a practical level Russia hoped to attain a dramatically higher level of cooperation in transport and communications, power production, agriculture, health care and elsewhere. The major emphasis, in cooperation, was to be placed on individual business and firms and entrepreneurship in that region. The Russian foreign ministry, and Russian legations abroad, were instructed to assist fledgling Russian entrepreneurs in their endeavours and to promote economic contacts in the region that would meet national interests and give a fillip to the progress in the southern regions of Russia.

Since then, Moscow has been paying substantial attention to the BSEC or, in a broader sense, to the Black Sea domain of Russian foreign policy. Thus the Russian National Committee for the Black Sea Economic Cooperation (RNCBSEC) was established, in March 1996, to coordinate and ensure the participation of Russian organizations, regions, business and research communities – those that wished to do so – in the BSEC. The committee was joined by government structures, larger banks, major companies and research institutions.[20] Participation in the BSEC is considered part of Russia's European policy. Russians have never questioned the European identity of the Black Sea region. These ideas were strongly voiced at the meeting of BSEC foreign ministers[21] and have been officially formulated as follows:

the BSEC is an integral element of twenty-first century European architecture open to cooperation with other European organizations and institutions;

the Black Sea region has every reason to be a fully-fledged member of the new Europe based on cooperation and partnership, part of the future integrated Europe. The BSEC is to find a niche in the system of European build-up;

the potential of the Black Sea region and favourable prospects for its development serve as a tangible basis for promoting comprehensive links with neighbouring and other regions of Europe.

The involvement of Russia in the BSEC is connected to its policy of promoting cooperation in the broad European context, which denies any new delimitation in this part of the world, including that emerging due to the relapse into the old bloc thinking.

The BSEC model is a unique and promising design for open international partnership, dovetailing mutual interests, which fits perfectly into the emerging system of common European security and cooperation. The experience accumulated to date enables nations to make a weightier contribution to the development of a new model of European security, promoting its economic component and civilian security aspects; the comprehensive process of the Balkan economic recovery would respond to the BSEC interests, as it would leave no void in the fabric of cooperation. Making use of its structures and mechanisms, the BSEC can supplement and reinforce the efforts made in the context of the 'Royamont process' and other cooperation initiatives. Russia supports the trends for collaboration between the EU and BSEC.

The European Commission's opinion[22] is that the European Union's approach to closer cooperation among the Black Sea states takes into account the common interests of the Black Sea states and of the European Union in the region. The Black Sea area is potentially an important market for EU export. Enlargement of the EC will further increase the Black Sea region's significance to the European Union, which proclaimed that it has a major interest in promoting political stability and economic prosperity in the region and stimulating the development of links, both within the region and with the EU.

The BSEC has expressed, more than once, its readiness for the development of relations with the EC. This idea was approved in the Moscow Declaration (1996) of the Heads of States or Governments of the Participating States of the BSEC. This point of view was reiterated in the final document of the Yalta summit (1998) which proposed to establish the common economic zone EURO-BSEC. Taking account of the natural relation between the Black and Mediterranean seas, Russia favours active and broad cooperation between Black Sea and Mediterranean nations, which may be facilitated by creating appropriate mechanisms. Naturally, it would be useful to arrange for the attendance of BSEC representatives at multilateral Mediterranean meetings and vice versa. This aspect acquires great importance in view of the Euro-Mediterranean cooperation under the EU auspices, announced at the 1995 Barcelona conference, together with the plans to establish a Euro-Mediterranean free trade zone by the year 2010. Russian experts and politicians generally share the view that it will be less than efficient to grapple with security, social and economic issues in the Mediterranean – specified in the resolutions of the Barcelona Conference – in isolation from the situation in the Black Sea region. It would be far more logical to establish ongoing contacts between the BSEC and Mediterranean structures.

Russia has made strenuous efforts to strengthen the BSEC. Russia has consistently advocated the identification of an international legal status for the BSEC. The BSEC is expected to become an equal partner among existing international organizations. So, in 1998 at the Yalta summit, the Charter of the Organization of the Black Sea Economic Cooperation was adopted – an act which transformed the existing intergovernmental mechanism into a fully-fledged regional economic organization.[23]

The current organization of the BSEC and its cooperation machinery constitute another area which is fraught with change. The Russian side believes that participating states should fine-tune and compare their approaches at the summit level more frequently, a procedure preceded by the preparatory work of experts, foreign and sectoral ministries. The main issue is to make the mechanism of the BSEC function more effectively.

Since the Parliamentary Assembly of BSEC (PABSEC) is an essential element of cooperation in the Black Sea and renders support to efforts aimed at augmenting useful cooperation between nations of this region, the Russian party stands for its stronger operational links with the BSEC. PABSEC could assist in the implementation of BSEC decisions in individual countries via national parliaments, while working bodies of BSEC and PABSEC may expand their contacts, exchange information and conduct requisite consultations.

One of the most significant measures designed to bolster the BSEC, and receiving special attention from the Russian party, is the effort to start up the Black Sea Trade and Development Bank (BSTD) which is regarded as a crucial tool and resource of Black Sea cooperation. Russia ratified this agreement in July 1996, with a proviso that the Russian federation reserves the right to restrict transactions of the BSTD in its territory or elsewhere, should these be denominated in Russian national currency. Unless otherwise restricted, the BSTD shall carry out its activities in compliance with Russian laws governing the operations of non-resident banks. The large amount of attention paid to the problems of the BSTD is explained by its obligation to finance crucial BSEC projects, among other operations – a mission that may be too difficult without connection to the European Bank for Reconstruction and Development (EBRD), the European Investment Bank (EIB), and other financial hubs. At the same time, there have been proposals to set up BSEC co-financing projects and to investigate opportunities for granting the EIB the right to branch out to all BSEC nations. Russia is one of the three states, together with Greece and Turkey, with the largest contribution to the BSTD (Russia, Greece and Turkey contribute 16.5 per cent each; Romania, Ukraine and Bulgaria contribute 13.5 per cent each; Moldova, Azerbaijan, Armenia and Georgia contribute two per cent each).[24] This is one reason why Russia will be paying considerable attention to all issues pertaining to the Bank's activities.

The identification of priorities in BSEC proceedings and the selection of the most essential and promising projects stands high on the agenda of participating nations. Russia has also become involved in these activities. The numerous ideas and proposals put forward by the Russian party contain a few of particular importance. Attracting investment to the Black Sea region is of paramount importance. Russian representatives work in the Group of Experts on Investment Problems. Together with the BSEC Secretariat, Russian and Ukrainian experts drafted 'Basic Principles of Investment Collaboration', which became the first multilateral BSEC document on investment protection. The Russian party notes the importance of encouraging international financial institutions (IBRD, EIB, EBRD, etc.) to participate in expanding investment opportunities in the BSEC area.

Being a country of tremendous distances, Russia is naturally interested in a road and conveyance project, especially taking into account a future role of the region as an transport bridge between the Caspian basin and different parts of Europe. BSEC projects of this kind envision the development of an infrastructure of regional transportation that would be hooked up to trans-European networks and provide transport linkage between Europe, the Middle and Near East, Central Asia, the Black and Baltic Seas. Transport routes in southern Russia will become an element of this huge new network. Russian experts were involved in the elaboration of detailed maps on rail and road transportation, and on ports and shipping lines in the BSEC Region. On the whole, Russia assesses transport coop-eration as having a huge potential that is yet to be fully deployed.

Power production is another priority that includes a project on the BSEC Interconnected Regional Power System (BSEC IRPS), open to integration with power systems of neighbouring countries and regions of the Central and Eastern Europe, Middle and Near East. In the future, the project may expand further to cover Northern Africa and hook up to the Euro-Mediterranean Power System.

The Russian Joint-Stock Company Russian Single Power System was among the authors of the idea of integrating power grids. The Russian party suggested that the European Union, Sofia-based Black Sea Energy Centre, international banking and financial institutions join in the project. According to Russian estimates, the Black Sea region has substantial opportunities for implementing major transregional projects of energy transportation and can play a significant role in tackling international energy security matters. Russia is also interested in promoting cooperation in industry and agriculture, communications and telecoms, which includes the establishment of transregional fibre-optic lines as part of interconti-nental mega-projects, for instance in pipeline projects, health care, and pharmaceutics. The Russian federation makes specific efforts to develop joint programmes to prevent pollution and preserve the biological poten-tial of the Black Sea.

The Russian party clearly understands that the economic progress of the region will largely depend on the active posture of the business communities in the BSEC member-states. In this context, Russian repre-sentatives at several meetings of foreign ministers spoke in favour of a more dynamic and active Business Council – a collective authority of the business people and entrepreneurs within the BSEC framework. Russia approves of the programmes for a better environment for small and medium-sized businesses, facilitating the free movement of entrepreneurs and business people, together with other similar efforts.

Recently Russia has put forward a new issue for the BSEC – coopera-tion of the BSEC nations in preventing and eliminating the consequences of natural calamities and technogenic emergencies – and has announced its readiness to share its experience in this sphere, including that related to combining bilateral and multilateral efforts.

Russia attaches a great priority to the involvement of researchers in grappling with Black Sea development issues. Southern Russia boasts a sizeable research potential in the form of universities, research institutes and centres staffed by skilled experts in Krasnodar, Rostov-on-the-Don,

Stavropol, Anapa, Gelenjik and other cities. In Moscow, St. Petersburg and other Russian cities there are many experts who are well-acquainted with Black Sea problems. The Council for the Mediterranean and Black Sea Studies (Moscow), established in 1989, brought together researchers from several academic institutes, university researchers and experts from various agencies. The Council's brief was to develop a concept of the Russian national interest in the Black Sea region, to promote the participation of Russia in the BSEC and to draft corresponding recommendations. This work is currently underway at several academic institutions under the auspices of the Institute of Europe (Russian Academy of Sciences), which has a Centre for the Mediterranean and Black Sea Studies.[25]

How can the current position of the BSEC be assessed? Russia has come to the BSEC to stay, as was necessitated by objective geopolitical factors on the one hand and today's development requirements on the other. The BSEC area represents a third market for Russia (after the EU and the Asian-Pacific area): approximately 16 per cent of total Russian foreign trade turnover.[26]

Even though the BSEC has already covered some ground in its evolution, it is still not far away from square one. Its interaction in various economic fields has been developing unevenly. In some fields visible results have been achieved, while in others progress is lacking in vigour. There is an impression that the BSEC is lagging behind regional requirements as indicated, for example, by the heated debates over the pipeline routes that may pass through its territory. The differences that divide participating nations on this issue may have compelled the BSEC to distance itself from it, though it is an issue that concerns almost all of the member-states in various ways.

It should be noted, however, that economic cooperation is accelerating and optimizing. Its obsolete mechanisms have been replaced by new ones which are more efficient and better adapted to resolving the tasks faced by the BSEC. The economic activities of the BSEC have become more effective and some are being successfully implemented. To put it in a nutshell, the BSEC has entered into an important phase where its performance is measured by economic growth indices for the region or individual nations or sectors.

The task of turning the region into a zone of peace and stability is a more challenging one. If the BSEC plays any role in this process, it is confined to that of creating economic prerequisites for tackling this whole issue. The BSEC is not to blame for its limited capacity. It is, rather, that participating nations may not be ready to make a joint effort in this direction.

The objectives proclaimed at the time of the BSEC's conception remain to be reached, as the region is still full of confrontation, hotbeds of tension and simmering conflicts. The Black Sea community tends to overlook the fact that peace in the region is, primarily, a cause for the region itself, its constituent states and nations, which have the BSEC as their only regional structure. It will obviously take some time before the participating nations can come close to implementing this stated objective.

However, interaction within the BSEC has helped the countries advance to the goal proclaimed back in 1992, that of ensuring good-neighbourly relations between participating nations. Though bilateral relations may differ in the region and range all the way from efficient cooperation to deep-seated rancour, communication within the BSEC framework is one which promotes negotiation, rather than force, in the resolution of disputes.

Thus, the Black Sea region becomes significant in both the European and the World area, uniting the efforts of such large regions as the Balkans, Transcaucasia, the Mediterranean, Russia and Ukraine, and cooperating with countries beyond the Danube and the Caspian and in Central Asia.[27] Given its historical traditions and geographical situation, its economic, human and natural resources and its new geopolitical role in a changing world, there is hope that the Black Sea region has a promising future.

Notes

1 *Moscow Times*, January 15, 1994.
2 *Nezavisimaya Gazeta*, March 25, 1998.
3 'Spornye Granitsy na Kavkaze' (Disputed Borders in the Caucasus), Moscow, 1996, p 225.
4 *Izvestia*, May 4, 1994.
5 *Segodnya*, October 13, 1994.
6 *Peace Courier* (Helsinki), September 1994.
7 *Nezavisimaya Gazeta*, September 6, 1997.
8 *Izvestia*, September 21, 1995.
9 *Acropol*, N 9, October 1997.
10 *Nezavisimaya Gazeta*, March 26, 1999.
11 *Finansovie Izvestia*, May 19, 1999.
12 Y. Valinakis, 'The Black Sea Region: Challenges and Opportunities for Europe', Institute for Security Studies (WEU), Paris, 1999, p 18.
13 Zb. Brzezinski, 'The Grand Chessboard: American Primacy and Its Geostrategic Imperative', New York, 1998. p 256.
14 See e.g. N. Broladze 'The US are interested in Georgia' in *Nezavisimaya Gazeta*, January 29, 1999.

15 Arcady L. Moshes, Russia and the Black Sea States of the CIS in the new military-political situation in 'Europe, The Mediterranean, Russia: Perception of Strategies', M. 1998. p 26.

16 *Segodniya* July 1, 1996.

17 *Gazeta*, February 15, 1997; January 20 and February 27, 1999.

18 *The Southeast Year Book* 1994-95. Athens, 1995. p 610.

19 Black Sea Economic Cooperation. Handbook of Documents. Volume One. Permanent International Secretariat. Istanbul, 1995. p 3.

20 In March 1996 the Russian National Committee for the Black Sea Economic Cooperation (RNCBSEC) was conceived at a constituent conference. Its founding members included the Russian Foreign ministry, the bank Russian Credit, Omskpromstroibank, Krasnodarbank, an association Scientific and Technological Progress, Rostelecom Company, Transstroi state committee, the Chamber of Commerce and Industry, the Institute of Europe of Russian Academy of Sciences, the Russian Association for European Studies, the government of Rostov region, the city government of Taganrog and other entities. As a non-profit and non-governmental organization, the RNCBSEC has to coordinate the involvement of Russian regions, business and research communities concerned in the BSEC.

21 See statements by Russian delegates at Meetings of the Ministers of Foreign Affairs in publications prepared by BSEC Permanent International Secretariat, Istanbul: BSEC, Report of the Meeting of the Ministers of Foreign Affairs.

22 Commission of the European Communities. Com (97) 507 final. Brussels. 14.11.1998.

23 *Nezavisimaya Gazeta*, June 6, 1998.

24 *Balkan Briefing*, EKEM. November 1995. p 29.

25 The results of research were published (in English) in 'Russia: The Mediterranean and Black Sea Region', ed. by Nicolai A.Kovalsky, Moscow, 1998, p 267; 'Europe, The Mediterranean, Russia: perception of strategies', ed. by Nicolai A.Kovalsky, Moscow, 1998, p 50.

26 Evgeny G. Kutovoy. Russia and the Black Sea Economic Cooperation. In 'Russia: The Mediterranean and Black Sea region', M., 1998. p 238.

27 E.N.Borisenko, A.P.Kononenko, I.V.Semenenko, 'Black Sea Economic Cooperation: From Regional Initiative to International Organization', Istanbul, 1998, p 167.

CHAPTER NINE

Cooperation and Conflict in the North Caucasus

Svante E. Cornell

The North Caucasus is a region known in the post-Soviet era for its political and social instability, and, among informed circles, for its remarkable ethno-linguistic diversity. In fact, over thirty distinct native languages from the Caucasian, Turkic, and Persian linguistic groups are spoken in this region. The geographical delimitation of the region is nevertheless debated. What is clear is that it composes the lands on the Northern slopes and foothills of the great Caucasian mountain range, and between the Black Sea in the West and the Caspian Sea in the East. The region is hence seemingly clearly naturally delimited in the East, South, and West. Some problems neverthe-less exist. The first regards the northern delimitation of the region: culturally speaking, the northern border of the areas of settlement of the peoples indigenous to the North Caucasus seems a logical answer. These borders nevertheless do not always conform with the boundaries of the autonomous units within the Russian Federation given to those peoples; rather, the northern boundaries of these units were drawn further northward in the Stalinist era in order to diminish the ethnic homogeneity of these units. Meanwhile, traditional areas inhabited by Caucasian peoples, primarily in the northwestern Caucasus, are left outside these territorial units. But more importantly, the Russian regions of Stavropol and Krasnodar are, from an especially economic point of view, closely linked to the North Caucasus. But as regards security concerns, the North Caucasian 'republics' form the core of the region and will be the unit of analysis here.

The area of overlap between the North and South Caucasus also poses a problem. In fact, some of the most conflictual areas in the Caucasus lie in the border area between the two parts of the Caucasus. There are in fact three locations where topography allows contact between the North and South Caucasus: in the West, along the Black Sea coast; in the East, along the Caspian coast; and in the central area of what is today North and South Ossetia. In the West, the main overlap between South and North Caucasus concerns Abkhazia. A part of Georgia politically for most of its history, Abkhazia's titular people are nevertheless related to the Circassian peoples of the North Caucasus ethnically, culturally, linguistically and to a lesser extent religiously. Given the cultural links and especially the political links in the 1990s that connect the Abkhaz with the peoples of the North Caucasus, the question of Abkhazia cannot be excluded from an overview of the region. For the purpose of this volume, moreover, Abkhazia is highly relevant in strategic terms as it forms the territorial link between the Black Sea—and thereby the outside world—and the North Caucasus. The next area of overlap is again an area between Georgia and the North Caucasus, that is the 'enclave' of Indo-European Ossetians in an area otherwise populated by Caucasian peoples. The belonging of North Ossetia to the North Caucasus is beyond question; nevertheless the inclusion of the area of what was the South Ossetian Autonomous Oblast would be somewhat of an exaggeration. Nevertheless the Ossetian question and its repercussions on North Caucasian affairs cannot be understood without reference to the problem of South Ossetia in Georgia, and will therefore be allocated certain attention. Finally, the Lezgin issue in the East between Dagestan and Azerbaijan represents, much like the Ossetian problem, a question of a people divided by a political boundary that gained importance in the 1990s.

In this chapter it is important to note that the analysis presented here is of the record of cooperation and conflict in the 1990s and covers the period up until 1999, because of the inevitable passing of time between the preparation of an article and its publication there will have been changes in the situations under discussion and events will have taken place that might change the emphasis of this discussion. In conducting this analysis, two fundamental axes of relationships can be identified, these are relations between the North Caucasian peoples and those between North Caucasian peoples and Russia. While the distinction is sometimes blurred politically, it is of relevance as it reflects the distinction between the two major political agendas in the region today, that of inter-ethnic relations and of the center-periphery relations within the Russian Federation. Firstly, the existing problems are analysed; then patterns of cooperation; and finally, the prospects for the future.

Problems: Actual and Potential

A section covering actual and potential problems in the North Caucasus is by necessity extensive. The region is among the most unstable areas of

Eurasia, particularly its central and eastern parts. In fact, it is a region undergoing a painful political and economic transition that moreover exists in an uncertain political status. This is especially true for Chechnya, which has achieved *de facto* independence; but it is also, to a certain extent, the case for the entire region. In fact the North Caucasian republics have most attributes of statehood while being a part of a larger federative state. In a sense, then, one can speak of the autonomous republics as being states within a state. For example, the Ingush-Ossetian conflict, described at length below, in many respects resembles an inter-state conflict, while still being subjected to the intervention of Russian Federal forces. The consequence of this is that this region has a sort of blurred constitutional status, sharing characteristics of intra-states ethnic relations but also of inter-state politics. What follows is that the politics of the region take place in the lack of a defined system of interaction; in fact the region itself may be in the process of defining its own political system, falling between the inter-state and intra-state levels of interaction. This factor should be borne in mind when analysing the different problems of the North Caucasus.

Due to the interrelated character of relations between the peoples of the region, no one conflict can be totally understood without a basic knowledge of the others. But fundamentally, one can note the existence of certain spheres of conflict. The Abkhaz conflict is clearly delimited, despite the extensive support for the Abkhaz rebels of large numbers of Circassians and Chechens. Similarly, the issues facing the northwestern Caucasus, that is the republics of Kabardino-Balkaria and Karachai-Cherkessia, can be seen in relative isolation from the rest of the North Caucasus. However, when one moves to the Central and Eastern part of the region, the matter becomes more complicated. Here, three zones of conflict can be identified. The first is the Ossetian question, which has two dimensions: a conflict with Georgia in the South, and a conflict with Ingushetia in the North. The latter is linked with the second question, that of Chechnya. The conflict between Chechnya and the Russian central government served as a catalyst for the emergence of what can be termed 'the Ingush question' – that is, the problem of carving out an Ingush republic out of a diminutive area in the North Caucasus, including Ingush claims on a traditionally Ingush-populated region of North Ossetia. The third zone of conflict is Dagestan. Dagestan itself is a republic with a multitude of issues, ranging from ethnic relations to the Lezgin problem, shared with Azerbaijan, as well as a religious revival with political undertones. As is clear from this brief enumeration, the problems facing the North Caucasus are multiple and often explosive in nature.

The Abkhaz Question

Of the conflicts that have plagued Georgia since before its independence, the war with Abkhazia has clearly been the most severe and the most intractable. Before Georgia's independence, Abkhazia was an Autonomous Soviet Socialist Republic (ASSR), as was Ajaria but unlike South Ossetia whose status was only that of an Autonomous Oblast (Region, AO). The Abkhaz, while being Georgia's arguably most troublesome minority among the over 80 ethnic groups living in the country, was by no means the numerically most important. The Abkhaz numbered only 95,000 in Georgia, out of a total population of 5.4 million. Composing only 1.7 per cent of the population of Georgia in 1989, the Abkhaz lagged behind the Armenians (8.1 per cent), the Russians (6.3 per cent), the Azeris (5.7 per cent), the Ossetians (3 per cent) and even the Greeks (1.8 per cent). However, in contrast to all of these, the Abkhaz differed by being indigenous and not having a homeland anywhere else in the Union. This is also the nominal reason why, despite their insignificant numbers, the Abkhaz were the holders of an Autonomous Republic. Following this logic the Georgian Muslims were given the ASSR of Ajaria whereas the Ossetians were given an Autonomous Oblast only, as North Ossetia was seen as their motherland. The Abkhaz also perceived their status differently for another reason: Abkhazia did not form a part of Georgia at the time of the Soviet Union's formation. In fact, Abkhazia was Sovietized after a period of Menshevik rule in March 1921 as the Soviet Socialist Republic of Abkhazia, a signatory to the Soviet Union in its own right.[1] In 1922 Abkhazia entered the Transcaucasian Federative Republic as an entity associated with Georgia, a 'treaty republic'. This position was lost in 1931 when Abkhazia was reduced to the status of an autonomous republic of Georgia (which was still part of the Transcaucasian Federation), apparently on the orders of Stalin.[2] When the Transcaucasian Federation dissolved in 1936, Abkhazia was a part of the Georgian SSR. The Abkhaz see this as the successful result of Georgian aspirations to incorporate Abkhazia into itself, and as a long campaign of violation of Abkhazia's sovereign rights, aimed ultimately at the destruction of Abkhaz ethnic identity and assimilation of the Abkhaz into a Kartvelian (Georgian) identity.[3] In this context Stalin is often seen as representing the interests of his native Georgia, which supposedly made him negative about the demands of the Abkhaz.

During the Stalinist years, both Abkhazia and Georgia suffered from the destruction of their cultural and political elites.[4] Abkhazia further suffered from the overwhelming pressure of Georgian migration into the Autonomous Republic. Whereas other national minorities in the Soviet

Union were forced to adopt a Cyrillic alphabet, a Georgian alphabet was imposed on Abkhazia, and all native language schools were closed, as was the case in South Ossetia.[5] Hence the combined effect of the deportation of certain Abkhaz from their native lands in 1864, the massive influx of Georgians, and the perceived efforts to destroy Abkhaz culture and society had a traumatic effect, although the Abkhaz escaped the wholesale deportations of the second world war.[6] The demographic structure is in retrospect the most lasting aspect of this 'campaign': In 1886, the Abkhaz constituted 41 per cent of the population of their present-day territory – hence it must be noted that Abkhazia *has* always to a great extent been multi-ethnic. But the figure for 1926 is 27 per cent, despite the fact that the Abkhaz population doubled from 28,000 to 56,000 in this time. By 1959, however, the Abkhaz share plunged to 15 per cent, in absolute numbers increasing only by 10 per cent in 33 years, whereas the population of the territory doubled from 201,000 to 404,000 in the same time span. Since 1959, the Abkhaz have somewhat recovered, their population now growing relatively rapidly, but still constituting only 18 per cent of the population of the republic in 1989, 94,000 out of a total of 525,000.[7]

The controversies between Abkhaz and Georgians were suppressed during the Soviet era, but without much success. Disturbances took place in 1957 and 1967, but came out into the open in 1977 with the constitutional reform under Brezhnev. A letter signed by 130 Abkhaz intellectuals was sent to the USSR Supreme Soviet in 1977 protesting against the influx of Georgians, assimilationist policies including Georgianization in Schools, and economic exploitation.[8] A commission from Moscow arrived to assess the Abkhaz grievances, and endorsed some of them, forcing the Georgian government to admit that some of the claims were legitimate.[9] Georgia's then President Eduard Shevardnadze takes pride in having prevented ethnic bloodshed from erupting at the time. So some concessions were made, including the institution of a university in Sukhumi, the Abkhazian capital, and further cultural rights. Nevertheless there was no fundamental change, and Abkhazia's autonomy, in the view of one Abkhaz analyst, remained largely theoretical.[10] The Abkhaz later termed it a 'total fiction'[11]; however in the Soviet era the question is whether this was specific for Abkhazia or the norm for all autonomous areas. Indeed, the autonomy of Georgia itself vis-à-vis the Soviet leadership was hardly absolute. However, the Georgians (Mingrelians) who were the largest population group in Abkhazia, reacted against the given concessions, feeling that excessive privilege was given to the Abkhaz. Notably, this period was also that of a Moscow-based attack on the Georgian language.

Certain Georgian forces put forward an argument which challenged the Abkhaz being indigenous to their lands, claiming that they had settled there displacing Georgians that had lived in the area[12] – an argument that has little scientific grounding. It should be noted that despite their minority position the Abkhaz were, after the concessions of 1978, in a position to secure control of the republican administration and the local economy: 67 per cent of government ministers and 71 per cent of Obkom department heads were Abkhazian. Hence the ease with which the Abkhaz could later use the state apparatus of their ASSR for their secessionist aims despite their demographic weakness.[13]

Nevertheless, the Abkhaz were not satisfied and public unrest erupted in October 1978, with troops being sent in to quell demonstrations and a form of martial law was imposed in Abkhazia for a while.[14] In 1981 tensions came to a head in Tbilisi as well, as demonstrations against Abkhazian privileges were held. Nevertheless open conflict was averted by the very authoritarian system that the Soviet Union was at the time; harder suppression of expressions of nationalism by both Georgians and Abkhazians in the Autonomous Republic are reputed to have been enforced by the KGB.

With the Georgian national movement gaining strength in the late 1980s during the policies of Perestroika under Gorbachev, its emerging leader Zviad Gamsakhurdia had focused his campaign on the rights of the Georgians in Abkhazia and South Ossetia, and hence his rise to power meant a deterioration of relations between the Georgian government and the minorities. Virtually all minorities, including the Armenians, Azeris and Muslim Georgians of Ajaria protested the new policies of homogenization, Georgianization and Christianization of Georgia announced by the Gamsakhurdia regime, which became increasingly radical with time. As a result the Ossetians and Abkhaz, who had a quasi-state structure in their autonomous region around which they could mobilize the people, felt that remaining within an independent Georgia would be unthinkable, as it would mean the destruction of their autonomy and possibly their cultural rights. Other minorities, possessing no official structures, had considerably greater difficulties in defending their rights than the smaller, autonomous minorities with the actual state structures they possessed.

However the main problem was the total lack of the will to compromise on both sides. The Georgians viewed the Abkhaz and Ossetians only as a tool and instrument of Russia in its attempts to destabilize Georgia and prevent it from acceding to independence. Despite the fact that the claims of the minorities to linguistic and cultural rights were very similar to those voiced by the Georgians themselves, the Georgian nationalists never recognized the demands or claims from the Abkhaz or Ossetians as legitimate: they were seen as artificially created by Russia, without any domestic roots of their own.[15] This extreme interpretation of the minorities' demands was not improved by the fact that these demands often centred on the role of the Russian language. As the Russian language had gained an incomparably stronger status in the autonomous areas as compared to Georgia proper – a considerable number of Ossetians and Abkhaz actually declared Russian as their first language – this further accentuated Georgian suspicions of Russia's hand behind every minority act. Furthermore, Georgians saw the minorities as either 'immigrants' or 'guests on Georgian territory'. As such it follows that they should have no rights except those granted to them by the Georgian 'hosts'. The term 'immigrants' was used for the Ossetians and Russians in particular; even the Abkhaz were not always recognized as the autochtonous ethnic group they actually are. In some of the Georgian nationalist literature, which seems to have been influenced by a Stalinesque writing of history, the Abkhaz are described as an originally Georgian tribe, which nevertheless through history has become a mixture of Georgians and Circassians. As such they are not seen as an indigenous ethnic group.[16] Hence the Georgian nationalists seem never to have understood that the centrifugal forces they represented at the union level, through their attempts to break away from the Soviet Union, spurred the creation of other centrifugal forces on the republican level, in the shape of the autonomous minorities. In a sense, the problem in Georgia is a problem of double minority status, sometimes even extending to triple minority status. For example, Georgians were a minority in the Soviet Union; Ossetians were a minority in Georgia; and Georgians in turn were a minority in South Ossetia. This complicated situation led to a security dilemma on the part of the minorities. If the status quo reigning in the Soviet Union was to be displaced, the Abkhaz would face the question of their status in the new Georgian state. As they saw this prospect as less than encouraging, they opted for an attempt to remain within the Soviet Union. This would in turn amount to secession from Georgia, which prompted a security dilemma on the part of the Georgians of Abkhazia, who were similarly worried about their position in an Abkhazia no longer part of Georgia.

The existing tensions between Abkhazia and Georgia were exacerbated by Perestroika, as both Georgians and Abkhazians, in the words of one analyst, found opportunities to 'revindicate their respective claims to independence'.[17] In June 1988, 60 leading Abkhazians signed a letter to the Soviet leadership enumerating their grievances with Georgia.[18] In March 1989, a petition was organized by the same forum, demanding the reinstitution of the Abkhaz Republic as a union republic of the Soviet Union, which would amount to secession from Georgia. The proposal received support from large sections of the non-Abkhaz population of Abkhazia as well. Nevertheless ethnic unrest spread in Abkhazia, with clashes in the summer of 1989 leading to over a dozen dead and several hundred wounded.[19] In August 1990 Abkhazia's supreme Soviet, following the predicament of the petition two years earlier, took matters into its own hands. The supreme Soviet proclaimed Abkhazia a full union republic, hence seceding from Georgia. However Abkhazia left the option open to restructure its relations with Georgia on a federative basis, as had been the case until 1931.

The main catalyst of conflict was the March 1991 All-Union referendum on the Union Treaty proposed by Gorbachev. The Georgian leadership prohibited the country's population from taking part in this referendum; nevertheless the Abkhaz and South Ossetians, favourable towards the preservation of the Soviet Union, organized the referendum and voted overwhelmingly in favour of it. This move seems to have been less conditioned by a positive desire to be tied to Russia than to a belief that, within the federative Russian state, minorities had a better chance than within a Georgia perceived as increasingly chauvinistic. The Georgian government declared these referenda null and void, and proceeded to declare Georgia's independence in April 1991. In January Georgia had been declared an unitary state with no internal boundaries, hence implicitly abolishing the autonomous status of all three autonomous entities of the country. The Abkhaz, in this context, ruled out the possibility of remaining within an independent Georgian state, and open conflict became a fact. War came to South Ossetia in January, which for some time attracted most of the Georgian leadership's attention. Abkhazia was, for the time being, spared large-scale ethnic unrest. Nevertheless, in the words of Paul Henze, 'amateurish military adventurism on both sides exacerbated the situation to the point where mitigation became impossible'.[20]

For some time the Abkhaz leadership attempted to negotiate a solution with Tbilisi. In June 1992, Abkhazia's President Vladislav Ardzinba sent a draft treaty to the Georgian State Council in which a federative or confederative solution to the problem was suggested, which would have safeguarded Georgia's territorial integrity. However, this conciliatory step was rejected by the new Georgian leadership. Meanwhile tensions again rose amid unproductive talks.[21] Abkhazia retaliated in July by reinstating its 1925 constitution which defines Abkhazia as independent but 'united with the Soviet Socialist Republic of Georgia on the basis of a special union treaty'.[22] Hence Abkhazia in practice declared its independence, despite warnings from the Georgian population's representative Tamaz Nadare-ishvili, who held the post of deputy chairman of the Abkhaz parliament.[23] However Abkhazia did so in a less provocative way than either Nagorno-Karabakh or South Ossetia had done, as it left open the possibility of staying attached to a restructured Georgia.[24] Nevertheless Ardzinba declared Abkhazia would independently seek membership in the CIS.

All this occurred at a time when Georgian President Eduard Shevard-nadze was highly unpopular in western Georgia, perceived (incorrectly in retrospect) as an agent of Moscow selling out Georgia. In mid-July, he had been greeted with stone-throwers and crowds calling him 'Judas' in Senaki, west of Kutaisi.[25] However, Shevardnadze openly opposed a suppression of the Zviadists, as supporters of the former President Zviad Gamsakhurdia came to be called, and even tendered his resignation should the state council take such steps.[26] By the end of July, Ardzinba's rhetoric had heated up, and he claimed Abkhazia was 'strong enough to fight Georgia' should that be necessary – indicating promises of outside support.[27] Meanwhile the very legality of the Abkhazian declaration of sovereignty was questionable. A quorum of two thirds of the total membership was needed for such a decision, which had not been the case as a simple majority had been present and voting.[28]

The Georgian response came on 14 August, in the form of military action led by Tengiz Kitovani, then defence minister and leader of a major paramilitary formation turned Georgia's national guard, and one of the men behind the coup against Gamsakhurdia. Kitovani apparently acted without Shevardnadze's explicit approval – who claimed not to have sanctioned such action.[29] In any case the Georgian forces advanced through Mingrelia, on the pretext of searching for a government minister kidnapped by Zviadists who the state council said had been taken to Abkhazia. As a result the forces advanced on Sukhumi and shelled the parliament, forcing the Abkhaz leadership to retreat to Gudauta in the Northwest of the republic.[30] Sukhumi was taken on 18 August. However at this point the retreating Abkhaz forces found support from the North, as North Caucasian volunteers, mainly Circassians and Chechens, came to their rescue.[31] The volunteers acted on behalf of the Confederation of Mountain Peoples of the Caucasus, of which Abkhazia was a member; Sukhumi had even been the seat of the organization.[32]

By early September, the intervention of Boris Yeltsin had led to a tripartite cease-fire agreement, also signed by Shevardnadze and Ardzinba which proved to be abortive; Shevardnadze's fragile position became obvious as Kitovani refused to retreat, and the Abkhaz took this as their pretext to embark on a reconquest of Abkhazia. The Abkhaz were very displeased with the agreement, which stipulated the deployment of Georgian forces in Abkhazia; hence only a pretext was necessary now that the Abkhaz felt strengthened by outside support. In a matter of weeks the Georgian forces were pushed back, with the assistance of Russian units, to the Abkhaz side, in particular air force units bombing Georgian positions.[33] On 1 October, the joint Abkhaz and North Caucasian forces launched an offensive on the city of Gagra, in Northwesternmost Abkhazia, which had been controlled by Georgian forces. This offensive led to the establishment of Abkhaz control over the strategic Abkhaz-Russian border. The interesting fact was that the Abkhaz troops were armed with T-72 tanks, Grad rocket launchers, and other heavy equipment that they had not previously possessed.[34] This heavy arsenal, which came to the rescue of the Abkhaz seemingly out of nowhere, was the first and primary cause of Georgian suspicions of Russian assistance to the Abkhaz rebels. The fact that over a hundred thousand landmines were laid during the war was another factor in proving Russian military support to Abkhazia, as there were simply no such amounts of armoury in the region.[35] The Russian factor became increasingly evident as unmarked Sukhoi fighter planes started bombarding the still Georgian-controlled Abkhazian capital Sukhumi, despite the fact that the Abkhaz possessed no air force at all. Abkhaz and Russian sources claim these raids were replies to Georgian bombardment of the (highly important) Russian military laboratory in Eshera, Abkhazia.[36] It is also necessary to note that the downing of a Russian helicopter by a surface-to-air missile emanating from Georgian-controlled territory – the helicopter was downed while evacuating refugees – was a key event which radicalized the Russian military in the conflict.[37]

Initially Russian support seems not to have been sanctioned at the highest echelons of power. For instance, during Yeltsin's intervention in early September, inviting Shevardnadze and Ardzinba to Moscow, the Russian President made it clear that Russia desired the preservation of the Georgian state, although he criticized Shevardnadze for deploying heavy arms against the Abkhaz. Nevertheless Russian involvement became increasingly obvious during the course of war.

During the winter, fighting temporarily died out. But by late February, bombing of Georgian-controlled Sukhumi gathered momentum, and Georgian forces shelled the Abkhaz stronghold Gudauta in response.[38] As the Georgian forces went on the offensive, they were soon countered by heavily-reinforced Abkhaz troops. The Abkhaz in fact rolled back the Georgian offensive and neared Sukhumi by mid-March.[39] Abkhaz forces incurred heavy losses in their attempts to seize Sukhumi and a cease-fire was agreed in Moscow on 15 May.[40] The cease-fire soon broke down as the Abkhaz continued their attempts to seize Tkvarcheli and Sukhumi. By June, both Tkvarcheli and Sukhumi were under Abkhaz siege, and the evacuation of civilians was undertaken, after diplomatic efforts.[41] The Abkhaz initiated another offensive in early July, in which Shevardnadze was nearly killed by an Abkhaz artillery shell.[42] Military observers deemed that over a thousand people were killed on the Georgian side in the first days of July, as the Abkhaz drive to capture the Ochamchira-Sukhumi road supplying the Georgian forces in Sukhumi intensified[43]. On 6 July Shevardnadze declared Martial Law in Abkhazia.[44] The Abkhaz forces then succeeded in cutting off the Ochamchira-Sukhumi road, and finally surrounded Sukhumi by 9 July.[45] Shevardnadze escaped death a second time as his headquarters were shelled on the same day, but pledged to stay with what he termed 'the heroic defenders of the city'. However, a Georgian counter-offensive was successful in preventing the Abkhaz from taking the city.

In the last days of July, a fragile cease-fire was reached through Russian mediation, the so-called Sochi agreement.[46] The agreement provided for the withdrawal of Georgian troops from Abkhazia, demilitarization of both sides, and the return of a 'legal government' to Abkhazia, the composition of which would be determined later. Russia took the role of guarantor of the agreement. As a result, Georgian heavy weaponry was shipped from the Sukhumi to the port of Poti further south on the Black Sea coast. The Abkhaz weapons, on the other hand, were stored near the front and were returned to the Abkhaz by Russian 'safekeepers' when hostilities restarted. To make matters worse for the Georgians, the cease-fire led to great disappointment among large parts of the population. In Mingrelia, this led to an upsurge of support for the Zviadists, and Gamsakhurdia reappeared on the political scene to 'reclaim' his position as head of state. A third of the Georgian troops fighting in Abkhazia went over to the Zviadists, who moreover took control over the weapons that arrived to the port of Poti from Sukhumi. The Zviadists explicitly tried to prevent the withdrawal of Georgian forces from Abkhazia, and captured several towns in Northwestern Georgia, including Senaki. As the Zviadist military challenge to Shevardnadze's government became stronger, the temptation to act became irresistible to the Abkhaz; indeed, the Zviadists presented the Abkhaz with a window of opportunity that few belligerents are given. Hence, in September, during a bout of intra-Georgian turmoil, the Abkhaz launched an offensive on 16 September and captured Ochamchira. On the 25th, Abkhaz forces surrounded Sukhumi, cut off the Georgian supply routes to the city at the Kodori river 25 km south of the city, and successively tightened the stranglehold.[47] By the following day, the Abkhaz had come within a few kilometres from the residence of Shevardnadze, who had come to lead its defence but was forced to escape by helicopter. Sukhumi was in the hands of the Abkhaz.[48] Yeltsin initially condemned the Abkhaz for breaking the cease-fire; however Grachev's statements displayed a totally different perception of events. Grachev claimed that only the 'immediate withdrawal' of all Georgian troops in Abkhazia could bring an end to the conflict.[49] As a result of the capture of Sukhumi, Abkhazia's whole territory gradually came under the control of the Abkhaz leadership, as Ochamchira and Gali fell only days later.[50] Russia 'condemned' Abkhazia and instigated economic sanctions on it, but did not step in to disengage the belligerents.[51] Most Georgians that lived on the territory of Abkhazia were forcibly evicted in a systematic campaign of looting and ethnic cleansing,[52] and UN observers have concluded that all sides were guilty of substantial Human Rights violations.[53]

Nevertheless Georgia's troubles were not over. The Zviadists now moved to capture the strategic port city of Poti as well as Samtredia near Kutaisi, and blocked food supplies to Tbilisi;[54] fighting approached the second city of Georgia, the Zviadists being only 20 km away on 20 October.[55] Russia made it bluntly clear that Georgia's problems would continue until and unless the country entered the CIS and accepted Russian troops on its territory. The Zviadists now threatened Kutaisi and seemed to plan an attack on Tbilisi itself.[56] As Shevardnadze was forced to accept Russia's *de facto* ultimatum (on 8 and 9 October respectively) with the prospect of Tbilisi starving and Georgia's complete disintegration nearing, Russian offered its assistance in a 'neutral military operation'.[57] This military assistance led to military advances in Mingrelia during October and November. Samtredia was taken back on 23 October, Senaki on 1 November, Poti on 3 November and Zugdidi three days later.[58] Zviad Gamsakhurdia fled to Abkhazia, but died in mysterious circumstances in a remote village in western Georgia in the final days of 1993. Most analysts believe he committed suicide, although the truth may never be known.

Fighting in Abkhazia ebbed out by the end of September, resulting in Abkhaz control over almost all of the Abkhaz ASSR's territory. The only exception was the Kodori Gorge in the east of Abkhazia as well as isolated areas in the Gali region. In fact over 70,000 Georgians left Abkhazia along the Kalasuri river through the Kodori gorge, into Svaneti and greater Georgia. Nevertheless Georgian forces kept control over parts of the area until March 1994, when the Abkhaz initiated a well-planned operation forcing the Georgian forces to escape through the gorge. The border area is populated by Svans, who captured many of the weapons the retreating Georgian forces were carrying; they also prevented and still prevent the Abkhaz forces from entering the Kodori valley. In fact, the Svans seem to control the region without much concern for the wishes of Tbilisi.[59]

A Russian-brokered cease-fire came into effect in late October 1993, which has endured with the exceptions of the above-mentioned fighting in the Kodori gorge; the renewed fighting in May 1998; and continuous terrorist activities on both sides that have been accentuated during 1998. It provided for the interposition of a 'CIS' peacekeeping force along a natural cease-fire line that would follow the Inguri river.[60] Buffer zones were created on both sides with only police units allowed in a 12-kilometre wide zone – only personal weapons would be allowed there. Beyond this zone, there is also a heavy weapons restricted zone.[61] Such rules have nevertheless been circumvented by both parties. In April 1994 an interim peace agreement was reached, which 'established general procedures for movement toward a political settlement'.[62]

The war led to perhaps 10,000 deaths. Beyond this, the hardest toll was borne by the Georgians that were systematically cleansed from mainly the Gali region in Abkhazia. This group of perhaps 200,000 people were subjected to a form of ethnic cleansing best described by the words of a UN official visiting Gali in early 1994, calling the area 'an empty desert'.[63] The presence of these refugees – or internally displaced persons, officially – can be felt by any visitor to Tbilisi; most noticeably through the fact that the once-famous hotel Iveria in central Tbilisi is now home to a large group of refugees.

The Abkhaz leadership under Ardzinba emerged strengthened from the war. With initial Russian support, Ardzinba installed an autocratic regime. The republic's infrastructure was heavily destroyed by the war, and the Abkhazian state's income sources, and especially sources of hard currency, have been very few. What helped the Ardzinba regime, nevertheless, was Abkhazia's socio-economic structure. Abkhazia is often described as a heaven on earth, where almost everything can be cultivated without much labour. As a result the regime does not need to import food; Abkhazia is self-sufficient in these terms. This is also true for electricity: several hydroelectric plants exist, and the population enjoys far better supplies of electricity than Tbilisi, for example. These factors have helped the isolated Ardzinba regime to stay in power without much opposition. It has also inhibited the settlement of the conflict as the Abkhaz leadership is not pressed domestically, to any considerable extent, to find a speedy resolution to the conflict.

The Northwestern Caucasus

Since the dissolution of the Soviet Union, the neighbouring republics of Karachaevo-Cherkessia and Kabardino-Balkaria have emerged as one of the potential trouble spots in the North Caucasus. There is a multiplicity of controversies in this region, primarily caused by the territorial delimitation of the North Caucasus in the 1920s and 1930s. Tensions exist between the indigenous peoples of the region, as well as a shared deep-rooted hostility towards Russia and the Moscow government. None of the conflicts have escalated but rather remain on low fire, occasionally stirred up by individuals and movements who find this to be in their interest. The region as a whole is volatile, located as it is between Abkhazia in the west, and Chechnya and the troublesome Prigorodniy district of North Ossetia in the east. At the same time there is clearly room for compromise and cooperation, especially as, despite their differences, there is no history of open conflict between the population groups and at base there is a common Caucasian identity which if emphasized can decrease the potential for conflict in the region.

The west-central part of the North Caucasus is inhabited by two groups of peoples. The first, the indigenous Circassian peoples, composed of the Adyge, (having their own republic centred on Maikop) the Kabardins and the Cherkess. The Circassian languages are divided by linguists into a western and an eastern family. The western is spoken by Adyge and Cherkess, while the eastern dialect is spoken by the Kabardins. The dialects are mutually intelligible, considered to be part of the same language.[64] Once a numerous and strong people, the Circassians now number less than 700,000 in the Caucasus, with a large Diaspora in Turkey and in the Middle East estimated at one million. The Kabardins are the largest of the subdivisions, numbering almost 400,000.

The second group, the Karachai and Balkars, live in the high valleys of the central North Caucasus, speak a common language, part of the Kipchak family of Turkic languages. They came to the mountain areas they presently inhabit in the thirteenth century, and number around 250,000, the Karachai being roughly twice as numerous as the Balkars.[65]

Throughout history, the Kabardins have been considered the most pro-Russian of all Muslim Caucasian mountaineers, and their feudal elite was co-opted to a great extent by the Russians during their conquest of the Caucasus.[66] The western Circassian tribes are substantially more anti-Russian in their attitudes than the Kabardins.[67] Islam is, generally speaking, stronger among the Karachai-Balkars than among the Circassians, particularly after the deportations. The position of the Qadiriya brotherhoods, which were imported from Chechen-Ingushetia, is strong. The Karachai-Balkars are also substantially more anti-Russian than the Circassians, to a large extent as a result of the second world war events.

The two groups roughly inhabit the same area, which since the 1920s is divided into two autonomous units within the Russian Federation: the Karachai-Cherkess and the Kabardino-Balkar republics. It is interesting to note that this division cuts across the ethnic divisions. As the Circassians typically live to the north, and the Karachai-Balkar in the mountainous south of both republics, it would actually have been possible to create two ethnically homogeneous, and in this sense potentially more stable units: for instance, a Karachai-Balkar and a Kabardino-Cherkess republic. Instead, Stalin's *divide et impera* policies saw fit to create two ethnically heterogeneous units. This naturally created trouble for the future; however the policies did not stop at this. The northern boundaries of these units was drawn further north than the territories actually populated by the Caucasian peoples. This led to the inclusion of heavily Slavic-populated areas; the situation was not improved by the fact that these Slavs were mostly Cossacks (especially in Karachai-Cherkessia) – having age-old animosities with the Muslims to the south. Hence the situation is that the Turkic side forms a plurality in Karachai-Cherkessia, and the Circassian in Kabardino-Balkaria. According to the 1989 population census, the demographic structure of the two republics was as follows:

Table 1: The Ethnic Composition of the Northwestern Caucasus

Republic	Karachai/ Balkar	Circassians	Russians	Others
Karachai-Cherkessia	31%	9.6% Cherkess 6.5% Abaza	42.5%	10.4%
Kabardino-Balkaria	9%	48%	32%	11%

Relations between the Karachai-Balkars and the Circassian peoples have been historically tumultuous – particularly due to the fact that the former were the vassals of the Kabardin nobility from the fifteenth century onwards.[68] On top of this lies the same distinction between foothillers and mountaineers that can be observed elsewhere, for instance in neighbouring North Ossetia and Ingushetia. The Kabardins, in particular, with their history of nobility and being one of the most advanced Caucasian peoples, look down upon the Balkars as inferior and primitive.[69] The Balkars, to be sure, have a generally lower level of education – which is no wonder given the disruption of the deportations. Nevertheless, it should be noted that there is no particular contentious issue of the magnitude of the Prigorodniy raion, which could escalate into conflict. However, that certain territories are disputed is a problem, mainly territories inhabited exclusively by Balkars before the deportations but now mixed, as the Balkars at their return were not resettled in their ancestral lands but in other parts of the republic. In the case of a division of the republic, these territories could become a conflictual issue.

Although these republics, in the words of one analyst, are 'situated in a region where conflicts rage with double the usual power, and there is a mountain "honour code" linking families, clans and regions in ways that supersede administrative divisions',[70] interethnic relations have on the whole been relatively harmonious. Even in the aftermath of the return of the Karachai and Balkars from deportation in Central Asia, these peoples have been able to live together without serious problems, and mixed marriages have not been uncommon.[71] At present, tensions exist on two fronts: between the two groups on the one hand, somewhat united, and the Cossacks on the other; and between the Turkic peoples and the Circassians on the other. Hence two potential conflicts exist, each of which falls into one of our two categories outlined above.

The Cossacks settled down in the area during the wars of the nine-teenth century, having been used by the centre as a form of watchdog over the Muslim peoples.[72] Recent discussions in Moscow about giving Cossack paramilitaries a semi-official status have prompted strong outcries from the side of the Muslim population. However it is clear that the Russian government is returning to its traditional policy of using the Cossacks as a tool and ally in the North Caucasus. In 1993 already some Cossack units were made part of the Russian armed forces. The same year, tensions rose in Karachai-Cherkessia as Cossacks were blamed for pig carcasses being put in Mosques; Cossack units even patrolled the streets at night.[73] The Cossacks' mobilization was prompted by the decrease of Russian influence in the Caucasus since the late 1980s and by the parallel process of increasing national consciousness of the Muslim peoples. The Cossacks fear a division of the Karachai-Cherkess republic into Karachai and Cherkess units, a division which would divide also the Cossack settlements. Such a development is feared as the Cossacks are afraid of discrimination on both historical and present grounds; instead the Cossacks would like to have their *stanitsy* (settlements) ruled from neighbouring Krasnodar, a Russian provincial centre.[74]

The possibility is not excluded that Russia is using the Cossacks as a lever against separatism on the art of the Karachai and the Cherkess.[75] According to this logic, the spectre of Cossack rebellion, possibly supported by Moscow, would deter the Muslim population from making their separatist claims more vocal. The Cossacks of northern Chechnya, for example, are encouraged by Moscow in their campaign to detach two districts from the semi-independent republic and join them to Russia.[76]

The present tensions between the Karachai/Balkars and the Kabardins/Cherkess exist in several dimensions. Basically, the main problem is the wish of certain groups in all communities to detach their people from the present administrative structure and form new, ethnically (more) homogeneous units. Such claims naturally have territorial implications, as no ethnically 'clean' division can be made of either of the two republics due to the overlapping settlement patterns.

The Karachai, led by a national movement named *Jamagat*, began lobbying for a division of their Autonomous Oblast in 1988. The centre answered by raising the status of the region to an ASSR; however the Karachai, in their quest for full territorial rehabilitation, saw a republic of their own – which they had enjoyed from 1926 to 1943 – as the only possible solution.[77] By 1990, the Cherkess had formed their own movement, called *Adygey-Khasa*, which defended the integrity of Karachai-Cherkessia, being anti-Russian rather than anti-Karachai in nature. A referendum held in 1992 showed that over 75 per cent of the population desires to retain a unified republic, hence proving that the Karachai demands had lost their following.[78] Many Karachai now see the possibility of a future majority position in an unified republic as more favourable than a smaller Karachai republic. Higher birthrates and limited Russian emigration may make this possible within a not too distant future.[79] At the time of writing, two developments deserve mention: first of all, there seems to be a regime change under way in Karachaevo-Cherkessia. Vladimir Khubiev, the incumbent president of the republic, has never been elected to the post but appointed to head of administration in 1979. Defying a supreme court ruling of April 1997, Khubiev is trying to cling to power and postpone elections.[80] By January 1998, Khubiev was the only non-elected republic leader, and public protests had emerged against the leadership, a new phenomenon in the republic.[81] Sixty thousand signatures have been collected to force elections by June 1998.[82] Secondly, the Karachai are now moving into the political sphere. A former army general and commander of Russia's ground forces, Vladimir Semenov after his resignation from the army announced his interest in running for president. This was greeted with enthusiasm from the people, as high-ranking military officers in general enjoy respect in the North Caucasus. In particular, members of deported nationalities reaching general's rank are seen with admiration as their origins were generally to their detriment in the Soviet army. Jokhar Dudayev, and to a certain extent Ruslan Aushev in Ingushetia, are examples of high-ranking officers who managed to rally their people around them; Beppayev has the potential to do the same among the Balkar. If Semenov does achieve a leading post in the republic, this could mean yet another leader hostile to Moscow and positive towards Chechnya in power in the North Caucasus.[83] For the time being however, both Karachaevo-Cherkessia and Kabardino-Balkaria are ruled by the Soviet-era nomenklatura, which explains the governmental submissiveness toward Moscow of both republics.

In Kabardino-Balkaria, it is again the Turkic people with their history of deportation which are most vocal. Whereas the Kabardins' political aims are restricted to more autonomy from Moscow and a proportional rather than equal distribution of political power with the Balkars,[84] (most political power is presently shared on a one-to-one basis) presently the Balkars seem to be the most determined trouble-makers of the two republics. Already heavily inferior in number to the Kabardins, the Balkars fear that the demographic changes in the republic, with lower growth of the Russian population than the natives, coupled with Russian emigration, will actually give the Kabardins a majoritarian position in the republic, something which by now (nine years since the last Soviet census) may very well be the case. The Balkars, just like the Karachai, claim full territorial rehabilitation, and some seem to envisage a separate Balkar republic, or at least a federative structure of the republic. The Balkars complain about being the 'poorest segment of the population of the republic', and the fact that all major political posts are held by Kabardins.[85] The primary claim of the Balkars nevertheless concerns certain territorial districts which before the deportations were inhabited by Balkars, but are now disputed by both peoples.[86] Simmering tensions first emerged in 1991, when a first Balkar Congress declared the creation of a Balkar republic which would remain in a federalized Kabardino-Balkaria. However, a referendum among Balkars showed a surprisingly low level of support for such demands, and the question lost its momentum.

Balkar grievances once again came out into the open in November 1996, when a congress of the Balkar people voted to establish a sovereign republic of Balkaria, requesting the Russian presidency to establish direct presidential rule in the region until necessary institutions were formed.[87]

The congress elected a former commander of the Transcaucasus Military District, Sufyan Beppayev, as chairman of the new Balkar state council. The Kabardin president of Kabardino-Balkaria quickly declared the decision unconstitutional, accusing the Balkar delegates of 'unbridled nationalist extremism' and of 'flagrantly flouting' the constitution of the republic.[88] Criminal proceedings were opened against the initiators by the procurator's office of the republic, while the central ministry of justice, while taking the matter quite easily, confirmed the unconstitutionality of the act. The situation was not improved, however, by the fact that the congress formed a 'Balkar ministry of internal affairs', which pledged to organize self-defence detachments in Balkar communities. These events took place only a week before the final date of submission of documents for the presidential elections in the republic, and should be seen as a political manifestation in light of this. As the Beppayev clique realized that their following was still low, Beppayev distanced himself from the earlier remarks.[89] The incumbent President, Valery Kokov, was the only candidate, and ran unopposed (which is by itself unconstitutional) in the elections which were held on 12 January.[90] Although the elections themselves took place without any misfortunes, at this point the situation in the republic does not seem to be very stable, as a bomb blast occurred four days before the election in the parliament building of the republic. No one was injured, but this event indicated the existence of political unrest.[91]

The west-central part of the North Caucasus, then, seems to be a place where the potential for further unrest is high. Certain elements in the two republics, especially among the Karachai and Balkar communities, are trying to stir up a conflict. This fact is largely due to their resentments from the time of deportations, with claims to rehabilitation that often impact upon the rights and territories of other communities, in this case the Circassians with which they have a historical uneasy relationship.

Then again, it is difficult to estimate the actual popular base of these demands. Referenda that have been held in the republics demonstrate one clear fact: the overwhelming majority of all the four peoples desire the preservation of the status quo. Furthermore, the spectre of Chechnya, and to a lesser degree of the Prigorodniy conflict, will probably keep some calm in the North Caucasus for some time; however this is valid only for the short term. And initial responses from Moscow on the unrest in Kabardino-Balkaria unfortunately do not seem to differ from past trends. As in other parts of the Caucasus, nothing positive is to be expected from Moscow. The potential of conflict in the two republics can be described as latent but not acute. It is possible that the Circassians and Karachai-Balkar peoples will continue living together – or rather side by side – with only minor disturbances; on the other hand, the ease with which tensions have escalated into conflict in other parts of the Caucasus does not look promising. One notable fact, however, is that both of these peoples are Muslim; and in the post-Soviet Caucasus, no serious conflict has so far pitted one Muslim people against another. Whether this is a variable to be reckoned with or a mere coincidence, however, remains to be seen.

The South Ossetian Question

South Ossetia, as opposed to Abkhazia, is by Soviet standards a territory with a substantial titular population. The South Ossetians formed just over two thirds of their AO's population in 1989, roughly 65,000 out of a population of 98,000. However, only 40 per cent of the Ossetians in Georgia lived within the South Ossetian AO; there were almost a hundred thousand Ossetians scattered in other regions of Georgia. As a result, the potential for fighting in South Ossetia was similar to that of Abkhazia: a comparatively small minority which, however, had ethnic brethren in the North Caucasus. The disturbances which came to a point in 1989 developed within a relatively short period of time. In November 1988, a law strengthening the position of the Georgian language in the entire territory of Georgia was enacted.[92] This can be seen as the preparatory stage in a 'war of laws' which began in earnest in the fall of 1989.[93] In the spring of 1989, the leader of the Ossetian popular front, the *Ademon Nykhas*, addressed an open letter to the Abkhaz people, supporting their secessionist claims. Isolated instances of violence started erupting in South Ossetia, and guerrilla attacks by both Ossetian and Georgian armed bands were reported in July, although the reliability of these reports is questionable. Many of them may have been spread by radical elements in order to fuel tensions. Nevertheless polarization was not total at this point; the *Ademon Nykhas* and the *Ilia Chavchavadze Society* made a joint statement calling on Ossetians and Georgians not to fall for extremism.[94]

In August, measures were taken to make Georgian the sole official language for use in public life.[95] Such a provision would have affected South Ossetia – where only 14 per cent of Ossetians knew Georgian – to a higher degree than Ajaria and Abkhazia, given South Ossetia's lower status in the hierarchy of autonomy. In early September, Ossetian authorities proposed giving equal status to Russian, Ossetian and Georgian in the Oblast; by the end of the month the Oblast Soviet decided to institute Ossetian as the state language of the region. This clearly marks the fact that September was the month in which the conflict escalated. In particular, it was in September that the movement for unification with North Ossetia gained strength. The *Ademon Nykhas* sent a petition to Moscow asking for the unification of North and South Ossetia. Excerpts of the appeal are quoted as follows:

> It seems to us politically and economically absurd that within the framework of a democratic state the small Ossetian people should be divided into two administrative units; and we demand that the question of the unification of North and South Ossetia be examined at the CPSU Central Committee Plenum on nationality questions.[96]

By late September, tensions had mounted to such a level that additional MVD troops were brought in to secure order. Inter-ethnic clashes began to erupt despite attempts to calm the situation, and on 10 November the Oblast Soviet demanded that South Ossetia be upgraded to an Autonomous Republic. Less than a week later, Georgia declared its right to veto all-Union laws, as well as affirming Georgia's right to secede from the union. This clearly exacerbated the tensions in South Ossetia. During Autumn 1989, inter-ethnic clashes left several dead, mainly Georgians, in the region.[97] What can be called the first stage of the conflict lasted from November 1989 to January 1990, and was prompted by the 'March on Tskhinvali' organized by Gamsakhurdia and Gumbaridze on 23 November, under the pretext of defending the Georgian majority population of the city.[98] The march was joined by between 12,000 and 15,000 people, but was met by an Ossetian mob while trying to enter Tskhinvali from the south. An armed clash was only prevented by armoured forces of the Soviet ministry of interior, which had been called in at the request of the South Ossetian Oblast Soviet, and which prevented the Georgian mob from entering the city. In the following two days, instances of inter-ethnic rioting led to the death of six people, and the injury of an additional 140.[99] Gamsakhurdia then pledged to drive out the entire Ossetian population of the region, and the first clashes erupted in villages on the outskirts of Tskhinvali.[100] Clashes went on until January 1990, when intra-Georgian feuding seems to have been the main reason for the calming of tensions.

In the first half of 1990, the situation remained tense, although a certain stability seems to have been reigning. In April 1990, the Supreme Soviet of the USSR enacted a law which generally enhanced the position of autonomous regions and republics vis-à-vis the central government. This law had the effect of increasing the polarization between the nationalist leadership of Georgia against the autonomies on Georgian soil, as it entailed the increased identification, in Georgian eyes, of the interests of the minorities with the interests of Moscow. In August, the Georgian law banning regional parties from the upcoming elections was enacted, and was instrumental in disrupting the delicate stability which had been building. The South Ossetian Supreme Soviet countered this move in mid-September by unilaterally upgrading its status, defining South Ossetia as an 'Independent Soviet Democratic Republic'. The Georgian parliament immediately revoked the decision, but the upcoming Georgian elections distracted the Georgian leadership from dealing with South Ossetia imme-diately. The elections were boycotted by South Ossetia as well as Abkhazia. When elections to the Supreme Soviet of the 'new' South Osse-tian republic were held in early December 1990, Gamsakhurdia turned his back on the declaration he had made that Abkhazia and South Ossetia would retain their autonomy – however he had shown intentions to revoke Ajaria's autonomy from the start, as will be seen below. Thus two days after the South Ossetian elections, the Georgian Supreme Soviet abolished the South Ossetian Autonomous Oblast on 11 December, instituting a state of emergency the next day in what was now called, the "Tskhinvali and Dzhava regions".[101] Simultaneously Georgia initiated a blockade on South Ossetia, which would last until July 1992, whereas USSR MVD troops were sent to secure order.[102] The response from Moscow came in early January, with Gorbachev annulling both the South Ossetian and Georgian decisions to alter the Oblasts' status. However, Moscow had obviously lost its ability to support its words with action, as it took none even when Georgia refused to comply, because Moscow's decision was considered a gross interference in internal Georgian affairs.

In early 1991, the Soviet military forces, present in South Ossetia despite Georgian protests, contributed to keeping the conflict down. This despite the fact that Torez Kulumbegov, chairman of South Ossetia's Supreme Soviet, was arrested during talks with Georgian authorities. As in the case of Abkhazia, the March all-union referendum took place in South Ossetia, and led to an equally resounding 'aye' as in Abkhazia – 99 per cent of the vote was in favour of the Soviet Union's continued existence – predictably, as those opposed to it obeyed the Government's boycott of the vote. Similarly, Ossetia refused to take part in the Georgian referendum on independence, as South Ossetia obviously no longer considered itself a part of Georgia. These developments contributed to the escalation of tensions. Ossetians complained of being evicted from villages around Tskhinvali; Georgians were complaining of similar practices by Ossetians. According to Alexei Zverev, the fighting on the Georgian side was done mainly by members of the Merab Kostava Society, allied to Gamsakhurdia, most of whose membership consisted of Georgian residents of South Ossetia. They were opposed by Ossetian self-defence forces which had rapidly organized.[103]

In any case Tskhinvali's Georgian population gradually began leaving South Ossetia, leading to accusations of ethnic cleansing. However, the refugee flow was not limited to Georgians. As low-intensity conflict plagued the enclave, the outflow of Georgians was accompanied by a flux of Ossetians to North Ossetia, variously estimated at between 30,000 and 100,000 people. These mainly included those Ossetians that lived in Georgia proper.[104] By mid-1991, the Georgians were bombarding the South Ossetian capital with artillery, in a manner intended to force the population to flee. In November, a series of hostage-takings took place, and Tskhinvali was surrounded by Georgian troops, which seemed poised to 'resolve' the question once and for all. The South Ossetian leadership declared full mobilization and a full-scale clash was prevented, as in many other instances in Georgia, by internal dissent in Tbilisi at the end of December.[105] The consequences for South Ossetia had this not happened can only be guessed at, but it is clear that had it not been for the internal Georgian problems, the conflict in South Ossetia would not have been recalled as the 'mildest' of the three conflicts in the Transcaucasus.

Meanwhile, Zviad Gamsakhurdia's position had become increasingly threatened as his presidency developed. To a great extent this was caused by his own erratic behaviour, his failure to manage the economic transition, and most of all his autocratic tendencies. In the words of Stephen Jones,

> Gamsakhurdia's other characteristics were a sense of paranoia, a conspiratorial frame of mind, virulent anti-communism, and a tendency to self-glorification. ... Gamsakhurdia viewed himself as the last in a long line of Georgian national heroes, all of whom, in his words, have embodied sacrifices on the altar of the fatherland. The struggle for Gamsakhurdia was between 'good and evil'. ... Comparing himself to de Gaulle, Gamsakhurdia argued that a strong presidency corresponded to the 'historical laws and characteristics' of the Georgian people.[106]

Gamsakhurdia's autocracy was then related to a perception of a need for strong governance for the fulfilment of independence. Ghia Nodia has placed this contention in the Georgian context in the following way:

> The rise of independence as a viable political project also put into question its putative harmony with democracy. Two opposing attitudes began to develop. One viewed democracy as an ultimate goal, but ranked it second behind independence. According to this way of thinking, a nation had to lay a solid basis

for its independence before it could build democracy. Until Georgia secured its territorial integrity and established a free enterprise system, it might be wise temporarily to prefer strong autocratic rule. Another view held that while Georgia could not be democratic without being independent, this did not imply that democracy was less important than independence. Democracy was not a kind of luxury to be achieved in the distant future: the way to democracy should be democratic too.[107]

Gamsakhurdia decimated democratic governance through a number of actions. For example, changing local government from being locally elected to centrally appointed prefectures; his ban on the communist party after the failed coup in Moscow of August 1991; or the break-up of an opposition demonstration by police the next month.[108] In retrospect, however, it is hard to disagree with observers like Nodia who feel that Gamsakhurdia's practical 'authoritarianism' was limited: 'it was his style more than his actions which gave him the image of a dictator'.[109] His main drawback was his equation of any opposition with KGB agents; Gamsakhurdia's evident identification of Georgia with himself led to the interpretation of almost everyone who disagreed with him as a traitor to the country. This in turn led to most of Gamsakhurdia's erstwhile allies turning against him and joining the opposition, which, it must be noted, was no more courteous in its attitudes and discourse than the president himself. In late 1991, the opposition had radicalized to a degree where civil war emerged, between armed formations led by Ioseliani and Kitovani and the government. Gamsakhurdia was forced to flee the capital in January, eventually being granted political asylum in Jokhar Dudayev's Chechnya. This time of turmoil was used by the Ossetian leadership to organize a referendum on 19 January, in which over 90 per cent of the voters expressed their wish to join Russia. This referendum received a mixed response in Russia, with some factions seeing it as a popular choice worthy of being supported – particularly as it suited the interests of the 'war party' in Moscow – and others seeing it as a complicating factor.[110]

The new Georgian regime, led by Shevardnadze since March 1992, initially seemed to adopt a more conciliatory stance vis-à-vis South Ossetia. In any case, Shevardnadze's advent to power, as in the case of Abkhazia, was thought to be instrumental in calming tensions. Whatever Shevardnadze's actual intentions were, he was never able to make them materialize. The new Georgian government showed signs of a conciliatory policy, with Shevardnadze visiting Vladikavkaz as well as Tskhinvali. There was also a decrease of hostilities in the early months of 1992 while the 'State Council', led by shady figures including Ioseliani, Kitovani, and

Tengiz Sigua, was establishing itself in power. A temporary cease-fire agreement was signed in May; however the calming of tensions seems to have been equally due to the Georgian forces loyal to the state council being busy with the civil war against the Zviadists (followers of Gamsakhurdia) who had staged an uprising in Mingrelia and parts of Abkhazia. In any case Shevardnadze soon proved unable to control the diffuse paramilitary forces which formed the Georgian army, loyal only to their respective leaders.[111] Hence, fighting re-emerged within a few months, with Georgian artillery attacks on Tskhinval picking up speed starting from late April; and as a busload of Ossetian refugees were massacred later in May, the situation continued to worsen.

At this point, several external factors intervened, which threatened to regionalize the South Ossetian-Georgian confrontation. These were the Russian, North Ossetian, and North Caucasian factors. Russian hardliners, including the speaker of the Russian parliament, Ruslan Khasbulatov (a Chechen) and vice-president Aleksandr Rutskoi, made harsh statements against the Georgian government, using terminology which defined the South Ossetians as Russian citizens, thereby implicitly recognizing South Ossetia's accession to Russia. While Yeltsin sought negotiated solutions, Russian helicopters attacked Georgian national guard armoured forces, and Russian troops were relocated into North Ossetia from other areas in Russia.[112] Khasbulatov reportedly threatened to bomb Tbilisi in a telephone conversation with Shevardnadze, and hence by June 1992 Russia was at the brink of war with Georgia.[113] This Russian response was very much dictated by North Ossetia. The North Ossetian government had cut off a pipeline carrying Russian natural gas to Georgia, and was applying strong lobbying efforts in Moscow. In addition, the Confederation of Mountain Peoples of the Caucasus in June brought a battalion of volunteer fighters to North Ossetia, ready to fight in the south. Although the North Ossetian leadership prevented it from actually travelling to South Ossetia, the gravity of the situation and its possible escalation of this hitherto localized conflict to a Caucasian war poising Georgia against Russia was instrumental in engineering a rapprochement between Shevardnadze and Yeltsin. On 22 June, the two leaders signed the Sochi agreement in the presence of the leaders of North and South Ossetia, who however did not sign it, the southerners especially being unhappy with its formulations. The cease-fire nevertheless came into effect on 28 June, and a peace-keeping force composed of Russians, Georgians, and Ossetians was set up. On 14 July the first peace-keepers were deployed, and the cease-fire has held ever since. Nevertheless no solution has been reached in this conflict either, although it would seem that this conflict has been the one of the three Transcaucasian conflicts to come closest to a solution, particularly because of the limited scale of warfare. In spite of this its estimated death toll of 700 people is terrifying enough for the participants.

The Ingush-Ossetian Conflict

Ossetians have been involved in two conflicts in the post-cold war era. In the conflict in South Ossetia, as detailed above, the Ossetians were the under-dogs, pitted against the much larger and potentially more powerful Georgians. However, in the other conflict, that with the Ingush, the Ossetians were in the opposite position as regards the conflict over the Prigorodniy raion in the borderland between North Ossetia and diminutive Ingushetia.

There are no records of specific conflict or hostilities between Ingush and Ossetians in the past. Of course, mutual suspicion may have existed to a certain degree, based on certain demographic circumstances. The first is that the Ingush, just like all other indigenous Caucasian peoples, are mountaineers; historically they have their home in the mountains, from which they have resettled to the valleys and towns only later in this century, partly due to Russian coercion.[114] By contrast, the Ossetians are so-called 'foothillers', people that live in the hills or in the plains, at lower altitudes. As in other parts of the Caucasus, foothillers and mountaineers are mutually suspicious of each other's life-styles, customs, and habits. Nowhere, however, have such tendencies resulted in organized violence – not to speak of war. Rather the mutual suspicion between Ossetians and Ingush led to them both minding their own business than anything else. A second consideration is ethnicity. As noted above, the Ingush are indige-nous to the Caucasus, while the Ossetians are 'immigrants' – albeit early ones, settling in the Caucasus in the sixth century AD.[115] The two peoples' languages are unintelligible to each other, Ossetian being distantly related to Persian and Ingush being a Caucasian language closely related to Chechen. This fact, at least until the advent of Russification, meant that the two peoples had difficulties in communicating with each other; and difficulties in communications is a factor which accentuates rather than attenuates tensions. A third point is religion: the Ingush are Sunni Muslims, with a strong Sufi influence, in particular in the form of the Qadiriya Tariqat; however Ingushetia was the last region of the Caucasus to be converted to Islam, due to its inaccessible location in the central Caucasian mountains. By contrast, most Ossetians are traditionally Orthodox Christian, although a Muslim minority exists, (only in the north) which seems to be relegated to the former feudal upper class. Thus historically the two peoples had not developed brotherly relations; although they were never at each other's throats either. What was to complicate their coexistence was foreign involvement. With the Russian advance in the North Caucasus, the Ossetians soon became Russia's main ally in the region, and to a great extent converted to Christianity; however the Ingush did not fiercely resist the Russian advance either, a fact which differentiated them from their Chechen kin.

The Soviet Era

At the beginning of the Soviet era, both Ossetians and Ingush were part of the Mountain ('Gorskaya') republic, which was subsequently dissolved in 1924. As the Ingush were allocated their own autonomous Oblast in 1924, the presently-disputed territory was a part of Ingushetia in its entirety and from the beginning; this did not change when the Chechen-Ingush Autonomous Oblast (later ASSR) was created in 1934. Naturally, the delineation between Ingushetia and North Ossetia was precarious, as the border passed through the densely-populated areas surrounding the city of Vladikavkaz (Ordzhonikidze)[116], North Ossetia's present capital and historically a city heavily populated by the Ingush. The root of the problem, however, lay in the events of the second world war, when the Ingush were among the peoples deported to Central Asia and Siberia. As the Chechen-Ingush ASSR was abolished in June 1946, its territory was broken up and distributed among its neighbours.[117] Most importantly, the Prigorodniy raion of Vladikavkaz, which surrounds the city on the north, east, and south, was given to North Ossetia. The region, prior to the deportations, had accounted for almost half of Ingushetia's territory.[118]

When the Chechen-Ingush ASSR was reinstated in January 1957, it actually gained some territory, to the north; however the Prigorodniy raion remained within North Ossetia. As the returning Ingush came to their former settlements, they found Ossetians living in their homes, who had themselves been (at least partially) forcibly resettled there.[119] As the Ingush tried to buy back their homes, they were counteracted not only by the local Ossetians but even more so by the North Ossetian authorities, who did their best to prevent the Ingush from returning to their places of residence. Even in later years, legal instruments were instituted to make their return impossible: in 1982 and 1990, decrees were signed limiting the issuing of the compulsory *Propiski* in the Prigorodniy.[120]

However, the Ingush defied all obstacles, and continued to move into the Prigorodniy, settling there both legally and illegally. The 1989 population census recorded almost 33,000 Ingush living in the entire North Ossetian ASSR, 17,500 of which in the Prigorodniy.[121] In reality, there were much more Ingush in the region. In certain areas of the Prigorodniy, they formed a huge majority of the population.[122] Relations between Ingush and Ossetians were not harmonious at this time; sporadic violence on ethnic grounds took place, and in January 1973, the Ingush staged a demonstration in Grozny regarding the Prigorodniy issue, forcing a candidate member of the Politburo to come and address the crowd.[123] Generally speaking, the Ingush were frustrated by their careers and academic lives being hindered in North Ossetia because of their ethnicity. In October 1981, widespread unrest erupted after the murder of an Ossetian taxi-driver by his Ingush passengers. As a response, the Ossetians demonstrated for the expulsion of all Ingush from the Prigorodniy. The reaction from Moscow was immediate; troops were sent in to restore order, and a curfew was instituted. The intervention succeeded in suppressing the demonstrations, hence preventing an escalation of the conflict. The North Ossetian republican leadership was blamed for having allowed the unrest to take place, and was replaced; a Russian (presumably less biased in the conflict) replaced the Ossetian republican head. However, the new leadership did not take any measures to solve the underlying problems – hence the problems were only allowed to worsen with time. And with Perestroïka, the general lighter atmosphere led to their breaking out, like so many other problems in the Union. In particular, the Ingush activists were now more free to voice their claims without having to fear the harsh repression of the Brezhnev era.

The Fall of the Soviet Union and the Escalation of the Conflict

In September 1989, the second congress of the Ingush people was held in Grozny, which reaffirmed the Prigorodniy's being an unalienable part of Ingushetia, while advocating the re-establishment of a separate Ingush territorial entity, apart from the Chechen-Ingush ASSR. Meanwhile, the North Ossetian leadership only stiffened their opposition to any territorial solution. These events also mirror the increased isolation of the Ingush in 1991, as the Chechen-Ingush ASSR seemed to turn into a Chechen-dominated and anti-Moscow institution, under General Dudayev's leadership. Hence the Ingush had double reasons to distance themselves from Chechen claims to independence: first, they were not represented in the all-Chechen congress which later replaced the Zavgayev government and feared being ignored in a Chechen state; and secondly they would have few hopes of regaining the Prigorodniy unless they kept good relations with Moscow. And the Russian leadership did not miss this chance to drive a wedge between the Chechens and Ingush: Boris Yeltsin, campaigning for his presidential election at a rally in Nazran in late March, expressed his tacit support for the Ingush claims – although this would hardly serve his election, as there are two times as many North Ossetians as Ingush. Hence the statements at least partly served a more complex purpose, that of trying to prevent unified resistance by Chechens and Ingush. Nevertheless by this time Ingushetia was one of the most pro-Yeltsin territories in the whole of Russia. By contrast, North Ossetia was one of the most conservative and pro-Soviet areas of the union, and seemed to rejoice over the August 1991 coup. Consequently both territories were in a precarious situation as the Soviet Union fell apart and the ultimate jurisdiction over them was replaced by the Russian Federation under Yeltsin. The Ingush pursued their pro-Russian policy, and had early on abandoned any hopes of reaching a solution through negotiations with North Ossetia, instead focusing their energy on achieving their goals through Moscow. Here, they were much more successful, at least initially. In March 1990 already, a commission (the 'Belyakov' commission) was set up to investigate the claims of the Ingush. Nine months later, it concluded that the Ingush claim was well-founded, and that the Prigorodniy ought to be restored to the Chechen-Ingush ASSR from the North Ossetian ASSR. It also requested the Supreme Soviet of the RSFSR to place the matter on its agenda.

North Ossetia, faced with this new political situation, became dominated by the communist forces wanting a return to the old order and has in fact kept its Soviet name until very recently.[124] As a Russian observer has noted, "the destruction of the Soviet statehood and the military-administrative system of the Soviet superstate was perceived within little Ossetia not as a liberation and the beginning of national revival, but primarily as the destruction of the complex of external security and internal stability".[125] With this logic, North Ossetia was one of the republics which was often named as seeking more autonomy in the immediate aftermath of the USSR's dissolution, confused as to what it actually wanted but distancing itself from the Yeltsin regime. However the Ossetian society in the first nine months was in crisis. Flooded by 100,000 refugees from the South Ossetian war with Georgia, and isolated in an Islamic North Caucasus with a religious revival brewing, Ossetia despite its aversion for democratic reform in Russia had few options but to seek an alliance with Moscow. This isolated feeling contributed to the importance accorded to the Prigorodniy raion, whose Ingush population was seen as a 'fifth column'. As Fiona Hill puts it, the Prigorodniy is a vital piece of real estate for North Ossetia, an alleviation to its high population density and served as a place to settle the refugees from South Ossetia. However, the territorial argument is true for Ingushetia as well; the Prigorodniy would represent fully a third of the non-mountainous Ingush lands and traditionally their main urban centre.[126] Meanwhile, the situation on the ground was getting worse. In March 1991, Ingush armed bands tried to forcibly take back their houses, and in April, clashes took place between Ingush and Ossetian paramilitaries, leaving one dead Ossetian and fourteen wounded Ingush. This resulted in a North Ossetian state of emergency the following day, which froze the situation temporarily.

The August coup in Moscow was detrimental to the Ingush in at least two dimensions. First, it led to a dramatic loss of Moscow's influence and power in the regions, hence the Ingush could not rely on the centre to resolve the issue in their favour; and secondly, the Chechen declaration of independence took place, and the Ingush, seeing no place for themselves in Dudayev's state, had no choice but to secede from it (in a peaceful way, negotiated with the Chechens despite the fact that the border between the two republics was undemarcated and thus subject to contention) and establish a 'republic' of their own. However this republic had no capital, no fixed boundaries, no administration, and no power structures of its own. As early as October, the Ossetians took advantage of the Ingush' weakness, and created a National Guard of around 5000 men, equipped with 20 armoured vehicles.[127] In November, the Ingush held a referendum which supported the establishment of a separate Ingush republic within Russia, but including the Prigorodniy. After the subsequent dissolution of the Soviet Union, and throughout 1992, the war of words between the North Ossetians and the Ingush escalated, however without any larger disturbances.[128] On 4 June 1992, a separate Ingush republic was officially declared by a Russian Supreme Soviet ruling, and a 'transitional phase' ranging until March 1994 was proposed to resolve all the questions related to it, including administrative issues but mainly its territorial delimitation:[129] the issue of the Prigorodniy but also the delimitation of its eastern border with Chechnya. A provisional administration was set up under a Russian General, Viktor Yermakov, but these decisions came much too late – no work had even begun on determining Ingushetia's borders before the clashes of November 1992 broke out.

Ever since 1989, then, both parties had been making themselves ready for a confrontation. According to Human Rights Watch/Helsinki, both the Ingush and the Ossetians were acquiring arms at a 'furious pace'.[130] Weapons, moreover, were readily available in the region. The Ingush got them through Chechnya, in particular after 1991, and the North Ossetians took advantage of the war in South Ossetia to arm themselves.

Russian weapons intended for support to South Ossetia or for peace-keeping operations there 'found their way' into North Ossetian hands.[131] Naturally, the Ossetians were in a more favourable position, as they could make use of their republican administration to legitimize the existence of rogue paramilitary units as different kinds of 'militias'.

Tensions between the two communities seem to have escalated since 1991, as crime became an increasingly serious problem – and often with ethnic undertones. The Ossetians complained of Ingush violence and extremism, while the Ingush alleged that their kinsmen were being harassed and killed by Ossetian uniformed men. As the Ossetians paramilitaries grew increasingly powerful throughout 1992, the Ingush in the Prigorodniy responded by arming themselves, organizing village guards, and constructing barricades. Clashes between these Ingush groupings and the Ossetians had become a serious problem by September/October 1992.

October 1992: War

On 20 October, a gas pipeline passing through the Prigorodniy (carrying Russian gas to Armenia and Georgia) was blown up, and North Ossetian officials were hinting at Ingush sabotage while explaining the event.[132] The same day, a twelve-year-old Ingush girl was crushed by an armoured personnel carrier from the North Ossetian OMON forces, in the settlement of Oktyabrskoye, whereby the local Ingush tried to take the law into their own hands and hang the soldiers in the tank, and an exchange of fire took place, however without any further casualties.[133] The next day in the village of Yuzhniy, two more Ingush were killed leading to clashes which left up to six dead. The Ingush in the Prigorodniy then established a coordinating council, which decided to organize self-defence units to patrol Ingush settlements.[134] The Ossetians naturally saw this as a threat to their sovereignty, and regarded it a *Casus Belli*. The North Ossetian leadership ordered all barricades set up by the Ingush to be removed, or else combat actions would be undertaken.[135] Nevertheless, the Ingush did not give in, as further killings took place in the following days. A mass meeting was staged in Nazran, which initiated a more or less spontaneous armed march on the Prigorodniy. The Ingush subsequently took control of most of the region, and marched on Vladikavkaz.[136] The North Ossetian authorities rallied a whole range of forces to push back the Ingush: Ministry of Interior troops, Republican guards, OMON special forces, as well as refugees from South Ossetia and local Cossacks. Interestingly, the South Ossetians (who had fled Georgia and been resettled in the Prigorodniy) were reputed among the Ingush for being significantly more ruthless and cruel than the

North Ossetians. By 30 October, violence on a large scale had broken out between armed Ingush and North Ossetian forces in several parts of the Prigorodniy. Meanwhile, Ingush bands from Ingushetia tried to break into the Prigorodniy, and succeeded in disarming a unit of Russian MVD troops in the village of Chermen.[137]

On 31 October around 3000 Russian paratroopers and MVD forces were flown in to 'restore law and order'. A state of emergency was issued by President Yeltsin to enforce the actions of the troops. The orders were clear: to separate the fighting parties from one another. However, many questions have been raised concerning the Russian intervention; the Ingush, in particular, argue that the Russians took the side of their 'fellow Christians', the Ossetians, and actually worsened the situation of the already weaker Ingush. What is clear, however, is that the Russian intervention failed to prevent the conflict from expanding. Quite the contrary: the death toll continued to rise in the immediate aftermath of the Russian forces' arrival.

As the Russian forces moved in, their headquarters were set up in Vladikavkaz – a fact which naturally compromised the Russians in the eyes of the Ingush. It has been alleged that the Russian forces were more or less coordinated with the Ossetian republican units.

The Russian 'peace forces' did not stop at controlling the Prigorodniy. Within a few days, they moved into Ingushetia proper, and by 10 November they had reached the (still undemarcated) border between Chechnya and Ingushetia. This in turn led to a stand-off with the forces of Chechen President Dudayev, who declared a state of emergency, fearing that this was a provocation which would enable Russia to attempt a reconquering of Chechnya. Only by the timely intervention of Russia's vice-premier of the time, Yegor Gaidar, did the situation de-escalate and Russian forces were withdrawn from, what the Chechens regarded as, Chechen territory.

According to official sources, a total of 644 people were killed in the conflict as of June 1994. The overwhelming majority perished between 30 October and 4 November: over 150 Ossetians and 300 Ingush.[138] However, it should be noted that significant numbers of people were killed even in 1993 and after, which tends to show that the conflict has not been settled. As Tscherwonnaja expresses it, the conflict moved from its acute stage to becoming a chronic one.[139] The state of emergency in the region was renewed consecutively until it was finally lifted as late as in February 1995.[140]

The Russian Intervention

The Russian intervention in the Prigorodniy to a great extent seems to follow – and confirm – the pattern of Russian activities in other parts of the

Caucasus. Hence it was instrumental in ensuring a permanent Russian military presence in the area, and was successful in re-establishing total control over this strategic part of the North Caucasus. As Julian Birch has noted, the Russian intervention can be questioned both regarding its motivation and its impact. The motivation can be seen as either pro-Ossetian, or neutral and peace-making; similarly the impact can be regarded as either positive, bringing about an end to the conflict, or as the cause of even more bloodshed.

As the Russian government had been rather favourable towards the Ingush claims to territorial rehabilitation, it might seem illogical to assume that the Russian intervention was pro-Ossetian. However, two circumstances shed light on this seeming lack of coherence. First, the activities of the Russian armed forces do not always represent the policy of the centre. This is a recurrent fact which has been observed in Abkhazia as well as in Chechnya. Hence the fact that certain formations of the army supported the Ossetian side might only mean that the commanders of that unit ordered this, not that the orders from the centre were to do such. This is all the more plausible as most of the military view the Ingush as a traditionally disloyal people, like their Chechen kin. The Ossetians, in contrast, have always been the established allies of Russia in the Caucasus. Hence it seemed logical for the Russian military to disregard Ingush claims, as the first priority was to secure the continuation of the age-old strategic partnership with Ossetia. A second element is that since mid-1992 a policy shift occurred in Moscow, which has been described by Mohiaddin Mesbahi as a switch from a Euro-Atlanticist to a Eurasianist perspective.[141] Suffice it to say here that the Russian policy shifted back toward a conservative, 'Great Russian' approach. And in this framework, Ossetia had an important position as a traditional pro-Russian and Orthodox bastion, while Ingushetia did not.

The argument that the conduct of the Russian forces may not have been sanctioned by the centre is strengthened by actual criticism coming from the Russian security council regarding the events in November 1992. According to the report, the troops did not disarm or liquidate armed formations, participated in looting, and were otherwise idle during the early days of their arrival. The security council report concluded that this amounted to a failure to prevent civilian casualties and hence a failure to fulfil their mission.[142]

Besides this later official acknowledgement of irregularities, the Ingush are supported in their argument by several facts. For example, the North Ossetian Supreme Soviet was quickly given complete power in the Prigorodniy, by an amendment to the state of emergency.[143] High Russian officials, such as deputy Prime Minister Khizha, also confirmed the policy of refusing to alter any borders within Russia, thus openly denying the right of the Ingush to territorial rehabilitation. But most of all, there is evidence suggesting the collaboration of Russian 'peace-keeping' troops with Ossetian formations. Indeed, the Ossetian forces operated together with Russian forces in the Prigorodniy,[144] patrolling together, both being directed from the Vladikavkaz headquarters. Russian officials also handed out weapons to North Ossetian authorities, which were subsequently redistributed to paramilitaries. Further, instead of separating the fighting parties as the situation was on the ground, the Russian forces either forcibly evacuated Ingush residents of the Prigorodniy or jointly attacked settlements controlled by Ingush paramilitaries with the help of Ossetian forces.[145] The forcible evacuation may have been intended to bring an end to hostilities, but in effect it accounted for an act on the behalf of and in the interest of the Ossetian side. Further, based on simple facts, one can observe that the death toll did not halt with the Russian intervention; quite the contrary, it went on increasing for a number of days, actually doubling before abating.[146] This is due to the fact that Ossetian irregular forces were actually enabled to operate freely in their objective to clear the Prigorodniy of Ingush.

Another argument that has been voiced is that the Russian troops took the conflict as a pretext to intervene and involve Chechnya in the conflict. According to this point of view, the main objective was to directly or indirectly force General Dudayev to intervene on the side of the Ingush, thereby giving the army a reason to invade Chechnya. The main evidence supporting this hypothesis is that the Russian forces, who entered the Prigorodniy from the west and north, actually crossed the border to Ingushetia, pushing eastward towards the still undemarcated Chechen-Ingush border, where they were countered by Chechen forces resulting in the stand-off mentioned above. An operation against Chechnya was halted by the threat of mobilization of the Confederation of Mountain Peoples of the Caucasus, which at that point could have led to a full-scale regional confrontation.[147]

The Outcome of the Conflict and its Aftermath

The Prigorodniy conflict led to the decisive victory – at least in the short term – of the Ossetian side. A solution, including the return of refugees, has not been reached. As Svetlana Chervonnaya notes, the Prigorodniy conflict is the Caucasian conflict where territory is the scarcest.[148] And considering the widely-accepted perception of the sanctity of territorial boundaries in the post-Soviet area and in the whole world, there is no pragmatic reason for North Ossetia to accept any alteration of its boundaries. Especially given the fact that North Ossetia has Moscow on its back, and that its people's attitude is as uncompromising as ever, there is no incitement on the Ossetian part to find a solution. The perpetuation of the *status quo*, then, is seen as both desirable and feasible. Negotiations, no doubt, have been undertaken since the spring of 1993 for the return of refugees, but the harsh conditions imposed by the Ossetian government ensures that no effective agreement on the issue will be reached in the near future. Accordingly, only people who have not been involved in the conflict and who possessed a valid residence permit (Propiska) at the time of the conflict have the right to return.[149] This has two implications: first of all, the practical difficulty of deciding who was and was not involved in the conflict; and second, the impossibility of the return of the Ingush who lived illegally in the Prigorodniy. The pace of repatriation falls short of even the expectations of the Russian government; the Ingush accuse the Ossetians of deliberately slowing down the process.[150] Only in June 1994 was a coherent agreement reached on the return of refugees; however this agreement did not lead anywhere either. In 1995, new negotiations were set up, but were broken off after three days as the parties were unable to agree.[151] Yeltsin himself tried to broker a deal between the two presidents, Ingushetia's Ruslan Aushev and North Ossetia's Aksharbek Galazov, without particular success.[152]

The war in Chechnya further complicated the situation, as Moscow's attention has been turned away from the Prigorodniy conflict, and as over 150,000 refugees have flown into Ingushetia. In the Prigorodniy itself, clashes erupted in the spring of 1995, when Ossetians tried to prevent Ingush returnees from settling.[153] Further casualties were claimed in May and June, pointing to a general instability and lack of law and order in the region. In Ingushetia, the existing tensions with Russia escalated in October 1995 in an odd event, where the Russian army attacked an airport, killing several civilians, due to an erroneous report that Chechen forces had occupied it.[154] Matters grew worse in February 1996, when withdrawing Russian troops killed seven civilians near the Chechen-Ingush border.[155] In July 1997, violence escalated again. This time, returning Ingush refugees were subjected to grenade attacks in the Prigorodniy,[156] despite Nazran's early warnings to the Kremlin that tensions were escalating and demands for presidential rule to be imposed on the Prigorodniy,[157] Yeltsin refused this option and instead imposed a 'joint action programme' which has been interpreted as heavily tilted toward the Ossetian standpoint.[158] Meanwhile refugee camps in the Prigorodniy were attacked by armed mobs, apparently including North Ossetian paramilitary forces, and refugees forced to flee back into Ingushetia.[159]

These events all indicate an increasing spiral of violence, and Moscow's amorphous policy towards the conflict enables the Ossetian leadership to hinder the return of the Ingush refugees both by overt and covert means. Hence, although (at the time of writing) organized warfare has not taken place since 1992, it is clear that this conflict has merely turned into a protracted one rather than abated. Tensions remain high, and the frustration on the part of the Ingush is only rising with the lack of attention for their grievances and the increasingly friendly relations between North Ossetia and the Kremlin. The harbouring of 35,000 to 65,000 refugees from the Prigorodniy had already taken a hard toll on the small Ingush republic, when an additional 150,000 Chechens sought refuge in Ingushetia fleeing the brutal Russian invasion of their lands. And given the fact the Chechen and Ingush languages and cultures are very similar, increased contacts on the grassroots level are likely to influence the way the Ingush view Russia.

Still in 1991, the Ingush saw Moscow as their ally and only means to achieve territorial rehabilitation and the return of the Prigorodniy. The events that have followed, both in the Prigorodniy itself and in Chechnya, have shown with all necessary clarity that Russia is not a friend nor ally of the Vainakh people. Quite to the contrary, the rulers in Moscow are still – consciously or unconsciously – prisoners of the age-old enmity which permeated Russian attitudes towards the Caucasian peoples, the Chechens and Ingush in particular. This fact is supported by statements of then Russian Deputy Premier Sergei Shakhrai and other high officials in the 'power ministries' which refer to the Ingush as a 'traditionally disloyal nation which has strong separatist feelings'.[160] This type of statement is all the more ironic as the Ingush refused to join the Chechen bid for independence, opting for remaining within Russia. Any separatist feelings have been reinforced by the Russian policy in the Caucasus. Indeed, today, many Ingush *do* regret their decision to separate from their Chechen kin in 1991.

The conflict over the Prigorodniy district is interesting in the sense that the two peoples party to it had no controversies to talk about.[161] The conflict, which can be termed an exclusively territorial one, can be blamed squarely on arbitrary Soviet and Russian policies in the Caucasus. Had it not been for the criminal deportation of the Ingush in the second world war, and the subsequent changes in the borders of the Chechen-Ingush ASSR, there would have been no reason for conflict between Ossetians and Ingush. But with the Prigorodniy conflict, a deepening rift between two Caucasian peoples has been created. Indeed, the conflict is likely to re-erupt in some form sooner or later, as the Ingush increasingly take matters in their own hands and 'illegally' return to their homes in the Prigorodniy, thereby being confronted by an Ossetian reaction. The impact of this conflict, however, goes beyond the two peoples involved. To a great extent, it has ruined the unity of the Caucasian peoples that was institutionalized in the Confederation of Mountain Peoples of the Caucasus. This confederation, before this conflict, had been successful in solving territorial disputes between Laks and Chechens in Dagestan; it had also demonstrated a considerable political influence by organizing and coordinating North Caucasian support for the Abkhaz in their conflict with Georgia. Indeed, North Ossetians and Ingush had worked together in this framework. However, the Prigorodniy conflict considerably reduced the power of the confederation, given the fact that two of its components were in direct confrontation with each other.

The Confederation's role has been minor in this conflict;[162] however it is important to note that it could actually be used as an institutional framework to find a solution to the Prigorodniy conflict. As Russian mediation is unlikely to be objective and disinterested, a local, Caucasian mediation could prove to have its advantages. The confederation has set up a committee to find a solution to the conflict and has also proposed to replace the Russian peace-keeping forces with a joint North Caucasian force, an idea which has been favourably viewed by most North Caucasians, and indeed by the Ingush.[163] Although the North Ossetian side may prefer Russian mediation – or rather no mediation at all – given the fact that it is the only Christian member of the organization and the closest to Russia, the confederation is an option that should not be underestimated in the quest for a resolution of the conflict.

For the time being, there is no solution in sight for the Prigorodniy conflict. As in so many other cases, the conflict is likely to continue simmering on a low heat, something which in the long run will only lead to worse confrontations whenever it is revived – which it is certain to be sooner or later.

The Chechen War

Although the Prigorodniy conflict was the scene of considerable levels of violence and ethnic cleansing, its consequences for the civilian population fade in comparison with the bloody war that was to begin two years later in the neighbouring republic of Chechnya, which had existed since 1991 in a precarious situation of factual independence.

Historically, the Chechens have been the Caucasian people who have had most difficulty accepting Russian overlordship. They are also the ones to have rebelled against Russia more often and longer than any other people, and have consequently suffered from Russian repression more than their neighbours.[164] This circumstance had already shaped the frame of mind of the Chechens before the deportations of the second world war – and indeed that of the Russians, whose contemptuous and condescending attitude towards the Chechens survives until the present day.[165]

The cruelty of the deportations was in any case a turning point, proving to the Chechens once and for all that they could not live under Russian rule.[166]Allowed to return in 1957, the collective experience of deportation is seen by most experts as having developed the feeling of national identity as well as religiosity among the Chechens, who hitherto had had mainly clan-bound allegiance rather than a feeling of common nationhood. Chechens were still suppressed, particularly during the Brezhnev era, but slowly rebuilt their roots and their social and religious networks, in particular through Sufi brotherhoods.[167] When the cavalcade of sovereignty declarations took place in 1989-90, the Chechens' reaction took on an entirely different dimension from that of the Volga Tatars, for example, or even of the neighbouring republics. The Chechen national movement became much more radical, much more emotionally laden than other 'popular fronts in the Soviet union'. As Abdurahman Avtorkhanov has expressed it, what took place was

> a revolt by children as revenge for their fathers' and mothers' deaths in the hell-like conditions of deportation in far-away, cold and hungry Kazakstan and Kyrgyzstan. It is a revolt by the whole nation against the enduring supremacy of the old power structures in Chechen-Ingushetia.[168]

Furthermore, the Chechens had the demographic strength of no other nationality in the North Caucasus, with close to a million people. This fact coupled with the determination of the Chechens, and the fact that the Chechen national movement immediately came to be dominated by the most radical forces, paved the way for the conflict with Moscow.

The Chechen Revolution

In November 1990 an all-Chechen National Congress was held in Grozny, which quickly came to be dominated by Jokhar Dudayev's charismatic personality.[169] Dudayev was a General in the Soviet air force who had developed an interest in his roots during his tenure as base commander in Tartu, Estonia, where he had found inspiration in the quest for independence of the Baltic peoples.[170] Dudayev was also advantaged by his coming from an insignificant clan in Chechnyan mountains, which enabled leaders of all clans to support him without fearing domination of another large clan. The congress – which importantly excluded the Ingush – under

Dudayev's leadership prompted the Supreme Soviet of Chehen-Ingushetia to proclaim sovereignty, which it felt compelled to do the next day. By spring 1991, Dudayev had taken full control of the congress and resigned from his military position. The August coup of August 1991 was the starting signal for Dudayev, who convened the national congress and condemned the coup which Chechnya's official leader, Doku Zavgayev, had silently supported. In September the supreme Soviet of the republic was forcibly disbanded, faced with popular demands and a raid against it conducted by Dudayev's forces.[171] Dudayev announced presidential elections for 27 October, and was duly elected president despite Moscow's denouncing the elections as unconstitutional. Only days later, on 2 November, Chechnya declared independence. To rein in the secessionists, Yeltsin had declared a state of emergency and attempted to crush the new Chechen government by force.[172] As this attempt backfired, the Russian parliament stepped back and ordered negotiations with Dudayev, which were however slow in taking place, and Chechnya was for all practical purposes left alone for three years.

During the three years of de facto independence, the economic and social problems of the republic led to internal conflicts among the Chechens which became increasingly harsh. Opposition to Dudayev grew and was countered by relatively insensitive policies towards the opposition, and by 1994 parts of the opposition had resorted to arms, in particular in the traditionally more pro-Russian northern parts of the Republic.[173] Doubtless, this opposition was supported and armed by Moscow.[174] In December 1994, when Russian involvement became obvious, Russia decided to intervene directly, not by proxy. Although meetings were held to try to defuse the escalating conflict, Russian forces invaded Chechnya on 11 December 1994, apparently in the belief that Chechnya would be easily subdued in a matter of days. According to the initial military plan, three detachments were to enter Chechnya from three different directions and move forward on Grozny. One detachment started from Mozhdok in northern North Ossetia, another from Vladikavkaz, and a third from Dagestan in the east. Ib Faurby outlines three phases of the offensive. In a first phase, these forces were supposed to encircle Grozny, leaving an opening to the south from which the Chechen forces could escape out of the city. In this phase, Grozny was not to be stormed. In the second phase, Dudayev's forces would be pushed southward and isolated in the mountains, while the Russian forces gradually established control over the lowlands, and instituted the Moscow-friendly opposition in Dudayev's place in Grozny. At this stage the Russians hoped to get popular support to switch to the opposition. The third and final phase was expected to be long-lasting, ranging up to perhaps three years, where the rebel forces in the mountains would gradually be isolated and eliminated.

The Russian Intervention and War

As the events were rapidly to show, this plan never materialized. As could have been predicted, the Russian forces soon ran into major trouble. Both in Ingushetia and in Dagestan, the Russian army was stopped or otherwise hindered by the local population. Confronted with this, Major General Ivan Barbichev, the commander of the western group, refused to use force against the civilian population, this slowed down the pace of the attack and led to the absence of coordination between the three forces. Interestingly, this refusal to obey orders proved no hindrance to the General's future career. However, the Russian forces did enter Chechnya, and once there, they faced a much stronger resistance from the Chechens than they had expected. Hence the Russian invasion forces were forced to ask for large reinforcements from other parts of the country. This embarrassing fact showed that the Russian army was guilty of one of the most dangerous mistakes in military planning – underestimation of the opponent. Grachev's 'prophetic' statement that Grozny could be taken in two hours by paratroopers proved to be a source of ridicule. Only by the end of December did the Russians reach Grozny; hence they had lost the main asset of an offensive war: the effect of surprise. However, the Russian advance did not lead to the rebels fleeing southward through the corridor that had been left for them. On the contrary, they used the corridor to receive reinforcements of troops and weapons. On 26 December, the Security Council decided that Grozny should be conquered promptly, despite objections from the military side concerning the readiness of their forces for such an attack. The city was to be attacked from four directions, and the four detachments would meet one another in the city centre.[175] The plan was carried out on New Year's Eve, in an attempt to regain an effect of surprise. However, this plan failed as well. Of the four main detachments, only one managed to reach Grozny's centre, while the three others barely managed to enter the city.

This was due partly to the harsh resistance by the Chechen forces, which were organized in groups of two to four men, equipped with anti-tank weapons. The Russians made a series of tactical mistakes, among which the gravest one was to try to occupy a city with tanks, unprotected by infantry. These unprotected tanks became easy targets for the small, mobile groups of Chechen defenders. The planning of the operation was dismal. In a detailed study of the battle for Grozny, Timothy Thomas quotes Nikolay Tsymbal as follows:

> As far as I can judge, we have an infamous operation that lacks even an integral plan. Military convoys are for some reason marking time on the approaches to the city and regrouping. Military commanders have not even worried about feeding soldiers. Nor about removing the dead and injured from the battlefield, something we made sure was done during the large scale World War II operations.[176]

As the storm of Grozny was a complete failure, the Russian army reverted to well-known tactics dating back to the siege of Stalingrad: to use heavy artillery and air to bomb the city, after which they conquered the city methodically block by block. Only after two months did the Russian army manage to establish control over the city – at a price of thousands of own casualties, over 20,000 civilians killed, total destruction of the city and hundreds of thousands of refugees.[177] Furthermore, the Chechen resistance was not crushed; as they lost control of the city, the Chechen defenders left it without a real fight and moved back to other major settlements such as Argun, Gudermes, and Shali, where heavy fighting continued. By May, the Russian army, with more support from air-force bombings, managed to take control of most of the lowlands of Chechnya, whereas the defenders were pushed back into the mountains. In June, the Russian advance continued and Russian forces even entered the mountains and attacked Chechen positions there.[178] At this point, the Chechens were on the verge of losing the war, and being forced to revert to becoming armed bands in the mountains while Russia consolidated control over Chechnya's lowlands.

At this point came the highly publicized hostage taking led by Shamil Basayev in a hospital in Budennovsk, deep inside Russia proper. Besides the political implications of this event for both sides, with discussions on Chechens resorting to terrorism among others, it resulted in the military accord of 30 July 1995, which led to leading figures proclaiming that the war was over.[179] According to the deal, an immediate cease-fire was implemented, while Chechen forces were supposed to surrender their weapons and Russian troops were partly to withdraw from Chechnya.[180] Whereas this accord did lead to a temporary cessation of hostilities, it could never be fully implemented. Few weapons were turned over, and the scheduled exchange of prisoners did not take place.[181] Furthermore the cease-fire never managed to prevent incidents from disturbing the process. Clashes still occurred, a Russian general was injured in an assassination attempt, and a bomb was disarmed at the presidential palace in Grozny.[182] According to Faurby, the main effect of the accord was to enable Chechen soldiers to travel freely within Chechnya without being attacked by Russian forces. Hence they were able to penetrate the Russian-held areas and regroup their forces.[183] This also meant that the fighters could melt into the population again, and any previous frontlines dissolved as the Chechen and Russian forces were to be found all over Chechnya.

Towards the end of 1995, the tensions started to escalate. In the middle of December, sporadic fighting in Gudermes started to escalate into open war.[184] The Chechen fighters first seemed to control the city, but soon lost it to the Russians. The war did not re-erupt on all fronts at this point, however. While incidents rose in number, talks were still going on, and the Russians managed to hold 'elections' in the republic, which although being heavily criticized and boycotted by all forces loyal to Dudayev, reaffirmed Zavgayev's prime ministership in Moscow's puppet government. From the middle of February, fighting intensified on several fronts, with Chechens blowing up gas pipelines as the Russians were pounding Dudayev's base in the mountains near the Ingush border, Bamut, with heavy artillery.[185] Within Grozny itself, the Chechens exposed the fragility of Russian rule by carrying out a six-hour-long battle in the city centre.

Following these developments, the Russian army staged a renewed offensive in March, only to experience Yeltsin's talk about withdrawal and peace negotiations in April. This led to heavy criticism and doubt concerning decision-making in Moscow, with speculations of the existence of several independent power centres in the Kremlin, acting without concert or even antagonistic to one another. General Aleksandr Lebed, among others, blasted the President for having betrayed the soldiers in Chechnya by sending them into battle with heavy casualties and then immediately withdrawing the forces from the areas they had just conquered. Lebed on another occasion alleged that Yeltsin was not even signing his own orders.[186] The month of April was also the time of an important incident in the war. On 16 April, Jokhar Dudayev was killed in a Russian helicopter attack on the settlement of Gekhi-Chu, not 100 km from Grozny.[187] Although Russian officials deny allegations that the attack was directed personally against Dudayev, evidence emerged almost immediately which proved Moscow's direct intent to kill the Chechen leader. In fact, Dudayev at the time of the attack was speaking with mediators on a radio telephone connection. It seems as if the Russians used high-technology equipment which enabled them to localize the village Dudayev was staying over in and thus launched an attack on the village, and succeeded in eliminating him.[188]

However great a blow this was for the Chechens, the loss of their leader did not change their determination to fight for independence, as the Russians might have thought. Rather, their determination became even stronger, although Dudayev's successor, Zelimkhan Yandarbiev, initiated negotiations very soon after coming to power. Yandarbiev had been the founder of the Vainakh Democratic party in 1991, and had from the start been Dudayev's chief ideologue.[189] His belief in independence and the struggle against Russia was as strong as Dudayev's. Nevertheless, although he was nominated as Dudayev's successor, his power over the military leaders such as Aslan Maskhadov, the chief of staff, or Shamil Basayev, was distinctively less compelling than Dudayev's. He also lacked the charismatic personality of Dudayev as well as his ability to make the people rally behind him, being rather a poet and intellectual by character.

Despite the negotiations, the war continued. At the beginning of May, Urus-Martan was shelled by Russian forces, which was significant since until then the population of the town had supported the opposition to Dudayev; however after this event the inhabitants sided with Yandarbiev. This is one of many examples of how Russia alienated the population which was not already against it, and pushed it into the arms of the rebel government.[190] Despite these incidents, a cease-fire was signed on 30 May, which was supposed to be followed by disarmament negotiations.[191] However, this cease-fire was not abided by, by certain elements on both sides, which again points to the lack of authority of both the Russian government and the Chechen leadership over their own forces. On 10 June, an agreement on Russian troop withdrawal was signed. This agreement and Yeltsin's willingness to compromise at the time in retrospect seems to have been highly circumstantial. Indeed, Yeltsin believed that unless he managed to bring an end to the highly unpopular war, he would not be re-elected in the June presidential elections.

On 17 June, Aslan Maskhadov announced that the Chechen leadership would not initiate any armed hostilities until after the second round of the Russian parliamentary elections.[192] However, by 23 June, tension started to rise as the Chechens protested against a Russian military build-up near Vedeno, in southeastern Chechnya. By the beginning of July, the Russians, who had profited from the truce by regrouping their forces and receiving reinforcements, started to provoke the Chechens, including issuing several ultimatums against the leadership. Meanwhile, the Russians began to shell Chechen bases in southern Chechnya. On 9 July, the settlement of Gekhi was heavily attacked by air, and Chechnya started to slide back into full-scale war.[193] At this point, however, it was quite clear even to international observers that Russia was the party that had provoked the fighting. With Yeltsin safely re-elected, the administration decided to take a different tack on the breakaway republic. This was heavily criticized by the US state department, among others.[194] As the fighting went on, the Chechen forces retaliated massively.

The Chechen Victory?

On 6 August in the worst outbreak of hostilities in several months, a Chechen force of almost 1500 fighters headed by Shamil Basayev launched a massive attack on Grozny. This attack was very awkwardly timed for Moscow, as Yeltsin was to be formally sworn in as President on 9 August, only three days later. Indeed, it seems as if the Chechens, who had already shown a certain quality in humiliating Yeltsin, chose this as a punishment for the latter's 'two-faced' behaviour during the Summer of 1996. The Presidential inauguration was indeed troubled by these events, and matters were only made worse as on that same day over 7000 Russian forces were surrounded by a far smaller number of Chechen rebels in Grozny. By 7 August, the rebels had established control over most of Grozny; by 12 August they controlled the whole city. Meanwhile, Yeltsin was forced to appoint Aleksandr Lebed, a known opponent of the war, as his personal envoy in Chechnya to find a negotiated solution to the conflict.[195] At his appointment, Lebed reiterated his belief that the conflict could by no means be solved by force. Quite quickly, Lebed was able to come to talking terms with Aslan Maskhadov, who personally headed negotiations on the Chechen side. On 23 August, a cease-fire came into effect, and on 31 August Lebed announced that he had reached an agreement in the Dagestani settlement of Khasavyurt with the Chechen leadership on pursuing peace.[196] The interesting point of this agreement is that it did not include any solution regarding the contentious issue of Chechnya's status vis-à-vis Russia. As Russia refused to accord Chechnya independence, and Chechnya refused to stay within Russia, the negotiators agreed to postpone this issue for five years, pending reconstruction and reconciliation. The Chechen side took this as a victory and interpreted it as a step towards Russian recognition of Chechen independence. Russia, however, refused this interpretation arguing that Chechnya has no right of secession under international law, a point on which most western observers agree although a few, including the present author, have argued that there is a legal basis for Chechen independence.[197] Whatever the case, no state has so far recognized Chechnya and it is highly unlikely that anyone will unless Russia does so itself. However, Chechnya has *de facto* acquired a level of self-determination which is noticeably larger than

Tatarstan, and in any case beyond autonomy. Chechnya has its own popularly-elected government, its own army controlling its borders, all crucial elements of an independent state. In fact, Russia seems to have no administrative control over Chechnya – nor can it enforce federal law there - and the peace treaty which was formalized in May 1997 can actually be interpreted as Chechnya standing outside of the Russian Federation. Indeed, at the time of writing an increasing number of statements from Moscow seem to indicate that Russia is becoming willing to concede Chechnya's independence. So, as Paul Goble has noted, the Russians and Chechens may be able to tacitly agree, for the time being, to a formula where Chechnya is independent in everything except in name.[198] Public opinion polls in Russia now show that numerous Russians would allow Chechnya to accede to independence.

Francis Boyle, a professor of international law, has concluded that the May 1997 treaty implies that Russia has recognized Chechnya as an independent state. First of all, Boyle notes that the title of the treaty is most revealing: "Treaty on peace and the principles of interrelations between the Russian Federation and the Chechen Republic of Ichkeria." The term 'treaty' is generally used for agreements between sovereign states, whereas the terms 'accord' or 'compact' are used for agreements between a federal centre and its component part. Hence the terms used, in particular the term 'treaty of peace', point to Russia's treating Chechnya as a *de facto* independent nation-state. Furthermore the words 'principles of interrelations' point to this fact, as normally interrelations between a centre and a region are laid down in the constitution of the federal state, which in this case is not mentioned (unlike the case of Tatarstan). Hence Boyle concludes that there is no reason why other states around the world and international organizations should not treat Chechnya as a *de facto* independent state now that Russia itself has done so.[199] Furthermore Chechnya, like Tatarstan, is speeding up its international contacts, setting up unofficial embassies around the world. Chechnya is also increasingly active as a key player in the Caspian oil politics, as the main pipeline through Russia passes Chechen territory. Chechnya has had tense negotiations with Russia on the division of royalties from Azerbaijani 'early oil' which started flowing late 1997.

Oil royalties or not, Chechens had now to contemplate what the results of the war have been. True, a *de facto* independence had been achieved, and it seemed unlikely that Russia would again try to subdue Chechnya militarily. The Chechens have proven their military abilities and their uncompromising sense of pride and honour once again, but must now show that they are equally skilled at domestic and international politics. For Chechnya is today in an abysmal condition, and reconstruction costs are far beyond Chechnya's capabilities, let alone what Russia could be expected to contribute.

Post-War Politics

The military victory of the Chechens was so sudden that they had hardly expected it themselves either in the first days of August or for that matter two weeks later, when Russian General Pulikovsky threatened to bomb Grozny. However by September the Chechen leaders understood that the war was over, and that they now needed to commence the transition into something they had fought for but were not prepared for: ruling Chechnya.[200] Elections were scheduled for January 1997, but the problem was to outline the structures of the Chechen state which came into existence *de facto* with the accords. Before the war, experiments had taken place regarding Islamic rule but had not received support from the population. Dudayev's Chechnya had undoubtedly been a secular state. But the war had changed this. As Dudayev often noted, Russia pushed the Chechens towards Islam, whereas their society actually preserved a number of traditions which were difficult to make compatible with Islam. The prime example is that Chechen customary law, *Adat*, was revered to such an extent that the imposition of Sharia seemed difficult. With the war, the religiosity of the people nevertheless skyrocketed, and demands for Chechnya to become an Islamic state ruled by Sharia gained salience. Many analysts have predicted that this is a passing tendency, a need for self-assertion after the humiliations of this war. Accordingly, Chechnya needed to impose a legal system different from that of Russia; what could be better than Islamic law, especially after a war which many people in their minds saw as a holy war? Whatever the case, another problem is that there is no consensus on *what* Islam to adopt. The official Hanafi Sunni version that Chechens nominally belong to would be the first answer; however this conflicts sharply with the tremendous importance of Qadiri and Naqshbandi orders in Chechen society, which virtually define most Chechens' understanding of Islam. The Sufi form is not suitable for state-building either, simply because of its secretive character which suits a movement in opposition rather than in ruling position. The third variant that has emerged in recent years, strongly so in Dagestan, is the so-called Wahhabite, purist version of Islam, officially endorsed in Saudi Arabia. However the term Wahhabite has been inflated in the Caucasus and Central Asia to define almost any non-indigenous forms of Islam. The self-designation of this group is *Salafites*, implying a tendency that has existed through Islamic history that calls on believers to return to the supposedly ideal and pure form of belief and way of life of the early Muslim communities.[201] The opposition to the Wahhabites is also very strong, as many Chechens see it as imposing an alien way of life not corresponding to Chechen tradition. As a result of this dilemma, President Maskhadov has paid lip service to the concept of an Islamic state, but has condemned Wahhabism as a destabilizing factor.

Presidential and parliamentary elections took place in Chechnya on 27 January 1997. Standing as main candidates were the incumbent Zelimkhan Yandarbiyev, Chief of Staff Aslan Maskhadov, and Field Commander Shamil Basayev. Maskhadov won an overwhelming victory, with 65 per cent of the vote. Basayev clinched 24 per cent and Yandarbiyev a mere 10 per cent. The elections then served to anchor the more moderate and peace-seeking policies of Aslan Maskhadov as compared to his main rival, Shamil Basayev. In elections that were unanimously described by international observers as fair and free, the Chechen people proved to the world that the Russian-inspired picture of the Chechens as violent, uncivilized, and unprepared for a democratic society that has been disseminated through the world was distinctively false. Observers noted with stupefaction that people were queuing peacefully since the early hours of the winter morning to vote. Many Chechens when questioned simply responded that this is what they had been fighting for, and why would they be violent now?

Whereas the main part of Chechnya's society set out to reconstruct their lives, the creation of a reasonably democratic state in Chechnya became the litmus test of a leadership which had shown its military capacity with little doubt. Maskhadov's most direct problem was how to assert central authority in a society split into many clans which had no history of ruling a state commonly. Observers quickly noted that Maskhadov's authority was limited. Real power, it seemed, remained in the hands of an 18-member council of former field commanders, headed by vice-president Vakha Arsanov. The existence of this council in a society saturated with arms, with few prospects for a return to normal life of the thousands of young men returning from the war is indeed crucial to the future of Chechnya. While the arguments that Chechnya will degenerate into civil war seem highly exaggerated, a potential for a certain level of chaos and a society with a high degree of violence and criminality is indeed present. While at the top a semblance of unity or at least a system for decision-making exists, the situation in society has worsened considerably since this war. The practice of hostage-taking has skyrocketed and

Chechnya has, together with Dagestan, acquired fame for being a region where westerners, or even Russians, should not venture. Despite Maskhadov's efforts to put an end to such terrorist acts, his failure to do so has only proven that the government in Grozny has limited control over its territory. The beheading of four British workers in late 1998 was indeed a severe setback in Chechnya's attempts to boost its international image. Indeed, Maskhadov described the gravity of the event by saying that 'we won a war; now we have lost another'.

A western analyst likened the power struggle in Chechnya to 'Wolf cubs fighting under a rug', paraphrasing Churchill's term for the struggle for power in the Kremlin after Stalin's death.[202] It is clear that governance, in particular democratic governance, will be a severe problem for Chechnya in the near future, as will the general lawlessness reigning in the republic. But these questions are crucial for Chechnya's development and reputation in the world. Unless Maskhadov, or the power centres in Jokhar-Gala, can bring a certain stability, order, and predictability into Chechen politics and society soon, Chechnya's image as comparable to the American wild west in a past century will increase, thereby obliterating any chances the republic has to receive foreign investments. Unfortunately, there are no particular reasons for optimism at present.

Dagestan

Since the first Russian attempts to conquer the Caucasus, the mountain peoples of Chechnya and Dagestan were consistently the most difficult to subdue, the most staunchly anti-Russian and the most conservative Islamic nations of the region. In history, these peoples periodically rose together in unified rebellions against the Russian overlord. Dagestan in fact often took the lead in these rebellions. The most well-known Caucasian mountaineer, Imam Shamil, was himself an Avar. The last North Caucasian rebellion of 1920-22, which has been termed 'the last *Ghazawat*' (holy war), took place mostly in Dagestan as the Chechens were considerably less involved in the matter.[203] Dagestani opposition to Soviet rule continued despite the defeat of the rebellion. Most notably, it is believed that the Dagestani peoples escaped the Stalinist deportations of 1943-44 by threatening the Soviet government with an all-Caucasian uprising, which the red army by experience knew would have been very lengthy and costly to suppress.[204]

In the post-Soviet period, however, Dagestan has been totally calm and quiet. Even with Russia's invasion of Chechnya, when many observers thought the Dagestanis would rebel in support of the Chechens, nothing happened − despite the fact that the north-eastern part of the republic, neighbouring Chechnya, had received its share of Russian bombs and missiles.

Dagestan is one of the most ethnically diverse and complex territories in the world. The largest republic of the North Caucasus with a population of roughly two million, Dagestan is home to over thirty indigenous peoples.[205]

This complex structure can be explained by the topography of the republic. Mountaineers settled in valleys isolated from one another by high mountains; hence through the centuries a large number of distinct, related but often mutually unintelligible languages developed.

In the Soviet era, when Dagestan was made into an autonomous republic, the issue of administration of the republic arose, and hence a system of distributing political positions among the ethnic groups was needed. The outcome was a system comparable to the Lebanese 'consociational' system prior to the civil war of 1975, with the only difference that in the Dagestani case the criterion was not religion but ethnicity, as defined primarily by language. This system, to a great extent, is still in place today.

As far as Dagestan is concerned, scholarly attention has been focused on three points: first, the possibility of a rebellion against Russia; second, the Islamic revival that has been observed in the post-Soviet era, and finally, last but not least, the fragile multi-ethnic stability of the republic.

Russia and Dagestan

The main difference between Chechnya and Dagestan in the post-Soviet period is that while in Chechnya, an anti-Soviet and anti-Russian leadership managed to grab power in the unruly days after the August 1991 coup, the Dagestani Soviet government was able to keep its hold on power until today. This fact can be linked to two main circumstances. First of all, the Chechen animosity towards Russia was exacerbated by the deportations of the second world war. As most Chechen leaders today were born in Kazakhstan or Siberia, they have first-hand experience of the horrors of deportation, which fuelled their traditional anti-Russian feelings. By contrast the Dagestanis' bitter memories date back longer, to the early 1920s. Secondly, the fact that Chechnya-Ingushetia was dominated by the Chechen people made the formation of a national front, the All-Chechen National Congress, easier. In Dagestan, the practical difficulties of politically uniting over two dozen peoples under a common framework resulted in no anti-Soviet popular front emerging – and the Sovietized government was able to stay in power without facing a credible challenge to its position. This government has remained true to Moscow despite the general quest for self-rule among the other North Caucasian territories. As Brian Murray has noted, 'the indigenous Sovietized elite within Dagestan maintains Soviet structures and Soviet power ... Soviet-ized Dagestanis are serving the role of an "absent sovereign" following the end of Soviet hegemony in the Caucasus'.[206] Similarly, Marie Bennigsen Broxup has argued that the Dagestani leadership 'subserviently voted in favour of remaining part of an "indivisible Russia" '.[207] Hence at the repub-lican level, the absence of Dagestani hostility to Moscow can be ascribed to the survival of old, pro-Russian power structures in the republic.

Compared to Chechnya, Dagestan is significantly more dependent on Russia for its finances. Over 80 per cent of the republic's funds are direct subsidies from Moscow;[208] the economic condition of the republic has also deteriorated considerably since 1991.[209] This gives an independent Dagestani state little economic viability, especially as Dagestan does not possess Chechnya's oil resources. This has certainly been a reason for the lack of enthusiasm for separatism.

At the popular level, an anti-Russian ferment certainly exists, although it is difficult to measure its extent and strength. The Russian army has not been careful in trying to prevent hostilities from spreading to Dagestan. In the initial phase of the invasion, the Russian forces on their way to Chechnya were stopped by civilians in Dagestan. In this case the Russian field commanders acted reasonably, choosing to make their way peacefully. In later stages, the Dagestani route was avoided, and most forces were chan-nelled through North Ossetia instead. The war actually spread to Dagestan on several occasions, most notably with the Chechen hostage-taking raid in Kizlyar and Pervomaiskoye, led by Salman Raduyev.[210] Whereas this event initially directed the Dagestanis' anger against the Chechens, the abrupt and bloody Russian intervention, which killed many hostages together with the Chechen rebels, certainly revived anti-Russian sentiments. Upon seeing the devastation of the village of Pervomaiskoye, one Dagestani member of parliament was even reported as cursing the Dagestani decision to side with Moscow and not with Chechnya in the war.

So far, Dagestan has remained comparatively calm, despite widespread criminality including the emerging practice of abducting people for ransom. No actual conflict has yet arisen between the Kremlin and Dagestan; however a change of leadership may be in the offing. The economic situa-tion of the republic, if nothing else, needs to be managed; foreign and domestic investments are needed; and in the long run the citizens will demand a more democratic form of government. If, furthermore, Moscow continues to disregard the popular will of the Caucasians – and there are no signals of the opposite – the Dagestanis might very well call for increased sovereignty. It is too early at this time to speculate on the outcome of such demands; however it should be noted that the Dagestani people are not susceptible to being significantly more pro-Russian than other Caucasian peoples. If history is of any guidance, the reverse is true. In this context, the religious awakening that is taking place in Dagestan is significant. Given Moscow's suspicious attitude towards Islam, the current tendency in Dagestan, which is truly growing to be – once again – the Islamic centre of the whole region, might very well cause Russia's discontent.

In May 1998, disturbances in Makhachkala erupted after Nadir Khachilayev, a member of the Russian State Duma and the leader of Russia's Muslim Union, whose brother heads the Lak national movement, apparently tried to stage a coup in the republic by occupying the building of the Dagestani state council.[211] Large numbers of Khachilayev's supporters emerged and demands were made for the resignation of Dagestan's leader Magomedali Magomedov. Negotiations resolved the immediate problems, but the event shed light upon Dagestan's present governance. The conflict had been prompted by the upcoming election to the state council's chairmanship. The chairman is currently elected by a constituent assembly, not by direct elections; strong forces, including the Khachilayev faction, demand direct elections to the post.[212] Only recently, Magomedov (a Dargin) had succeeded in removing the constitutional clause which stipulated the need of ethnic rotation for the post, hence enabling Magomedov to run for the post again.[213] Indeed, one of the main demands Khachilayev has made is for the post to be directly elected, and the rather drastic measures used can be seen as a way to create attention to the post-Soviet clique still ruling Dagestan. Nevertheless, Russian media as well as the Dagestani authorities have advanced the claim that Khachilayev's action is sponsored by Chechnya in an attempt to destabilize Dagestan. The impetus for such a move would be that a Dagestani government friendly to Chechnya would solve many of Chechnya's problems of contact with the outer world; indeed, Chechnya needs Dagestan for its access to the Caspian sea and to Azerbaijan.[214] Shamil Basayev, the Chechen field commander and current Prime Minister, indeed did support the action and Khachilayev is reputed to have good relations with Chechnya; furthermore Basayev has made no secret of his wish to create a unified and independent republic of Chechnya-Dagestan.[215] Perhaps Chechen involvement has been a factor, but it seems clear that the Dagestanis' leadership and its policies are by themselves sufficient to fuel widespread opposition. This was also the essence of Chechnya's foreign minister Movladi Udugov's reaction to the events.[216] The Khachilayev actions only prove that discontent with the government is growing. The later the real problems are dealt with, the more difficult will the 'de-Sovietization' of Dagestan be.[217]

The Return of Islam

The Islamic revival in the North Caucasus actually started long before Mikhail Gorbachev's advent to power, being traceable back to the 1970s.[218] Admittedly, even in the heyday of Soviet atheism, these religious practices were never eradicated; far from it, they flourished in the underground *Sufi* form. The Naqshbandya and Qadirya Tariqats, always powerful in the North Caucasus, became the focal point of Islam in the Soviet times, as official religion was persecuted by the authorities. What happened in the late 1980s was that religious practice came out in the open, finally even encompassing the indigenous Soviet elites. As Fanny Bryan has noted, the Islamic opposition underwent a strategic change with *Glasnost*. From being in latent opposition, it became an active, aggressive movement on the offensive against the system.[219] In 1989, the first religious demonstrations took place in Buinaksk and the capital, Makhachkala. The primary demand was the building of new mosques and the restoration of old ones. Before 1989, there were officially 27 functioning mosques in Dagestan, while by 1994 they were estimated at over 5000.[220] The Mufti of the Makhachkala 'spiritual directorate', accused of collaborating with the state security organs, was ousted by a popular revolt in May of the same year. It is believed that many of these revolts were initiated and conducted by the powerful *Tariqat* of the region. Furthermore, the *Haj* pilgrimage has been renewed on a large scale. Today, Arabic and Qu'ran classes are openly taking place in the schools of Dagestan,[221] and political leaders, riding on the Islamic wave, have proclaimed their intention to make Islam the state religion of the republic. The Islamic wind is blowing in the politics of Dagestan, too. The Islamic-Democratic Party decided to rename itself as the Islamic Party; its leadership has changed and become more religiously inflected.

As Vladimir Bobrovnikov has noted, in a rare field study on Islam in Dagestan, the Islamic revival has not taken place in a homogenous way. It has affected the northwestern part of the republic, populated by Avars, Dargins, and Kumyks, to a much larger extent than the central and southern parts, chiefly the places of residence of the Laks, Lezgins and Tabasarans.[222] The majority of newly-opened mosques and madrasahs are to be found in the northern and western parts of the country. The fact that the *Tariqat* have been strongest in these areas is probably an important reason for these regional differences. As we shall see in the next section, the religious movement, far from being united, has divided along national lines, with each of the larger grouping of peoples setting up a spiritual directorate, or Muftiate, of its own. Nevertheless this tendency is counteracted by currents which argue for unity in the name of Islam, currents which in the long run are likely to be victorious, at least if the religious movements are really such and do not turn out to be disguised nationalisms.

The Islamic revival in Dagestan is important as it is instrumental in tying the Dagestanis (and other North Caucasians) to the larger world of Islam. In particular, the performance of the *Haj* plays this role. The believers who, having performed the pilgrimage, return to their native lands can be presumed to work for the establishment of Islamic education there. Moreover, as has been the case in other areas such as in Turkey, their devotion entails a long-term objective of strengthening religion, completely independent from the short-term political struggle in the country – a strategy which has shown considerable success elsewhere.[223]

Hence in terms of identity, Islam – just as it has in the past – might become the unifying force of the North Caucasians. Whether this is a positive or negative development naturally depends on one's perspective on political Islam; Russia is likely to counteract this tendency, and even to use it as a pretext for re-establishing its hegemony over the region, reiterating its claim to be the defender of Europe and Christianity in face of an expansionist Islam. In Dagestan however, through its unifying power, Islam might be the main and crucial element in sustaining multi-ethnic peace and stability in the future. This logically brings us to our last point: multi-ethnic stability.

Multi-Ethnic Dagestan

The 'nationalities question' is more explosive in Dagestan than anywhere else in the Russian Federation, or for that matter in the whole of the former Soviet Union. Given the number of distinct nationalities, the size of the republic, and the overlapping settlement patterns, a territorial division of Dagestan is practically impossible.[224] For this reason, it is more imperative than elsewhere to prevent national movements from pronouncing territorial objectives, as such claims immediately would spur counter-claims and in the end a chaotic and conflictual situation.[225] It seems, however, that many Dagestanis are aware of this problem. The 'national question' is something people in the republic are reluctant to speak about.[226] However, past Soviet stirrings, as in the Prigorodniy and other places, have artificially changed the demographic structure of the republic. For example, as the Chechens were deported from their lands in, what was then, Eastern Chechnya, the territory forming the Aukhovsky district was given to Dagestan and a Lak community was forcibly settled on these lands with considerable loss of life. At the return of these Chechens, called the Chechen-Akkintsy, from deportation, this territory was not returned to the Chechen-Ingush ASSR. As the Chechens tried to settle in their native lands in the late 1980s, they came into a conflict with the Laks residing there, notably after the Aukhovsky raion had been re-established in May 1991 as a result of the April 1991 law on the rehabilitation of repressed peoples.[227] In this event, a solution was found to the conflict by the mediation of the Confederation of Mountain Peoples of the Caucasus as well as of the Dagestani government. The Laks, in a rare concession, agreed to resettle elsewhere in Dagestan, and funding for their new homes was to come from the central government. However, this concession was also due to the fact that Russian armed troops had been introduced in the region, troops which both population groups wanted to be withdrawn. The Akkintsy have also come into conflict with Avars who had been resettled in the Aukhovsky raion after 1944. The escalation of a conflict provoked by the Chechens threatening to move into two predominantly Avar villages in August 1992 was prevented by the intervention of Ramazan Abdulatipov and Ruslan Khas-bulatov, both widely-respected members of each community.[228]

Since the late Soviet years, popular fronts have emerged among most of the larger groupings of peoples of Dagestan. Among these, the most active and radical is clearly *Tenglik*, (Unity) the popular front of the Kumyk nation, founded in November 1989. The Kumyk people are the second Turkic-speaking people of the Caucasus after the Azeris, counting some 300,000 souls. The Kumyk traditionally live in the plains and foot-hills of the North Caucasus, in particular in the east of Dagestan, including the Caspian sea coast. Small communities exist in Chechnya and North Ossetia as well. The Kumyks' main grievance is that non-Kumyk peoples, primarily Avars and Dargins, migrated from the high-lands to settle in historical Kumyk lands during Soviet times.[232] The Kumyks also feel discriminated against in the government of Dagestan, as well as in higher education. The territorial issue nevertheless remains the key point of contention. Despite Kumyk protests, thousands of non-Kumyks were allowed to settle in Kumyk lands north of Makhachkala, lands from which Kumyks had been relocated to Chechnya in 1944.[233]

The demands of the Kumyks are unclear. According to Jibrail Khabibullah, a representative of *Tenglik*, the movement desires a form of local autonomy, with some radical groups even asking for a sovereign

Table 2: Dagestan's Demographic Structure[229]

Ethnic Group	Number	Percentage
Avar	495,000	27,5
Dargin	280,000	15,6
Kumyk	232,000	12,9
Lezgin	205,000	11,3
Russian	166,000	9,2
Lak	92,000	5,1
Tabasaran	79,000	4,3
Azeri	75,000	4,1
Chechen	58,000	3,1
Nogai	28,000	1,6
Rutul	15,000	0,8
Agul	14,000	0,8
Andi[230]	8000	0,4
Ukrainian	8000	0,4
Tses / Dido[231]	7000	0,4
Armenian	6000	0,3
Tatar	5500	0,3
Tsakhur	5000	0,3
Tat (Mountain Jews)	4000	0,3

Kumyk republic on the Caspian sea.[234] Moreover, the Kumyks want to restructure the whole of Dagestan. As pronounced by Kamil Aliyev, the foreign relations secretary of *Tenglik*, the Kumyk proposals to 'organize Dagestan's national problems' are as follows:

- National-regional autonomy (similar to Swiss cantons),
- Furnishing national minorities and national groups with land,
- Cultural autonomy.[235]

The Kumyks active in *Tenglik* seem convinced that such a restructuring of Dagestan, involving a new constitution and national parliaments, would ensure the 'multipartite and multinational unity' of Dagestan. They are equally convinced that an insistence on the part of the republican government on preserving the unitary structure of the country would lead to 'democratic struggle', whatever that entails.[236]

The arguments of *Tenglik* raise a very crucial and difficult question: which form of government is the most conducive to peace and stability in multi-ethnic societies? In reply to this question, two main models are advocated. The first, currently in place in Dagestan, preserves the unity of the state and provides for *power-sharing* mechanisms among the constituting peoples of the state. The second, as proposed by *Tenglik*, argues for a territorial delimitation and some kind of federal or autonomous structure.

The main contention hence lies between an approach which tries to integrate peoples of different ethnic groups in the management of a single state, and an approach which advocates that peace is best protected if groups stay apart and rule their own affairs to the greatest extent possible.[237]

The theoretical details of the different approaches are not our consideration here, however it should be noted that the power-sharing approach is divided into an 'integrative' wing, aiming at creating trans-ethnic political coalitions and alliances and intra-ethnic competition;[238] and a 'consociational' wing which accords more political importance in politics to the ethnic groups as such, involving minority vetoes, proportionality in allocation of civil service positions and funds, etc.[239] Basically, the integrative approach tries to cut through ethnic lines and diminish the salience of ethnicity in political and social life, whereas the consociational approach aims at protecting minorities and the achievement of consensus between the leadership of the respective groups. Dagestan has adopted a model reminiscent of the Lebanese one, with a division of political posts at the local and national levels based on ethnicity.[240]

In the Dagestani case, the 'cantonal' model proposed by *Tenglik* among others is, at a closer view, extremely dangerous. It is highly divisive, and what is more, impossible to translate into practice. Besides the number of ethnic groups and the problems arising thereof, as well as the problem of what to do with the smaller groupings of peoples, ethnically-mixed villages and cities would be cut into sections, one assumes, and the heritage of a *Dagestani* identity would fade away, leaving place for ethnic politics to fill its gap. Moreover the territorial claims of the many groups are overlapping, and hence a territorial delimitation would certainly lead to conflicts. Whereas most popular fronts in the republic accept these arguments and are against a territorial division, *Tenglik* has obstinately continued to advocate a revision of the republican structure, for example in a Makhachkala congress in March 1994.[241]

As Brian Murray has consistently argued, the presence of a Dagestani identity with the historical figure of Shamil as its primary figure-head, connected to the common Islamic identity of all peoples, makes a 'united Dagestan' a realistic objective. As he rightly notes, 'dividing Dagestan up into ethnic autonomous regions would repeat the mistakes of Soviet ethnic federalism and could have horrifying consequences given the republic's ethnic geography'.[242] To further Dagestan's peace and unity, however, the current power-sharing arrangement must be revised to answer to the post-Soviet reality. Many scholars in this respect would advocate the 'Lebanon-type' consociational approach. Given the complexity of Dagestan, some form of quota of ethnic groups in state service is probably inevitable; in this respect, the Kumyk claims might be satisfied to some degree. However, as far as it is possible, the ethnic differences should be bridged over rather than emphasized. The fate of the Lebanese consociational system is illustrative of this problemati. Brian Murray has highlighted the differences between multi-ethnic and ethnically bifurcated societies.[243] In particular, he emphasizes the dangers of ethnic federalism, which effectively bifurcate ethnic groups and hence aggravate rather than alleviate ethnic tensions.[244] Seen from a certain distance, Murray makes the point that Dagestan, despite its serious problems, has been the most peaceful republic in the post-Soviet North Caucasus. Does this not, then, support the argument that its policy of power-sharing (which existed only in Dagestan) in the place of ethnic federalism (practised elsewhere in the Soviet Union) is more conducive to peace than ethnic bifurcation?

What would suit Dagestan best, then, is a power-sharing agreement which is as integrative as possible, encouraging political movements in transcending ethnic differences and political competition within ethnic groups – all to prevent the salience of ethnic politics. Simultaneously, a certain consociational touch is necessary to protect the interests of the individual ethnic groups. A certain proportionality in parliament and in civil service could be desirable, as would cultural autonomy. Given the grievances of the Kumyks, a form of veto right over affairs that directly concern the ethnic group might be necessary.[245]

Here only an outline has been presented; however, the matter deserves further attention from conflict theorists. A study on a power-sharing model suitable for Dagestan is highly desirable.

In conclusion as far as Dagestan is concerned, the situation is worrying but does not give cause for alarm. The grievances of certain groups, such as the Kumyks, need to be addressed promptly to prevent further activism among the people. However, the proposals to split up Dagestan into autonomous units, cherished by *Tenglik*, indeed seem to be a recipe for disaster rather than a recipe for lasting peace. Dagestanis however share a certain overlapping common identity, heavily influenced by Islam, which may be capitalized upon to prevent communalism from expanding. Many

Dagestanis are aware of the danger of the national question, and efforts are being undertaken both by government and opposition to seek to promote inter-group cohesion.[246] These are promising trends, nevertheless the present structure of the republic needs to be revised sooner or later to cope with the new challenges that confront Dagestan in a new era. International support and counselling for models of power-sharing are therefore vital for the peace and stability of Dagestan.

Cooperative Efforts

Given the highly complicated pattern of open and potential conflicts in and around the North Caucasus, the prospects for creating a lasting cooperative environment in the region are indeed not evident. However, a number of attempts at cooperative organizations or movements have been made in the North Caucasus. The most well known of these is the Confederation of (Mountain) Peoples of the Caucasus, which is an all-encompassing organization; however other more limited attempts at cooperation include associations of repressed peoples (those that were deported during the second world war), of Circassian peoples (Adyge, Kabardin, Cherkess), of Turkic peoples (in the North Caucasus Kumyk, Nogai, Karachai, Balkar), of peoples of Chechnya and Dagestan.

The Confederation of Peoples of the Caucasus

The confederation's roots go back to 1989, when the tensions between the Abkhaz and Georgia were on the rise. The Abkhaz, aware of their demographic situation, realized the need for external support in their struggle. Hence they took the initiative in organizing a first congress of the mountain peoples of the Caucasus the same year, held in Sukhumi. The congress was attended by Abkhaz, Chechen, Ingush, Kabardin, and Cherkess participants. Within a couple of years, the Confederation of Mountain Peoples of the Caucasus had been established, with 16 'member peoples', including Abaza, Abkhaz, Akki, Adygei, Avar, Chechen, Cherkess, Dargin, Ingush, Kabardin, Lak, Lezgin, North Ossetian, South Ossetian, Rutul, and Shapsug. Four other peoples joined in as 'observers', namely the Cossacks and the Turkic Karachai, Kumyk, and Nogai. With the addition of these four, the term 'Mountain' was dropped from the name of the Confederation, which simply became the Confederation of Peoples of the Caucasus (CPC). The CPC created a parliament composed of three members from each group, members that were often close to government circles in their respective republic, occasionally even government officials.[247]

During its first years of existence, the confederation seemed to be developing into a coherent and credible political force. Its role first became apparent in the last phase of open hostilities in the Georgian-South Ossetian conflict in June 1992, as noted in an earlier section of this chapter. The Confederation succeeded in setting up a battalion of volunteers and bringing them to North Ossetia. The existence of this battalion exerted a significant influence on both the Russian and Georgian governments, in adding a North Caucasian factor to the conflict, thereby another danger of escalation. In fact the confederation's strong showing certainly had an influence on the cease-fire that was concluded later in the same month.

However, the main show of strength on the part of the Confederation was in the Georgian-Abkhaz war of 1992-93. The day after the Georgian attack of 14 June 1992, almost fifty South Ossetian volunteers set off for Abkhazia through the assistance of the Confederation.[248] Besides an estimated 350 Ossetian fighters, the Confederation was able to muster several hundred more volunteers, mainly Chechens and Kabardins. In fact, the later famed Chechen leader, Shamil Basayev received invaluable fighting experience as he led the Abkhaz forces in the battle of Gagra in August. Basayev later led his own battalion, the so-called 'International Battalion', in the war, which was one of the key fighting units on the Abkhaz side; nevertheless it nominally remained under the command of the Confederation. Several North Caucasian battalions in fact fought on the Abkhaz side in the war, and the Confederation's contribution to the Abkhaz war effort was crucial to the Abkhaz success.

As far as the Chechen war is concerned, the role of the Confederation was distinctively weaker. In fact, one could argue that Chechnya and Abkhazia have been the main pillars of the Confederation, perhaps with an emphasis on the former due to the simple fact that Chechnya is demographically ten times stronger than Abkhazia. The Circassians consider the Abkhaz a people closely related to themselves, something which is not true with the Chechens. As a result, the Circassian response that was forthcoming in Abkhazia was not reproduced in the case of Chechnya, although several dozens of Circassian volunteers did appear in Chechnya. An even larger number of Abkhaz travelled to Chechnya to support the Chechen war effort; however nothing close to the general Caucasian support that was forthcoming in Abkhazia manifested itself in Chechnya's war with Russia. There are several factors that help to explain this, all of which have a bearing on the future of the Confederation.

There are theories, especially in Georgia, that the Confederation was nothing more than a Russian stooge to prevent Georgia's independence and use Abkhazia and South Ossetia as levers against Tbilisi; being a Russian creation it would naturally not support Chechnya. According to this logic, the Confederation was an optimal tool for Moscow as it didn't publicly display Moscow's actions, but enabled a cover-up in the name of North Caucasian brotherhood. This theory is nevertheless contradicted by several factors. The first is that the Confederation's ultimate aim was to carve out a multi-ethnic independent republic from the Black Sea to the Caspian Sea from Georgian and Russian territory; 'from Sukhumi to Derbent', as Charles van der Leeuw quotes the Dagestani (Lak) secretary general of the Confederation Ali Aliev.[249] That Russia should be behind a movement that so openly represented a direct challenge to Russia's territorial integrity seems unlikely. What in fact does seem likely is that the interests of the Confederation and Moscow coincided as regards Abkhazia, and that Moscow used the Confederation, refraining from impeding its activities, as it served its purposes.

The real factors that have impeded the Confederation's working seem to be two-fold: a general decline of nationalism and the Ingush-Ossetian war. In fact, the same tendency can be observed throughout the Russian Federation's minority areas: a general upsurge of nationalistic fervour in the late 1980s, which however failed to survive into the mid-1990s. After the dissolution of the Soviet Union, the worsened economic situation in most peripheral areas of Russia led to a realization that the autonomous republics were dependent on Moscow for their survival. Also at the popular level a certain sobering, so to speak, has taken place; people are generally less preoccupied with political matters and have lost the euphoria of 1988-92, when many believed in the possibility of tangibly improving their own situation. As a result, by 1995 fewer people were prepared to go to war for the concept of Caucasian solidarity, at a time when the independence of the North Caucasus seemed unlikely but also economically non-attractive. Related to this, it was a substantial difference to fight the comparatively ill-trained and ill-equipped Georgian paramilitary forces, as compared to the massive Russian military forces that attacked Chechnya. The risks of joining a Chechen war effort that seemed poised to be bloodily defeated must have appeared much larger than the prospects of success that the Abkhaz adventure possessed. This said, the level of popular support for the Chechens in the North Caucasus was distinctive. Popular demonstrations hindered the movement of the Russian army columns on their way to Chechnya in the early stages of the war, in particular in Dagestan and Ingushetia.

With respect to the Confederation and its ability to coordinate support, the war between two members of the Confederation – that is the North Ossetians and the Ingush – seems to have carried great importance. In a sense, the war seems to have been instrumental in delivering a fatal blow to the power of action of the Confederation by causing a rift in the North-Central Caucasus that was vital for its cohesion. With a deep wedge between the Ingush and the Chechens on the one hand and the Ossetians on the other, with the Northwestern Caucasus seemingly rather indifferent to the controversy, the component pieces of the very diverse Confederation seem to have fallen into pieces. For example, the few South Ossetian volunteers that came to Chechnya to fight Russia were politely asked to leave, as the Chechens did not want to anger their Ingush brethren.[250] Instead of showing strength by mediating in the conflict, the Confederation allowed the Ingush-Ossetian war to ruin its foundations of Caucasian solidarity. As Dodge Billingsley notes, the Confederation is currently a non-player; however, the support for Chechnya on the grass-roots level is a sign that 'the spirit of the Confederation, if not the organization itself, lives on, perhaps to resurface in better times.'[251]

Other Cooperative Attempts

No cooperative attempt other then the Confederation has the capacity to encompass all nations of the North Caucasus at the highest level: that is what makes the Confederation so interesting. Basically, all other forms of cooperation fall into either one of the following categories: larger organizations that appeal to certain peoples of the region; and sub-regional cooperative attempts that appeal to certain but not all peoples of the North Caucasus. None hence has the prospect of uniting the North Caucasus as a whole to prevent the outbreak of new conflicts; in fact some have a potential to create rather than to impede further conflict.

The Assembly of Democratic Forces of the North Caucasus is an association of some 70 local non-governmental organizations of the entire North Caucasus and Kalmykia. It has tried to encourage peace initiatives in the Prigorodniy conflict, without particular success. However, the initiative is promising through its geographical extension, although its possibility to influence governmental bodies and hence to actually play a role is limited, given the weakness of civil society in the North Caucasus.

The Confederation of Repressed Peoples (CRP) is an organization that stretches over the entire former Soviet Union, comprising ten member peoples and striving to support the claims to full rehabilitation of the peoples that were deported and otherwise repressed in the Stalin era. As far as the North Caucasus is concerned, the four deported peoples (Chechens, Ingush, Karachai and Balkar) are represented in this organization. The CRP has supported the Ingush claim to the Prigorodniy raion, seeing it as a step towards full territorial rehabilitation. Obviously, the CRP is an interest group of a variety of peoples that have no regional connection; as such, it has little prospect of playing a stabilizing role in the North Caucasus

The Assembly of Turkic Peoples (ATP) is a worldwide organization of peoples claiming a Turkic heritage and thus connected by linguistic links. There are four members in the North Caucasus, the Kumyk, Nogai, Karachai, and Balkar. Among them, only the Karachai are significant demographically and by being the largest titular nationality in the republic of Karachai-Cherkessia. The ATP cannot, by the same token as the CRP, play any larger role in the North Caucasus given the comparative lack of Turkic peoples in the region. The ATP can nevertheless be expected to side with Kumyks if Dagestani politics were to take an ethnic turn, in which case the Kumyk would certainly be a major actor.

The Islamic Nation and the *Congress of Peoples of Chechnya and Dagestan* are organizations that seek to further a union of Chechnya and Dagestan, with the strong support of important Chechen figures such as Movladi Udugov and Shamil Basayev. After having made vague comments regarding the possible return of the Northwestern Aukovsky district of Dagestan to Chechnya, Udugov in 1997-98 clarified his political aims with the creation of the movement called the "Islamic Nation", unifying political forces from Chechnya and Dagestan, and aiming at creating an 'Imamate' of the type of Imam Shamil's nineteenth century state. During 1998, Shamil Basayev became a driving force behind the idea, and in May 1998 convened a 'Congress of the Peoples of Chechnya and Dagestan' with the support of Udugov, now foreign minister of Chechnya.[252] In July, Basayev resigned from his post as acting prime minister and claimed that he would now focus on building up an 'Islamic paramilitary brigade', intended to 'tackle the problems facing Muslims in the North Caucasus'.[253] The resignation seems also to have been prompted by disagreements with president Maskhadov, not least on the issue of Dagestan; Maskhadov does not seem to pursue the idea of stirring up Dagestan, but is rather trying to build friendly relations with the Soviet-time regime surviving there. In any case, the result has been a further destabilization of Dagestan, which already lived in a tense semblance of stability. The consequences of the unification attempts of Chechnya and Dagestan are difficult to assess. In the short term, they remain a factor of instability in the region and do not further North Caucasian security as a whole.

Conclusions and Prospects

In the discussion above, the concentration is, unfortunately, on conflicts as opposed to cooperation. In fact, the situation in the North Caucasus today is a situation marked by deep instability and a plethora of problems of all kinds – related to ethnic relations, governance, economic deprivation, widespread criminality, and difficult democratization, to name but a few examples. The region is formally littered with weapons of all kinds and calibres and the increasing number of abductions, especially of foreigners for ransom, has led practically all international organizations, private and public, to cease operating in the North Caucasus as the region is simply not safe. This has, in turn, led to an increased isolation from the outside world; almost all contact that the region keeps with the outside world is through Russia. Even cooperation with the Transcaucasian countries to the south is difficult; Azerbaijan and Georgia are worried about the instability in Chechnya and Dagestan especially, and do their utmost to prevent the instability to their north spreading into their territory. Georgia, for example, has long been contemplating opening its border with Chechnya and upgrading the existing road to a functional highway; however because of the spectre of Chechen criminal elements bringing unrest to Georgia, the project has been put on ice.

In the late 1990s the North Caucasus is, then, a region whose opening up to the world is delayed by its own problems. In turn, the lack of economic and other contacts with the outside world is likely to further delay the economic recovery of the region. Bearing in mind that most of the republics of the North Caucasus are financed to over 50 per cent, sometimes to 80 per cent, by subsidies from the Russian central government, the recent financial crisis in Russia does not bode well. In fact, it is possible, if not probable, that the subsidies from the centre will gradually be reduced. The result of such a development would be likely to lead to greater competition for the scarce government-provided resources in the region than is the case today. And given the high level of group cohesion and awareness of ethnic identity in the North Caucasus, such competition would in many instances be likely to take the shape of competition between ethnic groups, as has already been the case in Dagestan to a limited extent.

The situation in the North Caucasus does, definitively, not bode well. Most of the region, as it has been defined in this study, constitutes one of the most economically-deprived regions of a state (the Russian Federation) that is in a downward economic spiral. It is also a region in which, as has been discussed in detail above, a number of unsolved conflicts of which many have an ethnopolitical character exist. With the current isolation of the region, there is little that outside powers can or will do to prevent escalation of tensions. The future of the region is in the end to a large extent dependent on the policies of the Russian Federal government.

Notes

1   See Gueorgui Otyrba, "War in Abkhazia—the Regional Significance of the Georgian-Abkhazian Conflict", in Roman Szporluk, (ed.), *The International Relations of Eurasia, vol. 1: National Identity in Russia and the New States of Eurasia*, Armonk, NY: ME Sharpe, 1994, pp. 283-309.

2   A pro-Abkhaz account of the conflict's history is B. G. Hewitt, "Abkhazia: A Problem of Identity and Ownership", in *Central Asian Survey*, vol. 12 no. 3, 1993, pp. 267-323, here at p. 271.

3   For an Abkhazian perspective, see Stanislav Lakoba, "Abkhazia is Abkhazia", in *Central Asian Survey*, vol. 14 no. 1, 1995, pp. 97-105, here at p. 99.

4   See John Colarusso, "Abkhazia", in *Central Asian Survey*, vol. 14 no. 1, 1995, pp. 75-96, here at p. 78.

5   See Stephen Jones, "Georgia: A Failed Democratic Transition", in Bremmer and Taras, *Nations and Politics in the Soviet Successor States*, pp. 288-310, here at p. 291.

6   See Darrell Slider, "Crisis and Response in Soviet Nationality Policy: The Case of Abkhazia", in *Central Asian Survey*, vol. 4 no. 4, 1985, pp. 51-68.

7   See table in Philip Petersen, "Security Policy in Post-Soviet Transcaucasia", in *European Security*, vol. 3 no. 1, Spring 1994, pp. 1-57, here at p. 14; figures taken from Anzor Totadze, "Population of Abkhazia", in *Sakartvelos Respublika*, 17 September 1992.

8   See Stephen Jones, "Border Disputes and Disputed Borders in the Soviet Federal System", in *Nationalities Papers*, vol. 15 no. 1, Spring 1987, p. 56.

9   See Slider, "Crisis and Response in Soviet Nationality Policy: The Case of Abkhazia", op. cit.

10 Otyrba, "War in Abkhazia", op. cit [1], p. 285.

11 Hewitt, "Abkhazia: A Problem of Identity and Ownership", op. cit. [2], p. 282.

12 See Jones, "Georgia: A Failed Democratic Transition", op. cit. [5], p. 292.

13 See Darrell Slider, "Democratization in Georgia", in Karen Dawisha and Bruce Parrott, (eds), *Conflict, Cleavage and Change in Central Asia and the Caucasus*, Cambridge: Cambridge University Press, 1991, pp. 156-200, here at p. 170.

14 See Jones, "Border Disputes and Disputed Borders", op. cit. [8], pp. 56-57.

15 Interview with Avtandil Imnadze, one of the leaders of the Georgian National Movement since the 1970s, Tbilisi, October 1998.

16 Zviad Gamsakhurdia, "Istoricheskaia Spravka ob Abkhazii", in *Vestnik Gruzii*, October 1989, quoted in Gerber, *Georgien*, p. 207.

17 Quoted from Otyrba, "War in Abkhazia", op. cit. [1], p. 285.

18 See Elizabeth Fuller, "Georgia, Abkhazia, and Chechen-Ingushetia", in *RFE/RL Research Report*, 7 Februasry 1992, p. 5; Stéphane Yérasimos, "Caucase: Le Retour de la Russie", p. 63.

19 See *Current Digest*, vol. 41 no. 29, 1989, pp. 14-16.

20 Paul B. Henze, "Abkhazia Diary—1997", in Mehmet Tütüncü, *Caucasus: War and Peace*, Haarlem: SOTA; 1997, p. 105.

21 *BBC Monitoring Service: Former USSR*, 18 June 1992.

22 See Otyrba, "War in Abkhazia", op. cit. [1], p. 287; *BBC Monitoring Service: Former USSR*, 25 July 1992.

23 "Georgia: Georgian State Council Anxious About Abkhazia", BBC Monitoring Service, 2 July 1992; "Georgia: Abkhazia Declares Sovereignty", BBC Monitoring Service, 25 July 1992.

24 See "Abkhazia Declares its Independence, but Wants to Remain Within a Georgian-Abkhaz 'Federal State'", in *Current Digest*, v 44 n 30, 26 August 1992, p.24.

25 "Russia: Shevardnadze Ends Stormy Tour of West Georgia", *Reuters*, 24 July 1992; "Georgia: Shevardnadze Fears Georgian Disintegration", Reuters, 27 July 1992.

26 "Russia: Shevardnadze May Quit If Georgia Crushes Unrest", *Reuters*, 27 July 1992.

27 "Georgia: Abkhazia 'Strong Enough to Fight Georgia'", *BBC Monitoring Service*, 30 July 1992.

28 "Georgia: Deputies at Abkhaz Parliament Annul Decree on Constitution", *BBC Monitoring Service*, 1 August 1992.

29 "Russia: Georgia Lurches towards Civil War with Rebel Region", *Reuters*, 14 August 1992.

30 "Georgia: Georgia Sends Tanks Into Rebel Capital", *Reuters*, 18 August 1992; "Georgia: Abkhazian Separatists Maintain Defiance of Georgia", *Reuters*, 19 August 1992.

31 Mary Dejevsky, "Georgia: Caucasus Muslims Join Battle – Abkhazi Fighters Continue Armed Resistance", *The Times*, 20 August 1992.

32 "Mountain People Join the War on Abkhazia's side", in *Izvestia*, 26 August 1992, pp. 1-2, in *Current Digest*, 23 September 1992. On the Confederation, see Dodge Billingsley, "Confederates of the Caucausus", in *Jane's Intelligence Review*, February 1997. See also Otyrba, "War in Abkhazia", pp. 292-294.

33 For a relatively pro-Georgian perspective on this issue, see Svetlana Chervonnaya, *Conflict in the Caucasus—Georgia, Abkhazia, and the Russian Shadow*, (Translated by Ariane Chanturia) Glastonbury: Gothic Image Publications, 1994.

34 "Attack on Gagra Leaves Dozens of Dead and Wounded", in *Izvestia*, 2 October 1992, p. 2, in *current digest*, 11 November 1992.

35 See Alexei Zverev, "Ethnic Conflicts in the Caucasus 1988-1994", in Bruno Coppettiers, (ed.), *Contested Borders in the Caucasus*, Brussels: VUBPress, 1996, p. 49.

36 Viacheslav Chirikba, "The Georgian-Abkhaz Conflict and its Aftermath", in Mehmet Tütüncü, (ed) *Caucasus: War and Peace*, Haarlem: SOTA, 1998, p. 76

37 See Catherine Dale, "The Case of Abkhazia (Georgia)", in Lena Jonson and Clive Archer (eds.), *Peacekeeping and the Role of Russia in Eurasia*, Boulder: Westview Press, 1996, p. 126. On Russia's role, see Svante E. Cornell, *Small Nations and Great Powers: A Study of Ethnopolitical Conflict in the Caucasus*, Richmond: Curzon, 1999, chapter 9.

38 *RFE/RL News Briefs*, vol. 2 no. 10, 1993.

39 *RFE/RL News Brief*, 15-19 March 1993.

40 *Financial Times*, 15 & 16 May 1993; *Moscow News*, 21 May 1993.

41 Ibid., p. 54.

42 Helen Womack, "Georgian Leader Survives Shell Blast", *The Independent*, 6 July 1993.

43 *Svenska Dagbladet*, 7 July 1993.

44 *The Times*, 7 July 1993.

45 *Svenska Dagbladet*, 9 July 1993.

46 *Svenska Dagbladet*, 28 July 1993; *International Herald Tribune*, 29 July 1993.

47 *International Herald Tribune*, 27 September 1993; *Svenska Dagbladet*, 26 September 1993.

48 *International Herald Tribune*, 28 September 1993.

49 See "Russia Calls on Georgia Not to Fight Abkhazians", *International Herald Tribune*, 21 September 1993.

50 Anatol Lieven, "Georgian Forces Routed by Rebels", *The Times*, 1 October 1993.

51 For a short overview of the military events, see Christian Altmann and Frank Nien-huysen, *Brennpunkt Kaukasus*, Bergisch Gladbach: Bastei Lübbe, 1994, pp. 44-49.

52 See eye-witness accounts, e.g. Anatol Lieven, "Victorious Abkhazian Army Settles Old Scores in An Orgy of Looting", *The Times*, 4 October 1993; Lee Hockstader, "In Georgia, Tales of Atrocities", *International Herald Tribune*, 22 October 1993.

53 United Nations, *United Nations Peacekeeping*, 1994 update, p. 164.

54 *The Times, Svenska Dagbladet, International Herald Tribune*, 12 and 19 October 1993.

55 *Moscow News*, 22 October 1993.

56 See S. Neil MacFarlane, Larry Minear, and Stephen D. Shenfield, *Armed Conflict in Georgia: A Case Study in Humanitarian Action and Peacekeeping*, Occasional Paper no. 21, Watson Institute for International Studies, Providence: Brown University, 1996.

57 *The Times*, 10 October 1993.

58 *Svenska Dagbladet*, 7 November 1993.

59 See Dodge Billingsley, "Truce Means Nothing in Western Georgia", in *Jane's Intelligence Review*, June 1998, pp. 13-14.

60 See MacFarlane et al., *Armed Conflict in Georgia*, op. cit. [56], pp. 11-12.

61 Billingsley, "Truce Means Nothing in Western Georgia", op. cit. [59], p. 15.

62 Quoted from MacFarlane et al., *Armed Conflict in Georgia*, op. cit. [56], p. 12.

63 Quoted from MacFarlane et al., *Armed Conflict in Georgia*, op. cit. [56], p. 12.

64 See Alexandre Bennigsen and S. Enders Wimbush, *Muslims of the Soviet Empire: A Guide*, London: Hurst & Co., 1985, pp. 190-200, here p. 197. See also Rieks Smeets, Circassia, in *Central Asian Survey*, no. 1, 1995, pp. 107-125. Here p. 109.

65 Bennigsen and Wimbush, *op. cit.* [64], pp. 201-204.

66 For an overview of the co-optation of Caucasian elites, see Chantal Lemer-cier-Quelquejay, "Cooptation of the Elites of Kabarda and Dagestan in the Sixteenth Century", in Marie Bennigsen Brozup, (ed.) *The North Caucasus Barrier*, London: Hurst & Company, 1992.

67 Bennigsen and Wimbush, *op. cit.* [64], pp. 200.

68 *Ibid.*, p. 202.

69 See Sergei Arutionov, "Ethnicity and Conflict in the Caucasus", paper presented at a 1997 symposium of the Slavic Research Center, Hokkaido University, p. 8.

70 Marina Pustilnik, "Caucasian Stresses", in *Transition,* 15 March 1995, p.16-18.

71 See Arutionov, *op. cit.,* [69], p. 8.

72 See Tomila Lankina, "The Cossacks: A Guarantor of Peace or a Land-Mine in Russia's Federalism?", in *Nationalities Papers*, no. 4, 1996.

73 Pustilnik, *op. cit.,* [70], p. 18.

74 See Suzanne Goldenberg, *Pride of Small Nations: The Caucasus and Post-Soviet Disorder.* London: Zed, 1994, p. 206.

75 For details on the Cossack revival, see Roman Laba, "The Cossack Movement and the Russian State, 1990-96", in *Low Intensity Conflict and Law Enforcement*, vol. 5 no. 3, Winter 1996, pp. 377-408.

76 See Fiona Hill, *"Russia's Tinderbox": Conflict in the north Caucasus and its Implications for the Future of the Russian Federation*, Cambridge, Mass: Harvard University, JFK School of Government Strengthening Democratic Institutions Project, pp. 67-73 for the Cossacks' territorial demands and their implications.

77 See Goldenberg, op. cit. [74], p. 205.

78 See Hill, *op. cit.* [76], p. 63.

79 See Arutionov, op. cit. [69], p. 10.

80 "President of Karachayevo-Cherkessiya Postpones Elections", in *OMRI Russian Regional Report*, 8 May 1997.

81 "First Protest Meeting in Karachaevo-Cherkessia's History", in *The Jamestown Monitor*, 28 January 1998.

82 "Population of Karachaevo-Cherkessia Demand to Elect Their President", *The Jamestown Monitor*, 26 February 1998.

83 See "Former Russian Commander May Run for Presidency in Karachaevo-Cherkessia", in *The Jamestown Monitor*, 2 May 1997.

84 Helen Krag and Lars Funch, *The North Caucasus: Minorities at a Crossroads*, Minority Rights Publications, 1994, p. 32.

85 See Natalia Gorodetskaya in *Segodnya*, 23 November 1996, in *Current Digest of the Post-Soviet Press*, no. 47, 1996, p. 16.

86 Krag and Funch, op. cit. [84], p. 32.

87 OMRI Daily Digest, 19 November 1996.

88 See Dimitry Kamyshev, in *Kommersant*, 20 November 1996, in "The Chechen Example Could Become Contagious", *Current Digest*, no. 47, 1996, p. 15

89 See *OMRI Russian Regional Report*, 4 December 1996.

90 OMRI Daily Digest, 26 November 1996.

91 OMRI Daily Digest, 9 January 1997.

92 See Elizabeth Fuller, "Draft 'State Program' on Georgian Language Published", in *Radio Liberty Research Report*, 559/88, 12 December 1988.

93 See Catherine Dale, "Abkhazia and South Ossetia: Dynamics of the Conflicts", in Pavel Baev and Ole Berthelsen (eds), *Conflicts in the Caucasus*, PRIO Report 3/96, Oslo: International Peace Research Institute, 1996, pp. 13-26.

94 See Elizabeth Fuller, "The South Ossetian Campaign for Unification", in *Report on the USSR*, no. 49, 1989, pp. 17-20, here at p. 18.

95 See Elizabeth Fuller, "South Ossetia—Analysis of a Permanent Crisis", in *Report on the* USSR, 15 February 1991, p. 21

96 Fuller, "The South Ossetian Campaign for Unification", op. cit. [64] p. 19, quoting *Literaturuli Sakartvelo*, 20 October 1989.

97 Ibid., p. 21.

98 See Julian Birch, "The Georgian/South Ossetian Territorial and Boundary Dispute", in John F. Wright, Suzanne Goldenberg and Richard Schofield, (eds), *Transcaucasian Boundaries*, London: UCL Press, 1996, p. 182.

99 See Rachel Denber, *Bloodshed in the Caucasus: Violations of Humanitarian Law and Human Rights in the Georgia-South Ossetia Conflict*, New York: Helsinki Watch, April 1992, p. 7. Figures are from *Komsomolskaya Pravda*, 26 December 1990.

100 See Alexei Zverev, "Ethnic Conflicts in the Caucasus 1988-94",

101 See Elizabeth Fuller, "Georgian Parliament Votes to Abolish Ossetian Autonomy", in *RFE/RL Report on the USSR*, 21 December 1990, p. 8; Denber, *Bloodshed in the Caucasus*, p. 8.

102 See Zverev, "Ethnic Conflicts in the Caucasus 1988-94", op. cit. [35] p. 44

103 Ibid, p. 45

104 See Julian Birch, "Ethnic Cleansing in the Caucasus", in *Nationalism and Ethnic Politics*, vol. 1 no. 4, 1995, pp. 90-107. *Moscow News*, 19 November 1992, estimates a total number of 40-55,000 Ossetians from Georgia proper.

105 See Dale, "Abkhazia and South Ossetia: Dynamics of the Conflicts", p. 14-15.

106 See Jones, "Georgia: the Trauma of Statehood, in Ian Bremmer and Ray Taras (eds), *New States, New Politics—Building the Post-Soviet States*, Cambridge University press, 1997, p. 522.

107 Ghia Nodia, "Georgia's Identity Crisis", in *Journal of Democracy*, vol. 6 no. 1, 1995, p. 109.

108 Slider, "Democratization in Georgia", op. cit. [13], p. 162.

109 Ghia Nodia, "The Ethnic Policies of Zviad Gamsakhurdia", in Coppetiers, op. cit. [35], p. 80

110 See Zverev, "Ethnic Conflicts in the Caucasus 1988-94", op. cit. [35], p. 45.

111 See Charles H. Fairbanks, "The Postcommunist Wars", in *Journal of Democracy*, October 1995, for an overview of the peculiar, unprofessional character of guerrilla forces such as those of Ioselani and Sigua in Georgia, or those of Surat Huseinov in Azerbaijan.

112 See Birch, "Ossetia: A Caucasian Bosnia in Microcosm", p. 46-47.

113 See Zverev, "Ethnic Conflicts in the Caucasus 1988-94", p. 46.

114 Great Soviet Encyclopaedia, 1976, 'Ingush'.

115 See Julian Birch, "Ossetia: a Caucasian Bosnia in Microcosm", in *Central Asian Survey*, no. 1, 1995, p. 43-74; here p. 52.

116 The city was called Vladikavkaz (Roughly translated as 'Conquer the Caucasus') until 1931, when it was named Ordzhonikidze after one of the great Caucasian Bolsheviks, Georgiy Konstantinovich Ordzhonikidze. Perhaps as Ordzhonikidze came into conflict with Stalin in the mid-1930s and died of a 'heart attack', the city was renamed Dzhaudzhikau in 1945, only to receive the name back in 1954. In 1990 it was once again renamed Vladikavkaz.

117 See Alexandr Nekrich, *The Punished Peoples: the Deportation and the Fate of the Soviet Minorities at the end of the Second World War*, New York: Norton and Co., 1978, p. 91; quoted in Human Rights Watch/Helsinki, *The Ingush-Ossetian Conflict in the Prigorodnyi Region*, New York: Human Rights Watch, 1996.

118 See Birch, "Ossetia...", op. cit. [115], p. 53.

119 See Human Rights Watch/Helsinki, *The Ingush-Ossetian Conflict*, op. cit., [117], p. 12.

120 ibid.

121 *Natsiyonal'niy Sostav Naselenya SSSR Po Dannym Vsyesoyuzniy Perepisi Naselenya 1989*, Moscow, 1991.

122 See Swetlana Tscherwonnaja, "Der Ossetisch-Inguschische Konflikt im Nordkaukasus I", in *Osteuropa*, August (8) 1995 p. 741.

123 Human Rights Watch/Helsinki, *"Punished Peoples" of the Soviet Union—the Continuing Legacy of Stalin's Deportations*, New York: Human Rights watch, 1991, pp. 48-49. The 'visitor' from Moscow, Mikhail S. Solomontsev, was also the prime minister of the RSFSR.

124 Formerly the North Ossetian Autonomous Socialist Soviet Republic, in 1994 changed to the Republic of North Ossetia-Alania.

125 See Vadim Ogoyev, "The Ossetians' 'Loyalty' to Socialism as a Crisis of National Self-Awareness", *Nezavisimaya Gazeta*, 8 July 1992, in condensed form in *Current Digest of the Post-Soviet Press*, vol. 44 no. 27, 5 August 1992, p. 26.

126 See Fiona Hill, *"Russia's Tinderbox": Conflict in the north Caucasus and its Implications for the Future of the Russian Federation*, Cambridge, Mass.: Harvard University, JFK School of Government Strengthening Democratic Institutions Project, p. 49.

127 See Birch, op. cit., [115], p. 55.

128 Felix Corley, "The Inguish-Ossetian Conflict", in *Jane's Intelligence Review*, September 1994, p. 401

129 See Tscherwonnaja, "Der Ossetisch-Inguschische Konflikt", op. cit., [122], p. 744.

130 Human Rights Watch/Helsinki, *The Ingush-Ossetian Conflict*, op. cit., [117], p. 29.

131 *ibid.*, p. 30.

132 *Izvestiya*, 20 October 1992.

133 See Swetlana Tscherwonnaja, "Der Ossetisch-Inguschische Konflikt", op. cit., [122], p. 745, quoting *Izvestiya*, 21 October 1992.

134 Human Rights Watch/Helsinki, *The Ingush-Ossetian Conflict*, op. cit. [115], p. 33; Birch, "Ossetia...", op. cit., [115], p. 57.

135 Human Rights Watch/Helsinki, *The Ingush-Ossetian Conflict*, op. cit. [117], p. 34.

136 Zverev, *op. cit.*,

137 Human Rights Watch/Helsinki, *The Ingush-Ossetian Conflict*, op. cit. [117], p. 35.

138 Human Rights Watch/Helsinki, *The Ingush-Ossetian Conflict*, op. cit. [117], p. 60. The Ingush give totally different figures, according to which the death toll is counted in tens of thousands. However, all impartial sources seem to show that the official figures are at least a good estimation of the reality.

139 See Tscherwonnaja, "Der Ossetisch-Inguschische Konflikt", op. cit., [122], p. 750.

140 See OMRI Daily Digest, 17 February 1995.

141 Mohiaddin Mesbahi, "Russian Foreign Policy and Security in Central Asia and the Caucasus", in *Central Asian Survey*, nr. 2, 1993, p. 192.

142 For the full text of the document, see *Nezavisimaya Gazeta*, 23 March 1994; for discussion of the issue see Human Rights Watch/Helsinki, *The Ingush-Ossetian Conflict*, op. cit., [117], p. 68-69.

143 *Rossiyskaya Gazeta*, 6 November 1992.

144 Birch, "Ossetia", op. cit., [115], p. 60.

145 Human Rights Watch/Helsinki, *The Ingush-Ossetian Conflict*, op. cit., [117], p. 64-65.

146 Ibid., p. 60-61; Birch, "Ossetia...", op. cit., [115], p. 62

147 See Hill, *Russia's* Tinderbox, op. cit., [126], p. 50.

148 Swetlana Tscherwonnaja, "Der Ossetisch-Inguschische Konflikt im Nordkaukasus II", in *Osteuropa*, September 1995, p. 831.

149 Human Rights Watch/Helsinki, *The Ingush-Ossetian Conflict*, op. cit., [117], p. 79-81.

150 See FBIS-SOV, 21 August 1995, quoting *Ekho Moskvy*.

151 OMRI Daily Digest, 14 August 1995.

152 OMRI Daily Digest, 12 October 1995.

153 FBIS-SOV, 28 April 1995, quoting *Interfax*.

154 OMRI Daily Digest, 25 October 1995.

155 *The Washington Post*, 25 February 1996; OMRI Daily Digest, 26 February 1995.

156 "Grenade Attack on Ingush Refugees", in *The Jamestown Monitor*, 17 July 1997

157 See "Aushev Calls on Kremlin to Declare Presidential Rule in Conflict Area", in *The Jamestown Monitor*, 16 July 1997.

158 See "Ossetian-Ingush Crisis Puts Kremlin in Difficult Position", in *The Jamestown Monitor*, 28 July 1997; "Moscow Appears to Favor Ossetian Side in Ingush Conflict", in *The Jamestown Monitor*, 29 July 1997; and Liz Fuller, "Moscow's Ostrich Policy in the North Caucasus", *RFE/RL Report*, 11 August 1997. As for the proposed action programme, see "Diplomatic Victory for Vladikavkaz", in *The Jamestown Monitor*, 17 October 1997.

159 "Ingush Refugee Camp Attacked", *The Jamestown Monitor*, 31 July 1997.

160 OMRI Daily Digest, 2 February 1995.

161 For a discussion of the similarity of the political orientation of the Ingush and the Ossetians, see Tscherwonnaja, "Der Ossetisch-Inguschische Konflikt II", op. cit., [148], p. 825-829.

162 For an overview of the Confederation, see below.

163 Krag and Funch, *The North Caucasus* op. cit. [84], p. 30.

164 See Abdurahman Avtorkhanov, "The Chechens and the Ingush during the Soviet Period and its Antecedents", in Broxup, *The North Caucasus Barrier*, op.cit. [], pp. 146-194.

165 See chapter 5 in Svante E. Cornell, *Small Nations and Great Powers*, Richmond: Cuzon, 1999.

166 See Carlotta Gall and Thomas de Waal, *Chechnya: A Small Victorious War*, Basingstoke: Pan Books, 1997, pp. 56-75; James Critchlow, *"Punished Peoples" of the Soviet Union—the Continuing Legacy of Stalin's Deportations*, New York: Human Rights Watch, 1991, pp. 21-25.

167 See Michael Rywkin, "The Communist Party and the Sufi *Tariqat* in the Chechen-Ingush Republic", in *Central Asian Survey*, vol. 9 no. 1/2, 1991.

168 From Jokhar Dudayev, *Ternitsy Put' K Svobode*, Vilnius 1993.

169 See Christopher Panico, *Conflict in the Caucasus: Russia's War with Chechnya*, RISCT, London: Conflict Studies 281, Juy 1995.

170 See the short biography given in Gall and de Waal, op. cit. [166], pp. 83-90.

171 See Flemming Splidsboel-Hansen, "The 1991 Chechen Revolution: The Response of Moscow", in *Central Asian Survey*, vol. 13 no. 3, October 1994, 395-406.

172 See Marie Bennigsen Broxup, "After the Putsch, 1991", in Broxup (ed.), *The North Caucasus Barrier*, op. cit., [66]. Also Splidsboel-Hansen, "The 1991 Chechen Revolution: The Response of Moscow", op. cit. [171].

173 On the pre-war opposition, see Elizabeth Fuller, "Chechen Politics: A Murky Prospect", in *Transition*, 15 March 1995.

174 See, e.g., Panico, *Russia's War with Chechnya*, op. cit. [169], p. 14.

175 Ib Faurby, "Krigen i Tjetjenien: Baggrund, Operationer og Fremtidsudsigter", in *Kungl. Vetenskapsakademiens Handlingar och Tidskrift (Royal Swedish Academy of War Sciences, Proceedings and Journal)*, vol. 200, no. 3, 1996, p. 24.

176 Nikolay Tsymbal, in *Rossiiskie Vesty*, 10 January 1995, quoted in Timothy L. Thomas, "The Russian Armed Forces Confront Chechnya: The Battle for Grozny, 1-26 January 1995 (Part I)", in *Low Intensity Conflict and Law Enforcement*, vol. 5 no. 3, Winter 1996, p. 424.

177 Ingemar Oldberg, *Rysslands Krig mot Tjetjenien*, (Russia's war with Chechnia) Stockholm: Världspolitikens Dagsfrågor, Nr. 4, 1995, p. 17.

178 Ib Faurby, "Krigen i Tjetjenien: Baggrund, Operationer og Fremtidsudsigter", op. cit. [175], p. 27.

179 Open Media Research Institute (Prague, herefater OMRI) Daily Digest, 3 August 1995.

180 OMRI Daily Digest, 24 August 1995.
181 OMRI Daily Digest, 5 September 1995.
182 OMRI Daily Digest, 9 October 1995, 3 November 1995.
183 Ib Faurby, "Krigen i Tjetjenien: Baggrund, Operationer og Fremtidsudsigter", op. cit. [175], p. 27.
184 OMRI Daily digest, 18 December 1995.
185 OMRI Daily digest, 4 March 1996.
186 Robert Orttung, "Who Is Making Russia's Chechnya Policy?", OMRI Analytical Brief no. 300, 23 August 1996.
187 See, for example, Elizabeth Fuller, "Chechnya after Dudayev", OMRI Analytical Brief no. 81, 24 April 1996.
188 See, e.g., Turkish Daily News, 23 April 1996.
189 See Fuller, "Chechnya after Dudayev", op. cit. [187].
190 OMRI Daily Digest, 13 May 1996.
191 OMRI Daily Digest, 3 June 1996.
192 OMRI Daily Digest, 18 June 1996.
193 OMRI Daily Digest, 10 July 1996.
194 OMRI Daily Digest, 12 July 196.
195 "The Month in Review", Current History, October 1996.
196 See Elizabeth Fuller, "Whither Chechnya: Peace or Anarchy", OMRI Analytical Brief no. 317, 4 September 1996.
197 See Svante E. Cornell, "A Chechen State?", in Central Asian Survey, vol. 16 no. 2, June 1997. For a concurring argument, see Marie Bennigsen Broxup, "Thcétchénie: Une Guerre Coloniale", in Politique Internationale, no. 67, 1995, pp. 107-119. See also Soili Nystén-Haarala, "Does the Russian Constitution Justify an Offensive against Chechnia" in Central Asian Survey, vol. 14 no. 2, June 1995. For arguments defending the Russian position, see Tarcision Gazzini, "Considerations on the Conflict in Chechnia", in Human Rights Law jounral, vol. 17 no. 3-6, 15 October 1996. See also Christian Altmann and Frank Nienhuysen, Brennpunkt Kaukasus: Wohin Steuert Russland, Bergisch gladbach: Bastei Lübbe, 1995, pp. 140-144.
198 See Paul Goble, "How Independent is Chechnia?", Radio Free Europe/Radio Liberty Report, 11 September 1997. (Reproduced in Turkistan Newsletter, vol. 97:1/50, 15 September 1997).
199 See Francis A. Boyle, "Independent Chechnya: Treaty of Peace with Russia of 12 May 1997", in Turkistan Newsletter, vol. 97:, no. 50, 15 September 1997.
200 Maria Eismont, "The Signs of a Chechen Victory", in The Jamestown Prism, vol. 2 no. 15, 1 September 1996.
201 For an analysis of the phenomenon in the contemporary North Caucasus, see Igor Rotar, "Islamic Radicals in Dagestan", in Jamestown Prism, vol. 4 no. 6, 20 March 1998.
202 See Liz Fuller, "Wolf Cubs Fighting under a Rug", in RFE/RL Caucasus Report, vol. 1 no. 40, December 1998, p. 1.
203 See Marie Bennigsen Broxup, "The Last Ghazawat: The 1920-21 Uprising" in Broxup, op. cit., [66], pp. 112-145.

204 Marie Bennigsen Broxup, "Introduction: Russia and the North Caucasus", in *Broxup*, op. cit., [66], p. 15.

205 See Mike Edwards, "The fractured Caucasus", in *National Geographic* February 1996.

206 See Brian Murray, "Peace in the Caucasus: Multi-Ethnic Stability in Dagestan", in *Central Asian Survey*, v.13, nr. 4 (1994), p. 507-23.

207 See Marie Bennigsen Broxup, "After the Putsch", in Broxup, op. cit., [66], p. 237.

208 See Vicken Cheterian, "Les Mille et Une Guerres du Caucase", in *Le Monde Diplomatique*, August 1994.

209 See Ismail Özsoy, "The Socio-Economic Problems of Dagestan (1995)", in *Eurasian Studies* (Ankara), Winter 1995/96.

210 See Michael S. Serril, "Blown Away", in *Time*, January 29, 1996.

211 See Andrei Smirnov, "A State Duma Member Tried to Stage a Coup In the Republic", in *Segodnya*, 22 May 1998.

212 See *RFE/RL Newsline*, 27 May 1998.

213 See Smirnov, "A State Duma Member...", op. cit [211].

214 See the rather tendentious discussion in Julia Kalinina, "Chechnya Ready to Sever Dagestan from Russia", in *Moskovsky Komsomolets*, 26 May 1998.

215 See *RFE/RL Caucasus Report*, vol. 1 no. 14, 2 June 1998.

216 "Movladi Udugov: "We have nothing to do with it"", in *Moskovsky Komsomolets*, 22 May 1998.

217 For a recent overview of the most pressing problems of Dagestan, see Liz Fuller, "Fault Lines in Dagestan", in *RFE/RL Caucasus Report*, vol. 1 no. 14, 2 June 1998.

218 See Vladimir Bobrovnikov, "The Islamic Revival and the National Question in Post-Soviet Dagestan", in *Religion, State, and Society—The Keston Journal*, vol. 24, nos. 2/3, September 1996, p. 234.

219 See Fanny E. B. Bryan, "Internationalism, Nationalism and Islam", in Broxup, op. cit., [45].

220 See Bobrovnikov, op. cit. [218], p. 233.

221 See Cheterian, op. cit. [208].

222 See Bobrovnikov, op. cit. [218], p. 234.

223 See Tamara Sivertseva, "Cultural Transformation and Change of Identity in the Northern Caucasus", in *Religion, State, and Society—The Keston Journal*, vol. 24, nos. 2/3, September 1996, p. 239-40.

224 See, e.g., Anna Matveeva, *Dagestan*, Former Soviet South Briefing, Russia and Eurasia Programme, Royal Institute of International Affairs, London, May 1997.

225 On the conflict potential in Dagestan, see Robert Bruce Ware and Enver Kisriev, "After Chechnya: New Dangers in Dagestan", in *Central Asian Survey*, vol. 16 no. 3, September 1997.

226 Goldenberg, op. cit. [74], p. 203.

227 See Hill, op. cit. [126], p. 57.

228 Abdulatipov is an Avar and currently deputy prime minister of Russia; Khasbulatov is a Chechen and was at the time chairman of the Russian Supreme

Soviet. The two were the highest-ranking North Caucasians in the Russian Federation, a fact which contributed to their success in resolving the issue. See Clem McCartney, *Dagestan Field Report*, London: International Alert, 1995.

229 *Natsiyonal'niy Sostav Naselenya SSSR Po Dannym Vsyesoyuzniy Perepisi Naselenya 1989*, Moscow, 1991.

230 The Andi group is composed of the Andi and seven smaller peoples, the Akhvakh, Bagulal, Botlikh, Chamalal, Godoberi, Karata, and Tindi. These peoples have been registered as Avars since 1926.

231 The Dido group is composed of the Archi, Bezheta, Ginukh, Hunzal, Kapuchi, and Khwarshi. They have not been registered individually since 1926.

232 Kamil Aliyev, "The History of Kumyks and their Current Social Problems" in *Eurasian Studies* (Ankara), Summer 1995, p. 72-73.

233 *ibid.*, p. 73.

234 See Cheterian, op. cit., [208].

235 Aliyev, op. cit., [232].

236 *Ibid.*, p. 77.

237 See discussion in Timothy D. Sisk, *Power-Sharing and International Mediation in Ethnic Conflicts*, Washington, D.C.: United States Institute of Peace Press, 1996, pp. 34-45.

238 For an account of the integrative approach, see Donald Horowitz, *Ethnic Groups in Conflict*, Berkeley: University of California Press, 1985.

239 For the consociational approach, see mainly the writings of Arend Lijphart, for example "Consociational Democracy", in *World Politics*, January 1969, and *Democracy in Plural Societies*, New Haven: Yale University Press, 1977.

240 See McCartney, *Dagestan Field Report*, op. cit. [228], especially section 3, "Responses to Problems and Issues of Governance".

241 Bobrovnikov, op. cit., [218], p. 237.

242 Murray, op. cit., [206], p. 517.

243 *Ibid.*, p. 516.

244 For an overview of Soviet federalism recommended by Murray, see Philip G. Roeder, "Soviet Federalism and Ethnic Mobilization", in *World Politics*, January 1991.

245 See table in Sisk, op. cit., [237], p. 35 for a comparison of the two models.

246 Bobrovnikov, op. cit., [218], p. 237.

247 See Krag and Funch, *The North Caucasus*, op. cit. p. 30.

248 A rare overview of the Confederation is Dodge Billingsley, "Confederates of the Caucasus", in *Jane's Intelligence Review*, February 1997, p. 66

249 See Charles van der Leeuw, *Storm over the Caucasus: In the Wake of Independence*, Richmond: Curzon Press, 1999, p. 176.

250 Billingsley, "Confederates of the Caucasus", op. cit. [248], p. 67.

251 Billingsley, "Confederates of the Caucasus", op. cit. [248], p. 68.

252 *The Jamestown Monitor*, 19 May 1998.

253 *The Jamestown Monitor*, 10 July 1998.

Appendices

Map of Black Sea Region

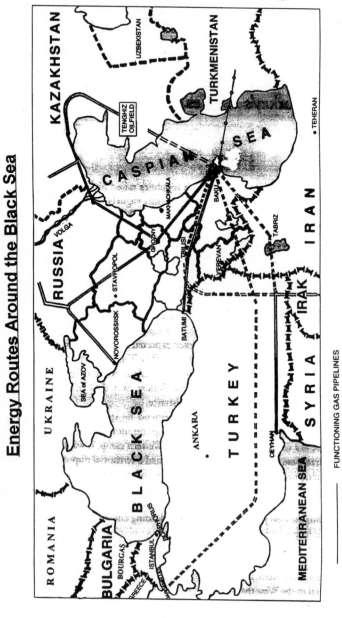

Energy Routes Around the Black Sea

FUNCTIONING GAS PIPELINES
FUNCTIONING OIL PIPELINES
PROJECTED OIL PIPELINES

Official Websites Related to the Black Sea Region

Black Sea Economic Cooperation
http://www.iews.org/srd.bsec.nsf
http://www.photius.com/bsec/bsec.html

The Black Sea Trade and Development Bank
http:www.bstdb.gr/about.html

Black Sea Regional Energy Centre
http://www.bg/

Black Sea Coordination Centre for the Exchange of Statistical Data
http://www.die.govtr/TURKISH/BSEC/

Black Sea Environmental Programme Coordination Unit
http://www.dominet.com.tr/black sea/

Black Sea Environmetal Internet Node
http://www.grid.unep.ch/bsein/

Protocol on Protection of the Black Sea Against Pollution from Land Based Sources
http://sedac.ciesin.org/pidb/texts/acrc/BlackSealBP.txt.html

East-West Institute Sub-Regional Cooperation Website
http://www.iews.org/srd.nsf

International Black Sea Club
http://www.friends-partners.org/ccsi/eeurope/bulgaria/blacksea.htm

Black Sea University
http://www.geo-strategies.com/romania/bsu.htm

The EU Homepage
http://europa.eu.int/

NATO Homepage
http://www.nato.int/

Western European Union
http://int-serv.weu.int/assembly

Council of Europe
http://www.coe.fr/index.asp

OECD
http://www.oecd.fr/

OSCE
http://www.osce.org

Central European Initiative
http://www.digit.it/ceinet/homepage3.htm

Council of the Baltic States
http://www.um.dk/english/udenrigspolitik/cbss

INDEX